65- 5108 (7-18-66)

RENAISSANCE DRAMA
VIII ∽ 1965

Woodcut from Vicenzo Cartari, *Imagini delli dei de gl'antichi* (Venetia, 1674). See p. 144 for a further description.

Renaissance Drama

VIII

Edited by S. Schoenbaum

Northwestern University Press

EVANSTON 1965

The front-cover illustration, from the title-page of the 1496 Strassburg edition of Terence's comedies, is reproduced by courtesy of the John M. Wing Foundation of The Newberry Library. The title-page device is taken from The Newberry Library copy of the works of Ruzzante (Vicenza, 1584).

TO THE MEMORY OF
R. C. BALD
1901-1964

Editorial Note

RENAISSANCE DRAMA, an annual publication, provides a forum for scholars in various parts of the globe: wherever the drama of the Renaissance is studied. Coverage, so far as subject matter is concerned, is not restricted to any single national theater. The chronological limits of the Renaissance are interpreted liberally, and space is available for essays on precursors, as well as on the utilization of Renaissance themes by later writers. Investigations shedding light on theatrical history and actual stage production are especially welcome, as are comparative studies. Editorial policy favors articles of some scope. Essays that are exploratory in nature, that are concerned with critical or scholarly methodology, that raise new questions or embody fresh approaches to perennial problems are particularly appropriate for a publication which originated out of the proceedings of the Modern Language Association Conference on Research Opportunities in Renaissance Drama.

Contributions offered for publication should be addressed to the Editor, RENAISSANCE DRAMA, Northwestern University, University Hall 101, Evanston, Illinois 60201. Prospective contributors are requested to follow the recommendations of the *MLA Style Sheet* (revised edition) in preparing manuscripts.

Contents

RENAISSANCE DRAMA
VIII ❧ 1965

The House of David
in Renaissance Drama
A COMPARATIVE STUDY
Inga-Stina Ewbank

Si j'avais à . . . [exposer sur le théâtre] . . . [l'histoire] de David et de Bethsabée, je ne décrirais pas comme il en devint amoureux en la voyant se baigner dans une fontaine, de peur que l'image de cette nudité ne fît une impression trop chatouilleuse dans l'esprit de l'auditeur; mais je me contenterais de le peindre avec de l'amour pour elle, sans parler aucunement de quelle manière cet amour se serait emparé de son cœur.[1]

I T IS HIGHLY UNLIKELY that when Corneille wrote the above words, in his *Examen de Polyeucte,* he should have known of an English play, written some sixty or seventy years earlier, in which the episode of King David watching the bathing Bathsheba is not just described but actually put on the stage.[2] Corneille was discussing how to deal dramatically with religious, and especially biblical, material; and he was doing so at a time, well over a hundred years after Buchanan's *Jephthes,* when humanists all over Europe had proved the possibility of christianizing the Tragic Muse, of serving both the ancients (but more specifically the not-quite-so-ancient Seneca) and the Lord. French dramatists in particular had been quick to see that the Bible contained as much potentially tragic material as classical myth;[3] but at about the same time as Corneille was working on his play

1. *Oeuvres de P. Corneille,* nov. ed. (Paris, 1873), II, 113.

2. Corneille presumably had in mind Montchrestien's *David,* which is discussed later in this essay. Cf. *Les Tragédies de Montchrestien,* ed. L. Petit de Julleville (Paris, 1891), p. 306.

3. Cf. the Introduction to *The Poetical Works of Sir William Alexander,* ed. L. E. Kastner and H. B. Charlton (Manchester, 1921), p. cxxxv. (This essay remains

about Polyeucte, saint and martyr, Milton was pondering over biblical topics for tragedy and noting down as possibilities, among others, "David Adulterous," "Tamar," and "Achitophel." The House of David might be as fruitful as the House of Atreus when it came to furnishing a tragic plot, and there was always the advantage that scriptural authority would, by definition, make the argument not less but more heroic.

> L'execrable Inceste d'Amnon
> Dont tu peints si bien la vengeance,
> Plus que la mort d'Agamemnon
> Tesmoigne de Dieu la puissance,

we read in a commendatory ode on N. Chrestien's play about how David's son Amnon raped his sister Tamar and was, in revenge, slain by his brother Absalom.[4] Corneille, too, assumes that biblical story has the sanctity of divine inspiration about it, so that a dramatist using such material may not change anything in his source. But his second point, and the one that leads up to the quotation above, deals with the *omissions* which may be made—provided always that one does not obscure "ces verités dictées par le Saint-Esprit." In the cause of dramatic decorum and unity of impact, he says, one must be selective. It is here that Corneille becomes immediately relevant to my main theme in this essay, because he shows how, in neoclassic theory, the standards of the "well-made" play are already looming up. He is in fact anticipating the criteria by which George Peele's play, *The Love of King David and Fair Bethsabe, With the Tragedie of Absalon,* is still most frequently judged—and by which,

---

the best work in English on the Renaissance Senecan tradition in Europe.) Cf. also Lancaster E. Dabney, *French Dramatic Literature in the Reign of Henri IV* (Austin, 1952), Chap. I; and Gustave Lanson, *Esquisse d'une Histoire de la Tragédie Française* (New York, 1920), pp. 15 ff.

4. "Ode" by O. du Mont-Sacré in commendation of *Tragédie d'Amnon, et Thamar,* in *Les Tragedies de N. Chretien* (Rouen, 1608).—In the case of both Chrestien and Montchrestien, whose names appear variously with or without an "s," I follow the spelling used by Raymond Lebègue in *La Tragédie française de la Renaissance,* 2nd ed. (Brussels, 1954).—This argument for the superiority of a biblical subject over a similar classical one was a commonplace. See, e.g., Christopherson on his *Jephthah* as against Euripides' *Iphigenia in Aulis.* (Quoted in F. S. Boas, *University Drama in the Tudor Age* [Oxford, 1914], pp. 48–49.)

inevitably, it is seen as the result of "shapeless unselectivity of incidents."[5]

There has always been disagreement as to what kind of a play *David and Bethsabe* really is. Peele's own title page shows a happy disregard of genres. Restoration play-lists call it a tragicomedy.[6] Thomas Warton places it in the medieval miracle tradition.[7] F. S. Boas veers between "revenge tragedy" and an almost Polonian labeling of the play as "Scriptural chronicle-history."[8] Lily B. Campbell is practically alone in taking it seriously as a new departure in drama, "a divine play conscious of its place in divine literature"; but even she finds the structure "cluttered with episodes."[9] Scholars are, perhaps, no longer as anxious as they once were to father onto Peele every shapeless Elizabethan play of unknown authorship, but he still tends to be used as an example of someone who "cared little for structural consistency."[10] We might do well to listen to Wolfgang Clemen when he says that, in order to do justice to Peele's plays,

dürfen wir sie nicht mit den üblichen Masstäben dramatischer Einheit und Komposition beurteilen, sondern müssen nach ihrer Eigengesetzlichkeit fragen.[11]

In this essay I propose to work toward a definition of that "Eigengesetzlichkeit" in *David and Bethsabe* and to do so by looking at other dramatic treatments of Peele's source (i.e., 2 Samuel XI–XIX.8), as well as at

5. Madeleine Doran, *Endeavors of Art* (Madison, 1954), p. 102.

6. See Francis Kirkman, *A True, Perfect, and Exact Catalogue of all the Comedies, Tragedies, Tragi-Comedies . . .* (London, 1671), and William Winstanley, *The Lives of the Most Famous English Poets* (London, 1687), p. 97.

7. *The History of English Poetry*, rev. ed. (London, 1824), IV, 153, note e.

8. *An Introduction to Tudor Drama* (Oxford, 1933), p. 157, and *University Drama*, p. 363.

9. *Divine Poetry and Drama in Sixteenth Century England* (London, Berkeley, and Los Angeles, 1959), p. 260.

10. Arthus M. Sampley, "The Text of Peele's *David and Bethsabe*," *PMLA*, XLVI (1931), 670.

11. *Die Tragödie vor Shakespeare* (Heidelberg, 1955), p. 146.—In his translation of Clemen's book, T. S. Dorsch renders this passage as follows: "To do justice to Peele's plays, we must not judge them according to the normally accepted standards of dramatic unity and structure; they must be judged by criteria that are appropiate to their special character" (*English Tragedy before Shakespeare* [London, 1961], p. 163).

nondramatic versions of the story, wherever they illuminate points in the plays under consideration.

Peele's is the only Elizabethan play on the subject of the House of David: if the fourteenpence paid by Henslowe in October 1602 for "poleyes & worckmanshipp for to hange absalome" were spent on a play other than Peele's, that play is now lost. We therefore have to go abroad for comparative material, and rightly so, for—as scholars like F. S. Boas, and more recently Lily B. Campbell and Marvin T. Herrick, have shown—the Renaissance desire to turn Bible story into drama was a European, rather than a localized, phenomenon.[12] If anything, the English dramatists, academic as well as popular, seem to have been more wary of tackling this type of drama than, for example, their Dutch and French contemporaries. Comparisons for comparison's sake are odious, but in this case I hope that a comparative method, while incidentally throwing some light on the ways in which the same source material is shaped by different individuals in different dramatic traditions, will mainly prove helpful toward defining the nature of the play we have before our eyes.

At the outset, however, something must be said about the *text* we have before our eyes.[13] There is no doubt that the text of the quarto of *David*

12. See Boas, *University Drama;* Campbell, *Divine Poetry and Drama;* and Marvin T. Herrick, *Tragicomedy: Its Origin and Development in Italy, France and England* (Urbana, 1955). See also Herrick's essay, "Susanna and the Elders in Sixteenth-Century Drama," in *Studies in Honor of T. W. Baldwin,* ed. D. C. Allen (Urbana, 1958), pp. 125-135.—I have been helped in my search for plays on the House of David by the bibliography in *Le Mistère du Viel Testament,* ed. James de Rothschild (Paris, 1882), IV, lvii ff.; and also by the list compiled by John McLaren McBryde, Jr., in his article, "A Study of Cowley's *Davideis,*" *JEGP,* II (1899), 454-527. Invaluable bibliographies of neo-Latin drama are Alfred Harbage's "Census of Anglo-Latin Plays," *PMLA,* LIII (1938), 624-629; and the two works by Leicester Bradner: "A Check-List of Original Neo-Latin Dramas by Continental Writers Printed before 1650," *PMLA,* LVIII (1943), 621-633, and "List of Original Neo-Latin Plays Published before 1650," *Studies in the Renaissance,* IV (1957), 31-70.

13. For the purpose of this essay I have used, and quoted from, the Malone Society reprint of the 1599 quarto of *David and Bethsabe* (ed. W. W. Greg, 1912). —To minimize the confusion which might arise from the fact that each author tends to use his own form of the biblical names (and that in Peele's play the spelling sometimes varies from scene to scene), I have in all cases, except in direct quotations, used the form and spelling to be found in the Authorized Version; thus "Bathsheba," "Hushai," "Absalom," "Ahitophel," etc.

and Bethsabe printed in 1599 is garbled. There are such flagrant corruptions and problems as the three misplaced lines, 1660–1662, which belong nowhere in the play as it stands; the "5. Chorus" which is the second, and last, in the play; and the reference in this chorus to "a third discourse of Dauids life," with its never fulfilled promise of showing us "his most renowmed death" (ll. 1654–1655). I cannot deal here with the textual riddles of the play, but for the purposes of my argument they seem to have been solved satisfactorily by A. M. Sampley's theory, which is that Peele originally wrote a five-act play dealing with the love of David and Bathsheba and the tragedy of Absalom.[14] This version was cut for stage performances and gradually got so mutilated that in the end it had to be revised to be brought back to a more reasonable length. The play, then, in its present form represents a drastically cut stage version of the play as Peele first wrote it, plus an addition (the Solomon scene) made by Peele before sending it to the printer. The important point, to my argument, is that we can be fairly certain, because of the homogeneity of the style throughout, that the final revision was carried out by Peele himself. That being so, the present text—apart from such obvious errors as undeleted lines—represents what Peele himself deemed ready for the stage and for the reader. To Sampley it stands as a proof that Peele was not interested in "structural consistency." I shall argue, however, that the play has virtues—a kind of imaginative shape and thematic unity—which have not been allowed for; and I hope to bring these out by discussing what qualities there are in Peele's play that are not also in others dealing with the same subject, and vice versa.

David and Bethsabe opens with a Prologue which takes the form of an epic invocation—

> Of Israels sweetest singer now I sing,
> His holy stile and happie victories—

but, as the "Prologus" *"drawes a curtaine, and discouers Bethsabe with her maid bathing ouer a spring: she sings, and Dauid sits aboue vewing her,"* it is hardly one of the happy victories he presents. Peele's audience would have been conditioned toward two kinds of response to this scene, and in his treatment of the love of David and Bathsheba, Peele draws on both.

14. See *PMLA*, XLVI (1931), 659–671.

Adam, Sansonem, Loth, David, sic Salomonem
Femina decepit . . .

we read in the neo-Latin *Comedia Sancti Nicolai*,[15] and here we have in a nutshell the first attitude to David the lover, one which the sixteenth century had inherited from the Middle Ages. David's *sin* is emphasized and seen as another version of the Fall, with Bathsheba as another Eve. The David and Bathsheba story had become an *exemplum* to illustrate one of the great medieval moral-satirical themes. As late as 1581 there was printed in London a collection of the dialogues of Ravisius Textor, where in the *Dialogus* between "Troia," "Salomon," and "Sanson" we find the following well with three buckets:

TROIA

Quis generi humano Paradisi limina clausit?

SALOMON

Foemina. Quis lyrici cantus Davida peritum
Fecit adulterium committere?

SANSON

Foemina. Sed quis
Aeneam valido fecit confligere Turno?

TROIA

Foemina. Qui veteres fecit pugnare Sabinos
Contra Romanes pastores?

SALOMON

Foemina . . .[16]

And so on, until the whole dialogue adds up to a flaming indictment of woman. Again, David's sin is linked with Adam's, as well as with that of the heroes of classical myth and history. David and Bathsheba form one of

15. This was written by a French Augustinian friar and printed about 1510. I have not seen this play but take my information about it, as well as the quotation, from Raymond Lebègue, *La Tragédie religieuse en France: les debuts (1514–1573)*, (Paris, 1929), p. 121.

16. *Ioan. Ravisii Textoris Nivernen Dialogi aliquot festivissimi* (London, 1581), fol. Cc 5ᵛ. The dialogues of Textor, written for his pupils at the Collège de Navarre, were well known in England; they were performed in Latin at the universities and in translations and adaptations elsewhere. Some of them were translated by Thomas Heywood as late as 1637 (*Pleasant Dialogues and Dramas, Selected out of Lucian, Erasmus, Textor, Ovid. & c.*).

the examples of the Triumph of Love in Petrarch's *Trionfi* (together with such figures as Alexander the Great, Pyramus and Thisbe, and Hero and Leander), and of adultery ("true," historical, adultery as against the fictitious sins of classical myth) in Brant's *Narrenschiff*.[17]

To the less sophisticated members of the audience the image of David as the adulterous sinner would come from more familiar sources, fictional and homiletic. In a "pleasant fable" George Gascoigne showed how insidiously a would-be adulterer could use the example of David to argue his case;[18] and Vives, in his *Instruction of a Christen Woman*, used David as a warning example in his chapter "Of Loving."[19] In 1589 Henry Holland published a moral treatise called *Dauids Faith and Repentance*, in which is described how David saw Bathsheba washing herself,

whereby his filthie lustes became so vehement, and kindled in him such a fire, that he could not, as in his former assaults, call for the presence of Gods spirit.[20]

Although the play entered on the Stationers' Register in 1561 as "an new interlude of the ii synnes of kynge David" is not extant, one can well imagine what it must have contained, especially as John Bale, in his *Tragedy or enterlude manyfestyng the chefe promyses of God unto men*, had shown the Lord rebuking David:

Of late dayes thou hast, mysused Bersabe,
The wyfe of Vrye, and slayne hym in the fyelde.[21]

But, as in Bale, David was not only the representative sinner but also the archpenitent. In his poem to the queen, "Of King Dauid," Harington stresses this side of the moral image:

17. See *The Tryumphes of Fraunces Petrarcke, translated out of Italian into English by Henrye Parker knyght, Lorde Morley* (1565?), fol. D 1ʳ; and *Narrenschiff* (Augsburg, 1498), fol. C 4ᵛ.

18. See *The Whole Woorkes of George Gascoigne* (London, 1587), pp. 195–196.

19. *A very Frutefull and Pleasant boke callyd the Instruction of a Christen woman* (London, 1541), fol. N 4ᵛ.

20. Henry Holland, *Dauids Faith and Repentance* (London, 1589), fol. C 3ʳ.

21. *A Tragedye or enterlude . . . manyfestyng the chefe promyses of God vnto man by all ages . . . Compyled by Johan Bale. Anno Domini 1538*, fol. D 1ʳ.

Thou, thou great Prince, with so rare gifts replenished
Could'st not eschew blind Buzzard *Cupids* hookes,
Lapt in the bayt of Bersabees sweet lookes:
With which one fault, thy faultles life was blemished.
Yet hence we learne a document most ample,
That faln by fraillty we may rise by fayth,
And that the sinne forgiuen, the penance staieth.[22]

Nathan's fable, as the Lord's method of rousing David's conscience, had attracted many; and both Harington and Sidney had seen in it the best mousetrap of all for catching the conscience of the king, and accordingly used it as a proof of the moral justification of fiction:

the applycation most diuinelye true, but the discourse it selfe fayned; which made *Dauid* (I speake of the second and instrumentall cause) as in a glasse to see his own filthines, as that heauenlye Psalme of mercie wel testifieth.[23]

As Sidney's words also suggest, it was natural to see David as an example of penitence when there were the Penitential Psalms as a constant reminder. The "miserere mei" of the Fifty-first Psalm had indeed become a universalized cry of confession and repentance; yet one also knew that it was "A Psalm of David, when Nathan the prophet came unto him, after he had gone in to Bathsheba." Many translators of, and commentators on, the Psalms had analyzed David's sin and repentance at great length, but perhaps the greatest literary expression of the connection between the Penitential Psalms and the love of David and Bathsheba is Wyatt's version, where his own links between the individual psalms describe the background story and David's progress in penance.

Indicative of the association of the Penitential Psalms with the love story behind them is the fact that in the late Middle Ages—and in France well into the Renaissance—a picture of Bathsheba bathing and David "above viewing her" would often be used in illustrating Books of Hours, as an

22. *The Letters and Epigrams of Sir John Harington,* ed. N. E. McClure (Philadelphia and London, 1930), pp. 223–224. The epigram "Of King Dauid. Written to the Queene" is in both the 1600 and the 1603 MSS.

23. Sidney, *An Apologie for Poetrie,* in *Elizabethan Critical Essays,* ed. G. Gregory Smith (London, 1904), I, 174.—Cf. Harington's *Briefe Apologie of Poetrie* (1591), in which Nathan's parable is used to defend the poet's right to "lie" (*Elizabethan Critical Essays,* II, 205).

introduction or frontispiece to the Penitential Psalms.[24] Here we are approaching the other form of response to the David and Bathsheba story —the delight in the sensuous beauty and sensual pleasure inherent in the scene as a human situation—for frequently the *Horae* illustrators seem to have taken more interest in the long, golden hair and other bodily charms of Bathsheba than in her representativeness as a vehicle of sin. In a typical Book of Hours, written in France in the early sixteenth century, we see David in contemplation of the carefully executed foreground figure of Bathsheba; she is standing in an ornate golden fountain, her equally golden hair falling over her shoulders, and with an arrow fired by a blind cupid heading straight for her breast (Figure 1). Bathsheba's bathing scene, we can see, was a natural meeting ground for Christian and pagan imagery. As Elizabeth Kunoth-Leifels has shown in her study of the David and Bathsheba motif in pictorial art, this motif—like its parallel, Susanna and the Elders—tended in the Renaissance to fuse with classical motifs, especially that of Venus and Adonis, into an image of earthly beauty.[25] The same tendency is obvious in verbal representations of the story: David appears torn between the Lord and Cupid, and Bathsheba's beauties are carefully catalogued. An English example of this is Francis Sabie's somewhat pedestrian epyllion, *Dauid and Beersheba* (1596), in which the poet, after entertaining us with Bathsheba's striptease act, cries out:

> O shut thine eies *Narcissus* come not neere,
> Least in the well a burning fire appeare.[26]

French poets were less restrained. In Remy Belleau's short epic, *Les Amours de David et de Bersabee* (1572), the emphasis is on the love story

24. Cf. Louis Réau, *Iconographie de l'art chrétien* (Paris, 1956), II, 273 ff. I have also found much valuable information on this subject in M. R. James, *The Illustration of the Old Testament in Early Times* (The Sanders Lectures for 1924; typewritten copy in the British Museum, pressmarked 03149.i.18).—In early printed books, a woodcut of the bathing scene was also extremely common. See Edward Hodnett, *English Woodcuts, 1480–1535* (London, 1935).

25. Elisabeth Kunoth-Leifels, *Über die Darstellungen der "Bathseba im Bade": Studien zur Geschichte des Bildthemas 4. bis 17. Jahrhundert* (Essen, 1962).—Cf. also Réau, *Iconographie*.

26. *Adams Complaint. The Olde Worldes Tragedie. Dauid and Bathsheba* (London, 1596), fol. F 1ᵛ.

(for all that the poem ends with David's repentance) and above all on the
bathing scene. The poet revels in Bathsheba's charms, and his lengthy
catalogue of them becomes increasingly detailed and warmly sensual as he
proceeds.[27] In Du Bartas, Bathsheba turns into an image of Venus:

> Elle oingt ses cheveux d'or: qu'elle plonge tantost
> De son corps bien formé l'albastre sous le flot,
> Telle qu'un lis qui tombe au creux d'une phiole,
> Telle qu'on peint Venus quand, lascivement molle,
> Elle naist dans la mer, et qu'avecques les thons
> Jà le feu de ses yeux embraze les Tritons.[28]

The same happens in the 1601 edition of Antoine de Montchrestien's play,
David ou l'adultère, where David describes how he saw Bathsheba—

> . . . telle comme on dit qu'vne belle Déesse
> Poussa des flots feconds le thresor de sa tresse,
> Quand sur vne coquille à Cithere elle vint,
> Seiour plaisant & beau que depuis elle tint—

but a sense of decorum has made him remove these lines from the 1604
edition of the play.[29] Peele here shows more decorum than his French
contemporaries, for, though his bathing scene is steeped in beauty, his
imagery is taken from the Bible and especially from the Song of Songs,
rather than from classical myth:

27. See *La Bergerie de R. Belleau* (Paris, 1572), p. 103.

28. *The Works of Guillaume De Salluste Sieur Du Bartas,* ed. Holmes, Lyons,
and Linker (Chapel Hill, 1940), III, 363 (*Les Trophées,* ll. 907 ff.).—Cf. the delight
with which Sylvester, translating Du Bartas, elaborates on this description:
"[Bathseba] Perfumes, and combes, and curls her golden hair; / Another-while
vnder the Crystall brinks, / Her Alabastrine well-shap't Limbs she shrinks / Like
to a Lilly sunk into a glasse: / Like soft loose *Venus* (as they paint the Lasse) /
Born in the Seas, when with her eyes sweet-flames, / Tonnies and *Tritons* she
at-once inflames." (Quoted from the 1613 ed. of Sylvester's translation, *Du Bartas
His Deuine Weekes and Workes,* p. 542.)

29. I quote from *Les Tragedies d'Ant. de Montchrestien* (Rouen, 1601), fol.
Q 2ᵛ. In the 1604 ed. (also Rouen), described on the title page as "edition nouvelle
augmentée par l'auteur," the play has lost its subtitle and become just *David.*

FIGURE 1. British Museum MS Kings 7, fol. 54ʳ. Reproduced by kind permission of the Trustees of the British Museum.

FIGURE 2. Liverpool City Museums MS Mayer 12001. (Book of Hours, Use of Paris, mid-fifteenth century.) Reproduced by kind permission of the Director of the Liverpool City Museums.

> Fairer then Isacs louer at the well,
> Brighter then inside barke of new hewen Cædar,
> Sweeter then flames of fine perfumed myrrhe.

(ll. 81–83)

I have already tried to show elsewhere [30] how much the opening scene of *David and Bethsabe* is in the tradition of Ovidian sensual poetry of the fifteen-nineties. No doubt the boy acting Bathsheba would have had to be dressed rather the way Bathsheba is in those Dutch sixteenth-century pictures where she is depicted as modestly washing her feet, her skirt pulled up to barely reveal her knees;[31] but Peele's poetry provides all the erotic atmosphere that later Rubens, for example, was to give to the scene. It may not be altogether fanciful to suggest that the play on sense impressions in Bathsheba's song—

> Hot sunne, coole fire, temperd with sweet aire,
> Black shade, fair nurse, shadow my white haire
> Shine sun, burne fire, breath aire, and ease mee,
> Black shade, fair nurse, shroud me and please me—

stems from the same impulse as that which introduced into paintings of the scene either a colored handmaiden or a black messenger boy, to set off the white-skinned and blonde-haired beauty of the bathing figure. There is no moral condemnation within Peele's scene; it would be "placed" only by the audience's awareness of its traditional moral implications. When David says of Bathsheba,

> Faire Eua, plac'd in perfect happinesse,
> . . . .

30. I-S. Ekeblad, "The Love of King David and Fair Bethsabe," *English Studies,* XXXIX (1958), 57–62.

31. See, for example, Hans Bol's "The Handing of the Message to Bathseba" in the Amsterdam Rijksmuseum (1568); the same painter's drawing, under the same title, in the H. Reitlinger Collection, London; and Maerten van Heemskerck's "The Handing of the Message to Bathseba." All these are reproduced among the excellent illustrations to Elisabeth Kunoth-Leifels' study (see her figs. 41–43). For a colored messenger, see the Rubens painting, Dresden Gemäldegalerie, and for a colored handmaiden, see Cornelisz van Haarlem, "Bathseba Bathing" (1594), Amsterdam Rijksmuseum (Kunoth-Leifels, figs. 50 and 48).

> Wrought not more pleasure to her husbands thoughts,
> Then this faire womans words and notes to mine,
>
> (ll. 57–61)

there is none of that irony in the image, placing the situation and anticipating its unhappy issue, which Marlowe uses so frequently—as when the Jew of Malta in Act I tells us that he holds his daughter as dear "As Agamemnon did his Iphigen." Like the illustrators of the Penitential Psalms, Peele is having his cake and eating it too: for, after using the first scene to celebrate the beauties of the flesh and the senses, he moves on to a strictly moral structure for the rest of the scenes dealing with the love story. Uriah is called home, and in a tragicomic scene (ll. 500–571) is made, ironically enough, to drink the health of "David's children"; and this is immediately followed by a chorus which underlines the sin of David—

> O prowd reuolt of a presumptious man,
> Laying his bridle in the necke of sin—

and goes on to point the general moral:

> If holy Dauid so shoke hands with sinne,
> What shall our baser spirits glorie in.
>
> (ll. 572–588)

The death of Uriah and the birth of the child, whether or not they had been enacted in an earlier version of the play, are summarized in the same chorus, leaving room for a scene of ritualistic lamentation of the sick child as a symbol of sin—

> The babe is sicke, and sad is Dauids heart,
> To see the guiltlesse beare the guilties paine;
>
> (ll. 625–626)

for Nathan's parable, which is taken almost verbatim from the Bible; and for David's penitence, with its echoes of the Psalms. Rapidly the rhythm of this scene brings David from penitence to purgation; as the child dies, retribution has been meted out, and David becomes the forgiven sinner:

> Let Dauids Harpe and Lute, his hand and voice,
> Giue laud to him that loueth Israel,
> And sing his praise, that shendeth Dauids fame,
> That put away his sinne from out his sight.
>
> (ll. 727–730)

The stage symbol of that forgiveness is the traditional *"Musike, and a banquet"*; its spiritual symbol is the conception of another son—

> . . . decke faire Bersabe with ornaments,
> That she may beare to me another sonne,
> That may be loued of the Lord of hosts.
>
> (ll. 735–737)

And so, by his treatment of the subject, Peele ultimately turns the love of King David and Fair Bathsheba into a kind of divine comedy.

We can find a very similar pattern in Hans Sachs's play on the same subject. His *Comedia: Der Dauid mit Batseba im Ehbruch* (written some time before 1561) follows the rhythm of sin, forgiveness, and ultimate triumph: he takes us from the adultery, via the death of Uriah, Nathan's fable, and the death of the child, to the birth of a second son, Solomon,

> Herr König / Bathsheba ausserkorn
> Hat dir ein andern Sohn geborn
> Dich wider mit zu trösten thon.
>
> (fol. 89ᵛ) [32]

Sachs treats the story with the same concreteness as in his *Fastnachtsspiele* he treated secular material—"dry brevity" is Creizenach's description of his style [33]—and so the total effect is much like that of a medieval mystery. There is none of the nymph-in-fountain atmosphere round Bathsheba's ablutions; they have the same style of domestic realism as in the second *Horae* illustration reproduced here (Figure 2):

32. *Das dritt vnd letzt Buch sehr Herrliche Schöne Tragedi / Komedi vnd schimpf Spil / Geistlich vnd Weltlich* (Nuremberg, 1561), I.

33. Wilhelm Creizenach, *Geschichte des Neueren Dramas* (Halle, 1903), III, 428.

Nun so hab ich gewaschen mich
Von meinem schweiss / nun so will ich
Mein hauss beschliessen.

(fol. 85ʳ)

As always in Sachs's plays, all moralizing is kept away from the characters'
speeches; it is left for the end, where the Epilogue warns against adultery
but, above all, stresses that man must not despair, however great a sinner,
but must trust to God's forgiveness. For, God

> . . . durchs heilig Evangelion
> Zeigt vergebung der sünden an
> Der Sünder wider thut begnaden
> Und wendet im ewigen schaden
> Dass auss verzweiflung im nit wachs
> Der ewig todt / das wünscht H. Sachs.

(fol. 90ʳ)

The same material that was shaped by Sachs into a homiletic *comedia*
was used, some forty years later, by Antoine de Montchrestien, writing in
quite a different dramatic tradition,[34] for his neo-Senecan tragedy, *David
ou l'adultère*.[35] His is also a play about sin and punishment, but with the
stress on the sin and only a final gesture toward contrition in David.
Where Sachs's five-act structure served him mainly to chop up the action
into equal parts, Montchrestien's follows a formal pattern of exposition,
development, and catastrophe. Act I, as we have already seen, is one long
monologue by David, relating how he saw Bathsheba bathing, lusted for
her, and satisfied his lust; at the end the news of her pregnancy is brought,
and Uriah is sent for. Act II is virtually given over to Uriah, who returns
with shrewd suspicions of what is going on; in Act III David debates with
Nadab whether he should send Uriah to his death, and Uriah himself has a

34. A recent and valuable study of that tradition is *Les Tragédies de Sénèque
et le théâtre de la Renaissance,* ed. Jean Jacquot (Paris, 1964). I am also indebted—
apart from the studies of sixteenth-century French drama already cited—to H. C.
Lancaster, *A History of French Dramatic Literature in the Seventeenth Century*
(Baltimore, 1929) and Kosta Loukovitch, *L'Évolution de la tragédie religieuse
classique en France* (Paris, 1933).

35. Cf. n. 29, above. In what follows, I quote from de Julleville's edition of
Montchrestien (cf. n. 2, above).

long speech in which he is shown as noble and loyal, as against the tyrannous king. In Act IV a messenger, in an elaborate account, relates the siege of Rabbah and Uriah's death. Act V opens with Bathsheba's lament over the death of Uriah and the sin of David, who "s'est montré trop homme et trop absolu Roy"; and David exhibits his hubris in sentences of extreme balance:

> On te rauit Vrie, et David t'est rendu;
> Tu gagnes beaucoup plus que tu n'auois perdu:
> Le Ciel t'oste vn soldat, vn Monarque il te donne.
>
> (p. 229)

But now the peripeteia occurs, as Nathan comes in and by his parable catches the conscience of David. The act and play end with Nathan's speech of absolution. A large proportion of the lines in each act is spoken by the chorus, which is significantly unspecified in nature and whose function is to provide lyrical-moralizing comments at the end of acts (or, in Act V, before the peripeteia). The subjects on which it meditates form, in order, a paradigm of the action. The chorus of Act I is on how *amor vincit omnia;* of Act II, on the sacredness of marriage; of Act III, on the terrible power of a tyrannical ruler; of Act IV, on the transitoriness of life; and of Act V, on how crimes will out and remorse will await the sinner.

As this will have indicated, in *David* the scriptural story has become purely a vehicle of moral generalizations. Nothing happens; all is said. Rhetoric is used to build the characters up into theoretically heroic positions. David in the first act, honor and love at war within him, has a lengthy, patterned sequence of lines, each starting "Suis-je ce grand Dauid qui . . . ?" which sets up the traditional figure of the Herculean hero conquered by love, and indeed the chorus comes in with the Hercules parallel:

> Hercvle auoit vaincu les monstres de la terre;
> Tout ce qui luy fist teste il le peut surmonter:
> Mais s'il fut indomptable au milieu de la guerre,
> Au milieu de la paix vn œil le sçeut donter.
> Amour n'est qu'vn enfant, mais sa puissance est grande.
> C'est vn aveugle Archer, mais il vise fort bien:
> C'est le plus grand des Rois puis qu'aux Rois il commande
> Et que de son seruage il ne s'exempte rien.
>
> (p. 207)

This is very much like the hubris of the David figure in one of Textor's dialogues, where David proudly declares his greatness and his scorn of any but divine love—

> Inter fatidicos prima est mihi gloria vates,
> Et mea prospiciunt praesagi verba prophetae,
> Ille ego sum David, tortae qui verbere fundae
> Magna Philistiae percussi membra gigantis.[36]

But there, too, Cupid shoots his arrow, and painfully David realizes, in the concluding words of the dialogue, that *Omnia vincit amor*. There is only one step from this image to the use of David in a *de casibus* tragedy; and thus we find him in Anthony Munday's *Mirrour of Mutabilitie* (1579), where he appears as a representative of the fall from high place through "Lecherye," warning the reader:

> You Princes great that rule in regall state,
> Beholde how I did blindly run astray:
> And brought my self unto destructions gate,
> But that my God redeemd me thence away.[37]

But Montchrestien does not seem to feel that the Fall of Princes is in itself a tragic enough subject, or that David is a satisfactory tragic hero, and so he places Uriah at the center of the tragic structure. He, even more than David, is allowed to build himself up to heroic stature:

> Mon cœur est grand et haut, mon ame ardente et pronte,
> Sensible au vitupere encor' plus qu'aux douleurs.

(p. 218)

The play, then, works as a kind of debate on the nature of heroism and of kingship, epitomized in the interchanges of David and Uriah and in the stichomythia between Nadab and David in Act III. Montchrestien did not want merely to teach a moral lesson. The biblical story would have appealed to him, too, because it was rich in situations of a potentially

---

36. *Dialogi* (cf. n. 16, above), fol. Bb 5ᵛ.

37. *The Mirrour of Mutabilitie, or the Principall Part of the Mirrour for Magistrates* (1579), fol. C 2ʳ.

antithetical kind—love versus honor in David, loyal soldier versus tyrannical ruler in Uriah's opposition to David, moral conscience versus exultant sinner in Nathan versus David.[38] The play becomes a pattern of antithetical positions, fine stuff for rhetorical monologues, sharp stichomythia, and choral meditations, but dramatically and spiritually stillborn.

What, in fact, we may see by comparing Montchrestien with Sachs, and with Peele, is something of the inherent weakness of a narrowly academic scriptural Seneca. The Senecan form was devised to accommodate the internal struggles of heroic minds, the stichomythic debates where such minds defined themselves more clearly, the violent physical actions which issued from them, and the remorse, torment, and punishment which followed. To achieve this out of the simple chronicle material of 2 Samuel would mean an inflation of figures, motives, and situations only possible if they were given a psychological depth which Montchrestien cannot master. (Later we shall see how another neo-Senecan, Honerdius, achieves this.)

What Montchrestien has also lost, because of his formal concentration on the single event, is the larger moral pattern which is implicit in the Bible and which is Peele's guiding idea: the effects of David's sin on his House. Seneca's is a drama of great individuals whose own tormented natures matter more than any hereditary curse over their House; and Montchrestien, as indeed his chosen structure forces him to do, treats David in isolation from his House. The play ends with Nathan's prophecy that the child of David and Bathsheba will die—thus not only before the first tangible occurrence of retribution but also well before the redemptory birth of Solomon which forms the "comic" conclusion of Sachs's play.

Montchrestien is here outside the main stream of sixteenth-century thought about David, for one of the fascinations his story held for the contemporary mind seems to have been its more extended moral perspective: the sin of the father being visited on the children and hence revisited onto the father himself. To some, David seemed the ideal hero of a moral tragedy; while on the one hand he was "a most mightie King, and . . . a

38. It is interesting to note that all the plays in Montchrestien's 1601 collection have exemplary subtitles—such as *Aman, ou la vanité* or *Les Lacènes, ou la constance*—but that in the 1604 ed. these have been removed: perhaps an indication that he did not want to think of himself as writing in a plainly homiletic vein. The sensuous delight with which he elaborates the bathing scene in *David, ou l'adultère* rather obscures the moralistic purpose.

most holie Prophet," the fortunes of his House, on the other hand, formed
an unequaled "monument . . . of so many and heinous crimes proceeding
out of one fact."[39] The connection between David's adultery, Amnon's
rape of his sister Tamar, Absalom's murder of Amnon, and finally
Absalom's rebellion and usurpation of the throne was used from the pulpit
as a stock example of the subtle way in which the Lord arranges his
retribution:

Even as he had dishonoured another mans childe / so sawe he shame upon his
owne children while he lyved / and that with greate wrechednesse. For Amnon
defloured Thamar his awne naturall sister. And they both were Dauids children
/ yet Absalom did miserably slaye Amnon his brother / for comytting that
wickednesse with his syster Thamar. Not long after / dyd the same Absalom
dryve his own naturall father Dauid out of his realme / & shamefully lay with
his fathers wifes. Whereupon there followed an horryble great slaughter / in
the whych Absalom was slayne with many thousands mo of the comen people.[40]

Peele's structure shows that this connection between David's sins and the
sexual disorders within his House, as well as civil strife within his realm,
was his organizing principle. In the Bible the rape of Tamar is subsequent
to the whole David and Bathsheba story, whereas in Peele's play it is fitted
in between David's adultery and the Lord's judgment, so that the thematic
link is implicit. It is also made explicit by David's reaction to the rape:

> Sin with his seuenfold crowne and purple robe,
> Begins his triumphs in my guiltie throne.
>
> (ll. 402–403)

Again with a modification of scriptural chronology, the news that Absalom has murdered Amnon is brought to David just after the capture of
Rabbah. This scene of victory is lamented by Sampley as a "digression,"[41]

39. *The Psalmes of Dauid . . . set forth in Latine by that excellent learned man
Theodore Beza. And faithfully translated into English, by Anthonie Gilbie* (London,
1581), p. 112.

40. Heinrich Bullinger, *The Christen State of Matrimonye*, trans. Myles Coverdale
(London, 1541), fol. 3^r–v.—Cf. the same Bullinger's *Fiftie Godlie and Learned
Sermons*, trans. "H. I." (London, 1587), p. 233, where the same point is made.

41. Arthur M. Sampley, "Plot Structure in Peele's Plays as a Test of Authorship,"
PMLA, LI (1936), 698.

and so it is from the "well-made" point of view; but it seems to me obvious
that Peele has here built up as effective a reversal—in visual and theatrical
as well as moral terms—as possible. David, having taken Rabbah (at whose
siege, we remember, Uriah was slain) and crowned himself with Hanun's
crown, is at the height of his power and glory—

> Beauteous and bright is he among the Tribes,
> As when the sunne attir'd in glist'ring robe,
> Comes dauncing from his orientall gate,
> And bridegroome-like hurles through the gloomy aire—
>
> (ll. 863–866)

when suddenly the glories of this Sun King are dashed by the message
that all his sons are dead. (A special poignancy is given here to that piece
of misreporting.) Similar reversals, theatrical and moral, form a leading
pattern in that part of the play which deals with Absalom's rebellion; and
I shall deal with these later on.

For the moment we must turn to the story of Tamar, Amnon, and
Absalom. Peele treats it concisely, with only two elaborations on the Bible
account. The first is Jonadab's speech while the rape is being committed. It
is out of character (as he had been the one to counsel Amnon to enjoy his
sister) and entirely choric; it aims not only to raise sympathy for Tamar—

> Now Thamar ripened are the holy fruits
> That grew on plants of thy virginitie,
> And rotten is thy name in Israel,
> Poore Thamar, little did thy louely hands
> Foretell an action of such violence,
> As to contend with Ammons lusty armes,
> Sinnewd with vigor of his kindlesse loue—
>
> (ll. 303–309)

but also, by implication, to relate Amnon's sexual crime to David's:

> Why should a Prince, whose power may command,
> Obey the rebell passions of his loue,
> When they contend but gainst his conscience,
> And may be gouernd or supprest by will.
>
> (ll. 296–299)

The second is Tamar's *Klagerede* after the rape, when she sees herself

> Cast as was Eua from that glorious soile
> (Where al delights sat bating wingd with thoughts,
> Ready to nestle in her naked breasts)
> To bare and barraine vales with floods made wast,
> To desart woods, and hils with lightening scorcht,
> With death, with shame, with hell, with horrour sit.
>
> (ll. 337–342)

The poetry here performs the function of realizing the emotional and moral state of a fall; and by the inversion of the Eden imagery from the bathing scene, the link with David's sin—as well as the sense that we are dealing with *all* sin—is kept.

Traditionally Amnon's rape was an *exemplum horrendum,* sometimes illustrating the Fall of Princes through lust,[42] sometimes a standard example of incest.[43] Peele, in concentrating on the plight of Tamar, shows more imagination. Dramatically his approach is a great deal more fruitful than that of Hans Sachs in his *Tragedia: Thamar die Tochter König Dauid mit irem Bruder Ammon vnd Absalom* (1556).[44] Sachs, too, connects the action with the David and Bathsheba story by giving David an opening speech about his guilt; and, as in Peele's play, the arrival of the news of the murder brings an ironic reversal into a scene where David muses on the happy and peaceful state of his kingdom. But his action leads up to an Epilogue which interprets the story typologically: David stands for God, who has two children; one—Tamar—is "die Christlich seel," the other—Amnon—is Satan. Absalom is God's vehicle of both retribution and consolation. The play is interesting to us chiefly, I think, as an indication that as late as 1556 a playwright could still ask his audience to keep together such (to us) disparate attitudes to a character as a cautionary and a typological one: David is, on the one hand, a human sinner and, on the other, a figure of God.

The story of David's children was obviously a subject which invited a

---

42. Munday, *Mirrour of Mutabilitie,* fol. I 3ᵛ.

43. Vives, *Instruction of a Christen Woman,* fol. M 1ᵛ.

44. *Das dritt vnd letzt Buch . . .* (1561; though the *Thamar* is dated, at the end, 1556), I, fol. 90ᵛ ff.

Senecan treatment of passion, incest, revenge, and fratricide, while at the same time it had a built-in opportunity for combining "tragicos cum pietate modos." [45] In three plays first published within a few years of each other, it was thus used. N. Chrestien des Croix wrote in French a tragedy, *Amnon et Thamar* (Rouen, 1608); and from the Low Countries there are two neo-Latin tragedies on the subject: *Thamara* (Leyden, 1611) by Rochus Honerdius (Roch van den Honert, *c.* 1572–1638), and *Amnon* (Ghent, 1617), by Jacobus Cornelius Lummenaeus à Marca (Jaques-Corneille van Lummene van Marcke, 1570–1629). [46] A detailed analysis of all these plays is out of the question here; all I want to show is how a comparison of structure and thematic emphasis in the three plays may bring out the different ways in which the same subject could be treated in what is, to a large extent, the same dramatic tradition. All three plays are neo-Senecan. They use a five-act structure with a chorus kept apart as commentator, a fairly unified action, and a relatively small number of characters. All are rhetorical rather than theatrical. In all, Amnon is given much scope to speak about the torments of his passion, Tamar to lament the outrage done to her, and Absalom to deliberate his revenge.

What initially distinguishes Chrestien's play from the two neo-Latin ones is that, while they put David at the moral center, Chrestien is writing a drama balanced between the two immoral individuals, Amnon and Absalom. David appears at the beginning of *Amnon et Thamar,* and is referred to throughout, as the godlike standard from which his two sons are aberrations. The pattern of concentration on villainy needs an ideal governor as a foil. Amnon wants his sister, Absalom wants the crown, to which Amnon is immediate heir; Amnon's rape gives Absalom the chance to combine moral revenge with the pursuit of political ambition:

> Dieu m'ouvre le moyen, & sans nul vitupere,
> De me deffaire en fin de ce pariure frere:

45. See the epigram by Hugo Grotius, in commendation of Honerdius' *Thamara* (Leyden, 1611), no page ref. Cf. n. 4, above.

46. In discussing these three plays, I use, and quote from, the following editions: *Les Tragedies de N. Chretien, Sieur des Croix Argentenois* (Rouen, 1608); *Rochi Honerdii . . . Supremi in Hollandia Consistori Senatoris, Thamara Tragoedia* (Leyden, 1611); *Amnon Tragoedia Sacra. Autore Rdo. Domino D. Iacobo Cornelio Lvmmenaeo à Marca* (Ghent, 1617).

> Frere mon premier né, & qui doit deuant moy
> Succeder à l'Estat de Dauid nostre Roy.

(p. 87)

Chrestien, then, has built out of the Bible story at least the beginnings of an intrigue play; the plot has some complexity, and motives and actions are neatly intertwined. Both Amnon and Absalom are Senecan heroes, contemplating with fascinated horror the deeds they are about to perpetrate. Amnon can no longer be interesting after the rape, so he is dropped—only to be brought on for a brisk on-stage murder in Act V—and Absalom comes to the fore in the second half of the play. All of Acts I and II are taken up with Amnon's struggles with his "Meurtriere Passion,"

> Qui condamne mon ame, & destruit mon honneur;

and in Act III he even reads his confidant a love poem he has written about Tamar.[47] In Act I, with a slight reminiscence of morality technique, he has a dream where an angel and a "Megere" appear to him, respectively to persuade him to sin and dissuade him from it. This parallelism of contrasted counsel is made a structural principle for the whole play, which is exceedingly symmetrically built up. Amnon has a good counselor—Ithai —with whom he debates in Act I the problems of love versus honor, good versus evil; he also has a bad counselor—Jonadab—with whom there is much stichomythic debating in Act III on the subjects of suicide and freedom of the will. Parallel to these deliberations are Absalom's two sets of stichomythia in Act II, with one good and one evil counselor. The dialogue between Absalom and Hushai becomes a debate on how to govern a state, with Absalom as the rebel and revolutionary and Hushai as the conservative speaker for king and country. In pointed contrast it is followed by the dialogue between Absalom and Ahitophel:

> ABSALON
> Mon Pere vit encor, & Amnon qui me passe.
> ARCHITOPHEL
> Il faut trouver moyen que ce frere trespasse.
> ABSALON
> Comment, tüer mon frere! ô forfait inhumain!

47. These "stances" use the image of Tamar as the sun and Amnon himself as an Icarus figure. Cf. the much more relevant use of this image in Peele's Prologue.

ARCHITOPHEL
Qui veut libre s'esbatre, oste le cruel frein.

ABSALON
Mais cest ébat, de Dieu le courroux nous attire.

ARCHITOPHEL
Ne desire donc point d'acquerir vn Empire.

ABSALON
Pourquoy, s'il est permis?

ARCHITOPHEL
Tu n'en as point de tel.

ABSALON
Mon Pere peut mourir, Amnon n'est immortel?

ARCHITOPHEL
La vie de ton frere est ta mort bien certaine.

(pp. 42–43)

This symmetry of contrasts is observed on the plane of sexual morality too. The first part of Act II presents Tamar as extremely pious, full of "l'amour vers Dieu" and ironically praying for her brothers' welfare, thus establishing a contrast with the ungodly passions of Amnon and also making the outrage on her more heinous; and we are also given a discussion between her and her women in which she appears as the mirror of chastity. The theme is taken up at the end of the act by the chorus of "Filles Iuifues," who sing the praises of chastity. Again, after the rape, there is a debate between her and her women about whether the violation of the body can also sully the spirit.

Altogether, then, *Amnon et Thamar* shows us a playwright interested in the Bible as Senecan raw material and (rather like Montchrestien) in this particular story for its possibilities as a scaffold for antithetical arguments. It brings home to one the weaknesses of the post-Garnier Senecan tradition in France: A subject that could have lent itself to the psychological and moral tensions of a *Phèdre,* or the examinations of divine justice of an *Athalie,* never rises in its execution above a chess play of moral axioms and rhetorical posturing. Chrestien's chosen scope does not allow him to show justice done on Absalom and his rebellious ambitions; the play ends as David has reconciled himself to the death of Amnon. Thus it remains morally lopsided.

If one sets side by side with *Amnon et Thamar* the *Amnon* of Lummenaeus à Marca, the difference in moral structure becomes imme-

diately apparent. Lummenaeus' scope is almost identical with Chrestien's:
He starts with Amnon lamenting his infatuation and ends with David's
reception of the news of Amnon's death at Absalom's hand. But his action
is firmly held in relation to David's own guilt. Act IV is largely one long
monologue of David's:

> Peccaui! & an diffitear? & crimen meum est,
> Quod fecit Amnon, publicum exemplum dedi,
> Et Bethsabea strauit incaesto viam;
>
> (p. 29)

and the chorus which follows takes up the same idea. There is little
theatrical interest in his structure. Everything happens offstage; the short
acts are made up either entirely of monologues (Acts I and III) or of a
combination of monologues and stichomythia; the choruses (by uni-
dentified speakers) are very long and meditate upon the situation by
giving examples—biblical and classical—of parallel situations. As in
Montchrestien's *David,* each act is in fact a static tableau. But within the
limits of a closet drama the play provides a dramatic tension between
human and divine revenge, Absalom's and the Lord's, with David as the
pivotal figure.

   Also, Lummenaeus à Marca's stichomythia, unlike Chrestien's, grows
from the situation rather than from theoretical concepts, and thus manages
to communicate a human content. In the following exchange between
Tamar and Absalom, the repetition of the words "frater" and "soror" is not
just rhetorical patterning; it acquires a symbolical value as an index to the
horror of the situation as it has to be spoken out by a sister and slowly
dawn on a brother:

> ABSALOMUS
> Quid me occupas insaniis? rursum iacet.
> THAMARA
> Crudelis Amnon!
> ABSALOMUS
> Tetigit.
> THAMARA
> Atrox, impie,
> Incæste, abominabilis semper mihi!
> Amnon! Iuuentæ carnifex turpis meæ!

ABSALOMUS

Frater?

THAMARA

Tacere liceat.

ABSALOMUS

& rursum implicas.

THAMARA

Frater pudorem rapuit incæstus meum.

ABSALOMUS

Frater? Sorori Virgini?

THAMARA

Parce obsecro.

ABSALOMUS

Amnon Thamaræ noxiam? & potuit ferus,
Et potuit? Amnon Virgini stuprum intulit?
Amnon? Sorori Virgini? . . .

(p. 16)

This exchange is, too, an ironic echo of Amnon's words in Act I, while he still struggles with his passion:

O sancta probitas! Virginem vt stupro occupem?
Frater sororem?

(p. 8)

The repetition of the phrase "Absalom omnes tulit," when in Act V David has got the false news that Absalom has killed all his sons, has the same quality of expanding the Bible story not just into rhetoric but into fully realized human moments.

Honerdius, in *Thamara*, carries this psychological probing one step further—so that Leicester Bradner can, with some justification, speak of him as a forerunner of Racine.[48] With even less external action than Lummenaeus à Marca, he has concentrated on the tension inside his characters even more, humanizing them rather than merely making them vehicles of rhetoric. The difference in titles between the two plays is significant, and is reflected in the way identical material has been handled. In *Amnon* the rape takes place between Acts I and III—before Tamar has appeared on the stage—and the revenge is thus made the central element in

48. "Latin Drama of the Renaissance," *Studies in the Renaissance,* IV (1957), 42–43.

the action. In *Thamara* the rape is delayed till between Acts III and IV, and the action stops short of the retributive murder of Amnon. (The last speech is Absalom's vow to avenge the crime against "nobis, sorori, legibus, regi, deo.") The structure thus gives a different emphasis to the story: Amnon's act is one which he has fought hard against and which, when it comes, is seen as done on a girl who is innocent, tender, and sympathetic. Also, unlike the case in *Amnon,* David impresses his sense of sin on the reader *before* the crime has been committed. Act II consists of a six-and-a-half-page monologue in which he speaks of the expiation of his sin; ironically he fears a fate for Amnon similar to that of his firstborn child with Bathsheba:

> Et morte pueri credidi falso scelus
> Satis piatum. poena sic iuxta suum
> Nefas stetisset . . .
>
> (p. 21)

The play's emphasis, then, is thrown on Tamar, in herself innocent, expiating David's sin. This, together with the central position of David in the play, confirms the didactic purpose which Honerdius states in his preface "Ad Lectorem":

Tota namque haec actio nihil aliud est quam implexa disciplina. Quid enim? . . . Thamarae injuria, parentum libidinem, liberorum contumelia plerumque expiari?

Honerdius was not a professional divine, and, as far as I am aware,[49] he wrote only one other play, and that also a neo-Latin biblical one, *Moses nomoclastes* (Leyden, 1611). I have not seen this tragedy, but the title suggests that he may have chosen the subject for its moral, rather than inherently exciting, nature. On the other hand, Lummenaeus à Marca, who was first a Capuchin and then a Benedictine monk, was a prolific writer, especially of scriptural plays; and in the collection of his works published as *Musae Lacrymantes* (Douai, 1628), we find not only the almost inevitable *Jephtha* but also plays on such topics as *Bustum Sodomae* and *Samson.* He seems to have had a good eye for a sensational biblical

---

49. I take my information on Honerdius from the *Biographie Universelle* (Paris, 1857), XIX, 387.

subject. That, however, he combined this with an interest in moral themes can be seen from his *Dives Epulo*—one of his *Tragoedia Sacra* (Ghent, 1617)—in which, though presented in richly classical imagery, all the characters apart from Dives and Lazarus are personified abstractions: Voluptas, Desperatio, Poenitentia, and so on.

After Chrestien's *Amnon et Thamar,* the two neo-Latin plays from the Low Countries would seem to go some way toward justifying a Christian Seneca. The tight form makes for a solemn, almost ritualistic acting out of the doom on the House of David; moral emphasis grows out of the action itself and is, especially in the case of Honerdius, supported by psychological realization of the human problems involved.

In his lines "Ad Lectorem" Honerdius also speaks of Absalom's *ambitio* as another of David's punishments, and thereby he provides a link with the next, and last, group of plays I want to deal with—plays treating the rebellion of Absalom, his usurpation of David's throne, David's flight, and Absalom's death. (This is the story of 2 Samuel XIV–XIX.) Obviously these events contain much material that is naturally dramatic—from the hubris of Absalom to the pity and terror of David's lament over his son.

In Peele's play, as I have already said, it is made clear that Absalom's insurrection is part of a pattern of personal guilt and civil disorder evolving from David's adultery and his misuse of kingly power in having Uriah killed. The pattern is emphasized by the very abruptness—a structural flaw if we look at it from the viewpoint of the "well-made" play—with which we move from the scene where David forgives Absalom's fratricide (scene ix) to that which follows: *"Enter Dauid . . . with others, Dauid barefoot, with some lose couering ouer his head, and all mourning"* (S.D., ll. 1020–1022). It is one of the many sudden and morally effective reversals typical of the play. David's opening speech here is a confession of sins, in which the body politic and the individual conscience are fused into one image:

> And to inflict a plague on Dauids sinne,
> He makes his bowels traitors to his breast,
> Winding about his heart with mortall gripes.
>
> (ll. 1033–1035)

By the use of Gospel imagery, Absalom is seen as the type of an anti-Christ:

> Ah Absalon the wrath of heauen inflames
> Thy scorched bosome with ambitious heat,
> And Sathan sets thee on a lustie tower,
> Shewing thy thoughts the pride of Israel
> Of choice to cast thee on her ruthlesse stones.
>
> (ll. 1035–1040)

David's guilt, then, in all its aspects—personal, domestic, national, and moral-allegorical—is the thematic unifier which makes the Absalom scenes an essential part of Peele's play. It functions in the totality of the play somewhat as the usurpation of Henry IV functions in the three *Henry VI* plays.[50] As in Shakespeare's trilogy, the underlying moral-political cause may be lost sight of within the individual scenes, but it is brought up at key points and it forms the framework of the whole. Some of Peele's scenes, like Ithai's demonstration of faithfulness or the cursing of Shimei, are in themselves moral tableaux, but they are not "digressions." Shimei's cursing, in particular, is very effectively and cogently handled: Not only is Shimei himself made the voice of David's conscience (unlike the source passage in the Bible where he merely refers to vengeance for the blood of Saul)—

> Euen as thy sinne hath still importund heauen,
> So shall thy murthers and adulterie
> Be punisht in the sight of Israel,
> As thou deserust with bloud, with death, and hell—
>
> (ll. 1363–1366)

but he also gives the king the opportunity of appearing as David Penitens—

> The sinnes of Dauid, printed in his browes,
> With bloud that blusheth for his conscience guilt—
>
> (ll. 1374–1375)

and above all as the Christian figure of Patience. The various episodes of this part of the play are, in fact, devoted to bringing out David's patience, as a refusal to despair:

50. Cf. E. M. W. Tillyard, *Shakespeare's History Plays* (London, Penguin, 1962), p. 147.

> I am not desperate Semei like thy selfe,
> But trust vnto the couenant of my God,
> Founded on mercie with repentance built,
> And finisht with the glorie of my soule.
>
> (ll. 1382–1385)

Most clearly the juxtaposition of despair with patience is brought out in the contrast, implied by the structure, between David and Ahitophel. In the Bible Ahitophel's suicide is dealt with very briefly:

And when Ahitophel saw that his counsel was not followed, he saddled his ass, and arose, and gat him home to his house, to his city, and put his household in order, and hanged himself, and died.

In Peele he is given a scene to himself (xiii), in which he makes a speech of nihilistic despair, leading up to the climax,

> And now thou hellish instrument of heauen,
> Once execute th'arrest of Ioues iust doome,
> And stop his breast that curseth Israel. *Exit.*
>
> (ll. 1502–1504)

The "hellish instrument of heaven" is explained by the stage direction: *"Achitophel solus with a halter."* The halter, the instrument of Judas' self-destruction, was well known as a symbol of despair, from pictorial representations and from dramatic as well as nondramatic literature.[51] As Ahitophel exits, he is like Despayre in *The Faerie Queene,* who, from a collection of murderous instruments,

> . . . chose an halter from among the rest,
> And with it hong himself, unbid, unblest.
>
> (Bk. I, canto ix)

Another moral contrast theatrically pointed throughout these scenes is that between Absalom's pride and David's humility. We move, for example, from David's laudable *apatheia*—

51. See S. C. Chew, "Time and Fortune," *ELH,* VI (1939), 83–113.

> Here lie I armed with an humble heart,
> T'imbrace the paines that anger shall impose,
> And kisse the sword my lord shall kill me with—
>
> (ll. 1114–1116)

to the next scene: *"Absalon, Amasa, Achitophel, with the concubines of Dauid, and others in great state, Absalon crowned"* (S.D., ll. 1160–1161); and it becomes obvious that even without Absalom's proud and self-infatuated speeches this would have struck the audience with the force of a visual emblem—just as the sight of Absalom hanging by his hair hardly needs Joab's words to point the irony of moral retribution:

> Rebell to nature, hate to heauen and earth,
>
> . . . .
>
> Now see the Lord hath tangled in a tree
> The health and glorie of thy stubborne heart,
> And made thy pride curbd with a sencelesse plant.
>
> (ll. 1579–1585)

Similar in many ways to the Absalom section of Peele's play is a *Tragedia Spirituale* by an Italian Franciscan friar, Pergiovanni Brunetto. *David Sconsolato* was first published in Florence in 1556 and appeared in several later editions.[52] In external shape it is a regular five-act tragedy, but its internal form is almost as episodic as the Bible story. Brunetto starts with Absalom's recall from banishment, expanding the scene of the widow from Tekoah; in Act II we see Absalom's growing rebelliousness; and only in Act III does the rebellion proper break out. Between David's flight from Jerusalem and his encounter with Shimei, the Bible has the episodes of Ittai, Zadok, Hushai, and Ziba. Out of these Peele has only included that

---

52. I have used, and quoted from, the 1586 edition. There were at least three separate editions: 1556 (though Rothschild, *Le Mistère du Viel Testament,* IV, lxxii, disputes its existence), 1586, and 1588; and the play was also published in Vol. III of *Raccolta di Rappresentazioni sacre* (Venice, 1605 and 1606). Despite the kind assistance of Professor Carlo Dionisotti, I have been able to find out very little about Brunetto. The title page of *David Sconsolato* describes him as "Frate di S. Francesco osseruante"; and Mazzuchelli, in *Scrittoria d'Italia,* II (1758 ed.), p. 2178, only adds that he flourished around the middle of the sixteenth century and wrote poetry in the vernacular. The bibliographical information above is also taken from Mazzuchelli, who lists no further works by Brunetto—whom, incidentally, he calls Brunetti.

of Ittai, the Gittite. He combines the others into the ritualized lamentation scene, ll. 1050–1071, where he gets the effect of a crowd of faithful followers round David, by lyrical rather than narrative or dramatic means. Brunetto, however, in a series of short scenes in Act III, includes and expands all the biblical episodes. In some ways, then, his structure is closer than Peele's to that of the mystery type of religious drama. But Brunetto's unifying theme, like Peele's—and as his title indicates—is that of David's sin; and here he makes effective use of a popular Senecan device. *David Sconsolato* opens with a prologue spoken by "Ombra del Figliuolo adulterino di Dauid," who expounds the whole tragic context in an atmosphere that is as much Senecan as biblical:

> Da le dannate grotte vscit' à luce
> Men vengo à voi presente ombra infelice,
> Del figlio adulterin, del Gran Dauide;
> Grande per certo per valor', & forte,
> Temuto, & ammirato in ciascun' Clima:
> Ma s'à le gent'indomite preualse,
> Epost'ha'l freno à molte ampie prouincie;
> Vinto si diede pur al van diletto,
> De le brutte bellezze d'vna Donna,
> Ne pote ritener in vita il figlio
> Che egli contra'l mondo, e contra'l Cielo
> Acquistò bruttamente, e chi puo mai
> Il voler impedir del grande Dio?

(no sig.)

He also dwells on the intermediary tragedy—

> Amnon Tamarre stupra sua sorella
> Et Absalon l'vccide per vendetta—

and predicts "La morte d'Absalon ch'ambizioso." And the curse on David's House, and its origin in the adultery, is harked back to throughout the play—notably by Bathsheba on her first appearance (I.iii).

Despite the Senecan opening, the play does not develop into a horror tragedy: Absalom's death is reported; Ahitophel—though, Timon-fashion, he gives us his epitaph—hangs himself offstage. It is, though, a strongly emotional play, with a great deal of human interest gained out of the many episodes. Unlike the more formal French tragedies we have looked at, this

play, with its wealth of characters and incidents, does create a strong sense
of context—House and city—for David. Contributing to this effect is the
chorus "di donne Gierosolimitane," which is used not only to provide
meditative odes (like the "O' miseri mortali" at the end of Act II) but also
to take part in the conversation and the action. Brunetto shows how
effective, in relation to this material, is the tendency of Italian humanist
tragedians of the sixteenth century to combine Senecan and Grecian
dramatic techniques.[53] His moral theme also forces him toward a tragedy
of double issue rather than a plain unhappy ending, in that the outcome is
a fall for Absalom (and Ahitophel) but is at the same time ultimately
happy—that is purgative—for David and his House. In the end David
himself takes the place of the chorus:

> Mal può letizia dar trafitto core
> Dicesi, & è ben vero,
> Spesso'n cibo soaue
> Mosca noiosa, & importuna cade,
> Dauid tropp'era liet'hor è beato,
> Al Regno ritornato,
> Se non moriua'l figlio,
> Ma così'n questo esiglio
> Il mal si purga, e illustrasi bontade.

Good has ultimately issued from evil, David disconsolate has become
David consoled; and in Hans Sachs's terms the play would be a *Comedia*,[54]
but like Peele's it remains formally the tragedy of Absalom. Yet its real
nature is best indicated by the woodcut which, twice repeated, illustrates
the play in the 1586 edition—one often used, too, to illustrate the Penitential Psalms in *Horae* (cf. Figure 2). It represents David kneeling in
contrition, his crown laid humbly aside, with God's grace, symbolized by
the sun, streaming down upon him. Brunetto could be used by either side
in the debate about the possibility of a Christian tragedy.

53. Cf. Kastner and Charlton, *Works of Sir William Alexander,* pp. lxiii–xciv;
and Herrick, *Tragicomedy,* pp. 93 ff.

54. Sachs himself did write a play on the Absalom story: *Ein Tragedi . . . der
auffrhüriske Absalom mit seinem Vatter König David (Das ander Buch . . .*
[Nuremberg, 1560], I, fol. xvii[r] ff.). This is an allegorical morality about good
fathers and bad children, good kings and rebellious subjects. The play itself is
dated 1551.

Clearly the ambitious Absalom, rather than the contrite David, was the more stimulating figure to anyone wanting to pour this particular biblical story into a neoclassical mould. We see this exemplified in the Latin MS play *Absalon,* of unknown authorship and date.[55] Whether it is by Bishop Watson or not is immaterial here, though it seems to me that the careful metrical annotations on the autograph manuscript would fit in with an author "who to this day would never suffer yet his *Absalon* to go abroad, and that onelie because, in *locis paribus, Anapestus* is twise or thrise vsed in stede of *Iambus.*"[56] Boas, who compares this play with Peele's, thinks that it "profits by comparison," for "in dexterous arrangement of material, in concentration of interest, and, above all, in psychological insight, *Absalon* is the work of an abler and more original playwright than Peele." [57] Boas' comparison, however, neglects the fact that Peele's whole intention and direction in this, the third, movement of his play were different from those of the classical scholar who penned *Absalon* into a neat five-act structure. Though the author of *Absalon* has not pressed his material into artificial conformity with the unities—like Brunetto he starts with Absalom's return from exile and ends with David's lament over Absalom's death—he has yet treated the Bible chronicle very selectively. According to the plan of a "well-made" play, he has subordinated the chosen events to an over-all study of rebellion and of the casting out of a tyrant. Absalom emerges as a typical Senecan tyrant figure; Ahitophel, as the bad counselor hoist with his own petard, who wittily rationalizes his particular form of suicide:

> Ergo nocentis vinculo vocis viam
> Obstingere est equū. scelus cōcepit hec,
> Periat eadem. solū placeat suspendiū.

(fol. 24ᵛ)

55. There is a unique manuscript in the British Museum: MS Stowe 957. It is discussed most fully by G. R. Churchill and Wolfgang Keller, "Die lateinischen Universitäts-Dramen in der Zeit der Königin Elisabeth," *Shakespeare Jahrbuch,* XXXIV (1898), 229–232, and by Boas, *University Drama,* Appendix I.—Unfortunately, a recent critical edition and translation of the play came to my notice too late for me to use it for this essay: John Hazel Smith, *A Humanist's "Trew Imitation": Thomas Watson's "Absalon"* (Urbana, 1964).

56. Ascham, *Scholemaster,* in *Elizabethan Critical Essays,* I, 24.

57. *University Drama,* p. 365.

We need only compare this situation to Peele's Ahitophel and his morally emblematic halter to see that the author's dramatic conception (as indeed Boas points out) is pagan rather than Christian. Although David is at one point (II.ii) made to recognize that what is happening is part of a retributive pattern, the structure itself does not bear out such a pattern. Although David is consoled at the end, he is so because Absalom deserved death rather than because Absalom's death was part of the ways of God to David. The author of *Absalon,* then, has admirably fulfilled his plan of constructing a classical tragedy out of biblical material; what he has not achieved, because he had no intention of doing so, is the creation of a spiritual pattern where, as in both Peele and Brunetto, divine comedy emerges out of tragedy. That this is the final direction of Peele's play becomes obvious when we turn to the scene which neither of the other Absalom plays dramatizes: that involving the accession of Solomon (xvii). To Boas and most other Peele critics, Peele's introduction of Solomon is particularly obnoxious; it "mars the emotional effect of Absalom's tragic fate and diverts the interest at a culminating point." [58] I would argue that, rather, it *directs* the interest—once we know what the interest is—*to* a culminating point.

Once we are clear—and I hope the preceding discussion has made that point—that it is not "the emotional effect of Absalom's tragic fate" Peele is primarily after, but the working out of moral and civil disorder within the House of David, then it also becomes clear that Solomon at the end of *David and Bethsabe* has a function that can be compared, however cautiously, with Richmond's at the end of *Richard III* or even Fortinbras' at the end of *Hamlet.* After the disorders in the House and the strife within the kingdom, here is the good son, figure of the future. Solomon's establishment in the succession of David means not merely the rooting out of evil from the House and realm of David but also the enthronement of good. Yet the use of Solomon, with the distortion of biblical chronology which it involves, has reverberations of a more general moral significance. Solomon is the son whom David begot on Bathsheba, with the Lord's blessing, after the child of adultery had died. We have already seen how his birth forms the resolution of Hans Sachs's *Comedia* on the adultery and how the conception of "another Sonne, That may be loued of the Lord of

58. *Ibid.*

hosts" formed the happy resolution of the first movement of Peele's play. Nor would the audience have forgotten that this was the son who was to carry on the line of Jesse—the House of David—toward the Messiah. In Bale's interlude, *The chefe promyses of God unto men,* the Lord turns from rebuking David to his promise:

> A frute there shall come, forth yssuynge from thy bodye,
> Whom I wyll aduance, vpon thy seate for euer.
> Hys trone shall become, a seate of heauenlye glorye,
> Hys worthy scepture, from ryght wyll not dysseuer,
> Hys happye kyngedome, of faythe, shall perysh neuer.
> Of heauen and of earthe, he was autor pryncypall,
> And wyll contynue, though they do perysh all.[59]

Of this fruit, Solomon is a prefiguration; the promise embodied in him reaches forward to the end of all sin. But we have also seen how, through the imagery of the play and through the traditional associations of the audience, David's sin reaches back to Adam's, to the beginning of all sin. At this point, the particular form of the Solomon scene becomes of interest. It has long been known that Peele here shamelessly incorporates a large number of lines almost literally translated from Du Bartas' *Les Artifices.*[60] In *Les Artifices* Du Bartas presents Adam in a state of poetic-prophetic "fureur secrete," in which he sees the future of his race and describes it to his son Seth. Now, Seth was the son of Adam and Eve who represented *their* special promise:

For God, said she, hath appointed me another seed instead of Abel, whom Cain slew.

(Genesis IV.25)

And so Peele is not just plagiarizing when he modifies Du Bartas' words into what he would see as a parallel situation—for Adam showing the future of the world to Seth is like David handing over to Solomon his House and his vision,

---

59. *The chefe promyses of God,* fol. D 2ʳ.
60. See P. H. Cheffaud, *George Peele* (Paris, 1913), esp. p. 131; and H. D. Sykes, "Peele's Borrowings from Du Bartas," *NQ,* CXLVII (1924), 349–351, 368–369.

Of all our actions now before thine eyes,
From Adam to the end of Adams seed.

(ll. 1821–1822)

He is using Du Bartas' material more organically than Du Bartas himself
had done, for the "fureur secrete" which seizes Du Bartas' Adam is
spiritually less motivated than the fury that moves David to prayer—

Transforme me from this flesh, that I may liue
Before my death, regenerate with thee.
O thou great God, rauish my earthly sprite,
That for the time a more then humane skill
May feed the Organons of all my sence—

(ll. 1829–1833)

and that "ravisheth" the soul of Solomon. Peele has given us the Psalmist,
the inspired David of the Psalter, and in so doing he has linked the scene
up with the invocation to the play:

And when his consecrated fingers strooke
The golden wiers of his rauishing harpe,
He gaue alarum to the host of heauen,
That wing'd with lightning, brake the clouds and cast
Their christall armor, at his conquering feet.

(ll. 10–14)

He has not simply improved on his source in using it; he has also given us
an indication, by the Adam-David analogy, of the dramatic structure
which his contemporary audience—whether they knew Du Bartas or not—
would, I think, have sensed in the "epic" drama on "Israel's sweetest
singer": the rhythm of God's promises, of Paradise lost and regained. It is
at this point, I think, that we can see why Peele inserted the succession of
Solomon before the reception of the news of Absalom's death: The final
part of this scene gives in an epitome the spiritual progress that the whole
play acts out.

With one of the sudden reversals which we have seen as typical of the
play, Absalom's death sends David from the highest celestial communion
to the lowest human despair, in which he sees his poetry, the link between
him and God, as shattered:

Then let them tosse my broken Lute to heauen,
Euen to his hands that beats me with the strings,
To shew how sadly his poore sheepeheard sings.
He goes to his pauillion, and sits close a while.

(ll. 1908–1911)

In the Bible, Nathan is not in this episode (2 Samuel XIX), but in the play he is, to echo and complete his role as a moral conscience. It is he who points out to David that he is sinking into the sin of despair:

These violent passions come not from aboue,
Dauid and Bethsabe offend the highest,
To mourne in this immeasurable sort.

(ll. 1922–1924)

And after Joab's persuasion (which follows the Bible in appealing on the point of national unity), in defiance of psychological probability but in fulfillment of the spiritual pattern, David "riseth up," to pronounce a *Lycidas*-like apotheosis of Absalom. Boas finds this last move on Peele's part "still more incongruous with the general scheme and spirit of the play" and speaks of "David's amazing final rhapsody upon Absalom's joy in the beatific vision of the Triune Deity."[61] But David's restoration to spiritual health, and his vision of a forgiven and beatific Absalom, both summarize and complete what I hope we have by now seen as the over-all "scheme" of the play. Though infinitely more inarticulate, intellectually and structurally, than Milton's mighty edifice, Peele's *David and Bethsabe* yet anticipates the epic on the Fall and the Redemption.

In the end the closest parallel to *David and Bethsabe* among all the documents I have discussed here may be the *Horae* illustration reproduced in Figure 2: Both consist of fragments from the story of David, held together under the one unifying vision of sin and grace. By the standards of "well-made" structure, smooth-flowing story, and consistent characters,

61. *University Drama,* p. 365.—I should not like to conclude this essay without thanking all the friends and colleagues who, over the last few years, have helped me to collect David material—especially Mr. Bernard Harris, Professor G. K. Hunter, Miss Joan Grundy, and Mr. Brian Nellist. I should also like to thank Mr. David Cook for discussing *Horae* illustrations with me, and the staff of the Warburg Institute for letting me look at the Institute's collection of Renaissance biblical pictures.

Peele's play is clearly inferior to the humanist tragedies on the same biblical subject written in other languages. But by the standards of its own elastic pattern—glorying in the sin as much as in the redemption—it is not less but more humanist. Perhaps his position in time and space, and the freedom from the tyranny of external form which it implied, gave Peele a better chance than any of the others who dramatized the story of the House of David—a chance to embody in a dramatic structure, however badly made, the glory that was the Renaissance.

Forms and Functions
of the Play within a Play

Dieter Mehl

T|o trace the development of some particular dramatic convention or element of style throughout the Elizabethan and Jacobean period is a critical method that can often produce illuminating results and contribute much to our understanding of dramatic art in the Renaissance. There have been very useful and stimulating studies of the development of dramatic speech, of the ghost scenes, of dramatic exposition, and of the play metaphor; I have myself attempted to describe the history of a minor dramatic device, the dumb show.[1] One conclusion reached by most of these studies seems to be that each one of these dramatic conventions underwent remarkable changes, which in turn reflect general changes in dramatic technique and literary taste, and that they can therefore be understood only within their context. The latter point seems to me particularly important, although it has not always received due consideration, or has been evaded

---

1. See W. Clemen, *English Tragedy before Shakespeare: The Development of Dramatic Speech* (London, 1961); G. Dahinten, *Die Geisterszene in der Tragödie vor Shakespeare* (Göttingen, 1958); E. Th. Sehrt, *Der dramatische Auftakt in der Elisabethanischen Tragödie* (Göttingen, 1960); A. Righter, *Shakespeare and the Idea of the Play* (London, 1962); and my *The Elizabethan Dumb Show: The History of a Dramatic Convention* (London, 1965).

41

by a limited selection of material, e.g., by excluding certain types of plays.

It is by now a commonplace that the device of the play within a play enjoyed particular favor with English dramatists throughout the Renaissance period. It is employed, in some form or other, in a great many plays and by widely differing playwrights, but it is also much more complex and less easily defined than many other dramatic conventions, such as the dumb show or the prologue, and this is perhaps the reason why there has been much incidental comment on plays within plays but hardly any attempt to treat the subject comprehensively.[2] I am not even sure whether it would be possible at all, because such a bewildering variety of forms would have to be included, making fruitful comparison very difficult indeed. Rather than outline once more the history of the play within a play, I shall therefore try to indicate briefly the wide range of this convention and its affinity to other dramatic devices employed by English playwrights. Such an unsystematic and necessarily incomplete survey may perhaps lead to further investigation along similar lines.

It is hardly surprising to see that the convention of the play within a play is to be found mainly in periods when not only dramatic literature but also theatrical practice was flourishing, when dramatists experimented with established forms, and—perhaps most important of all—when the purpose and function of drama and its illusionary character were subjects for searching discussion. All this is particularly true of the Elizabethan period. Drama then was entertainment for the masses as well as for the "judi-

2. There are some useful surveys: H. Schwab, *Das Schauspiel im Schauspiel zur Zeit Shaksperes* (Wien-Leipzig, 1896); F. S. Boas, "The Play within the Play," *A Series of Papers on Shakespeare and the Theatre* (The Shakespeare Association, 1925-1926), pp. 134-156; A. Brown, "The Play within a Play: An Elizabethan Dramatic Device," *Essays and Studies* (1960), pp. 36-48. Some aesthetic and philosophical implications are discussed by J. Voigt, *Das Spiel im Spiel* (Diss., Göttingen, 1954); R. J. Nelson, *Play within a Play: The Dramatist's Conception of His Art: Shakespeare to Anouilh* (New Haven, 1958); and, with special reference to Shakespeare, by L. A. Fiedler, "The Defense of the Illusion and the Creation of Myth," *English Institute Essays* (1948), pp. 74-94, and W. Iser, "Das Spiel im Spiel. Formen dramatischer Illusion bei Shakespeare," *Archiv für das Studium der neueren Sprachen und Literaturen,* CXCVIII (1961 / 1962), 209-226. See also my article "Zur Entwicklung des 'Play within a Play' im elisabethanischen Drama," *Shakespeare-Jahrbuch,* XCVII (1961), 134-152, on which some parts of the present essay are based.

cious"; it supplied uninhibited fun as well as moral instruction and questioning. Above all, the stage was but an emblem of the world at large; it was understood to "hold a mirror up to nature," not only by the subject matter of the performance but also by being a continual reminder of the discrepancy between appearance and reality.[3]

All this seems to me to bear directly on the many-sided use of plays within plays in English Renaissance drama. Just as numerous plays contained scenes of crude merriment and of dry moralizing side by side, we find inserted plays that take the form of tragedies within comedy, or vice versa. Indeed, perhaps the first thing that must be said about the play within a play is that it was not confined to any particular dramatic type. We find it in comedies, histories, and tragedies. Similarly, the plays inserted can be anything from a short dumb show to a complete little tragedy. They can be pure entertainment, literary parody, or moral exemplum. Without attempting a systematic classification, which would probably not be very helpful, I wish to point out some distinctly different types of plays within plays that were developed by Elizabethan and Jacobean dramatists to suit their particular dramatic purposes.

The simplest and most obvious device is of course the introduction of a company of actors within a play, who then perform some kind of play themselves before an audience made up of characters from the "main" play. *Sir Thomas More* (*c.* 1595) is a good example of this type. Here the actors are separated completely from the other characters of the drama, and the play performed by them, a scene from *Lusty Juventus,* seems to bear no obvious relation to the main action. The device is employed chiefly to provide some comic relief after some more serious scenes of state and to give an illustration of More's buoyant sense of fun and his love of the theater.[4] It is he who links the two planes of action by suddenly joining in the play to replace some actor who has failed to appear. It becomes clear, even from this somewhat heavy-handed use of the play within a play, that for the author the main interest of this device lay in the interaction

3. See M. C. Bradbrook, *Themes and Conventions of Elizabethan Tragedy,* 2nd ed. (Cambridge, 1957), pp. 75 ff.; M. Doran, *Endeavors of Art* (Madison, 1954), pp. 93 ff.; and Righter, *Shakespeare and the Idea of the Play, passim.*

4. Cf. the brief discussion by Brown, "Play within a Play," p. 39. The dates given in round brackets are those suggested in Alfred Harbage, *Annals of English Drama, 975–1700,* rev. S. Schoenbaum (London, 1964).

between the two levels of dramatic performance. The attention of the audience in the theater is directed not so much at the inserted play for its own sake but at the reaction of the spectators on the stage. The more skillful dramatists often took care not to make the inserted play too absorbing, so as not to distract the audience. This applies to many of the plays discussed here, particularly to *The Murder of Gonzago,* which technically also belongs to this first and most simple type of play within a play: A group of itinerant players arrives and performs a tragedy which is completely different from the "main" play in tone and character.

A thorough discussion of the play scene in *Hamlet* is beyond the scope of this paper.[5] It is enough here to emphasize how skillfully the play is integrated into the context of Hamlet's tragedy. Again it is chiefly the impression made on the spectators that is the center of dramatic interest, and here also lies, I believe—apart from some incidental satire—the reason for the introduction of a dumb show which gives a brief outline of the play that is to follow and thus largely satisfies the audience's curiosity as to its plot. After the dumb show the attention of the spectators can be focused on Hamlet and the court, who watch the performance. Another important aspect of this scene is that here drama is employed not so much as entertainment but as a moral weapon. Every serious Elizabethan dramatist hoped that his tragedies would "make mad the guilty and appal the free." In *Hamlet* this moral function of drama is put to the test in full view of the audience and is at the same time used as a means of creating a maximum of dramatic suspense. It is hardly necessary to point out how masterfully the attention and sympathy of the audience (in the theater) is manipulated here. Like Hamlet we are watching the king very closely, but we are at the same time following Hamlet's own movements and speeches with great excitement until, in the end, we know that his device has only partly succeeded because he has betrayed himself more than the king and has done nothing toward achieving his revenge.[6]

5. Cf. my chapter on *Hamlet* in *The Elizabethan Dumb Show,* pp. 110–120, where the most important studies of the play scene are listed. See also F. Fergusson, *The Idea of a Theater* (Princeton, 1949), pp. 120–127, for a more general discussion.

6. "His triumph in unmasking the King has led to no practical decision. The mountain has laboured and brought forth a mouse. . . . His [Hamlet's] principal task is forgotten." L. L. Schücking, *The Meaning of Hamlet* (London, 1937), pp. 135–136.

In *Hamlet* as well as in *Sir Thomas More* the play is performed by a group of professional actors. This of course gives the author a particularly good opportunity to comment on contemporary stage practices and to define his own views about the proper function of drama—as could also be illustrated by quotations from many other plays, although there are very few in which these problems are discussed so seriously as in *Hamlet*. In several others the play that is introduced serves mainly as an entertainment.

As an example of a quite different kind one could mention Beaumont and Fletcher's *The Maid's Tragedy* (*c.* 1610). Here we are not explicitly told who actually performs the masque in the first act; it is at any rate quite separate from the rest of the play. We watch all the bustle of preparation, the spectators crowding to get to see the performance; an atmosphere of intense expectation is created. There is also, at the very beginning of the play, some rather scornful criticism of the whole practice of such masques; they are said to be "tied to rules of flattery."[7] The masque that is then presented is quite long (nearly two hundred lines) and is played through without any interruption from the spectators. Its main dramatic function seems to be to provide a vivid contrast between the first act, with its festive court setting, and the second, far more intimate and intense act in which the hideous truth behind the gay façade is revealed. The masque evokes an impressive if conventional picture of the happiness in store for the newlyweds; in the light of the following events this turns out to be ludicrously inappropriate. The play within the play here is an instrument of Fletcher's overdeliberate, almost brutal irony, his often somewhat strained hunting for sensational surprises. As such it is very much in keeping with the dramatic technique employed throughout *The Maid's Tragedy*.

If we turn from this play to Shakespeare's *The Tempest* (*c.* 1611), however, we find that the wedding masque conjured up by Prospero, so different from Fletcher's, again fits in particularly well with the general tone of the play and its theme. It is an elaborate demonstration of Prospero's magic art and a most appropriate tribute to the marriage of Ferdinand and Miranda, who watch the performance and only once interrupt it to voice their admiration and astonishment. As well as

---

7. Cf. C. Leech, *The John Fletcher Plays* (London, 1962), pp. 120–122.

emphasizing that nothing but perfect harmony will be the result of the lovers' union, the masque contributes to the airy and fleeting character of the play, in which there are several such apparitions and in which the illusionary character of dramatic performance is several times insisted on.[8]

In the plays discussed so far—and several others could be cited—the inserted play was performed either by actors who had nothing to do with the other characters of the play or by spirits conjured up for the purpose. The two levels of acting were kept entirely separate, and no confusion of identities, of the part acted and the character behind it, was possible. Another type of play within a play is that performed by characters from the "main" play itself. This device appears to have been far more frequent than the first because it was particularly flexible and could be adapted to almost any type of play. It also enabled the dramatist to make the interrelation between the two planes of dramatic action far more subtle and intriguing.

Shakespeare's *A Midsummer Night's Dream* (*c.* 1595) is a comparatively simple case. We watch the preparations for the play to be performed, and the rehearsals as well as the performance itself are full of amusing comments on acting and dramatic art in general. Moreover, the play of Pyramus and Thisbe not only parodies certain dramatic conventions, but, as has often been noticed, bears an obvious relation to the "main" play by giving, in grotesque distortion, another example of romantic love.[9] There even seems to be some good-humored satire on dramatic conventions employed quite seriously in the "main" play. On the other hand, there is not very much interaction between the two sets of characters. Except for "Bottom's Dream," they are practically kept separate throughout the play, and the inserted tragedy is distinctly different from the rest of the play.

A much more complicated, though perhaps not very subtle, use of the same device occurs in Kyd's *The Spanish Tragedy* (*c.* 1587). It is one of the earliest examples, if not the earliest, of the play within a play. Here the play

8. See the interesting chapter on *The Tempest* in J. Kott, *Shakespeare Our Contemporary* (London, 1964), pp. 174–216, where it is called a "play within a play" (p. 180). I find Nelson's interpretation less convincing (*Play within a Play,* pp. 30–35).

9. See the discussion by Brown ("Play within a Play," pp. 47–48) and the edition by Clemen (The Signet Classic Shakespeare [New York, 1963]), pp. xxxiv–xxxvii.

to be performed is devised and prepared by the play's protagonist, Hieronimo, who acts as Master of the Revels and plans to carry out his revenge under the guise of a courtly entertainment.[10] The main interest of the scene lies, I think, in the deliberate blurring of the dividing line between reality and dramatic illusion. When Hieronimo announces, "I'll play the murderer" (IV.i.133), we already suspect a double meaning in the phrase. The king and the court, however, suspect nothing. When the play is performed, Hieronimo and Bellimperia are still applauded for their realistic acting, when in fact they have already overstepped the limits of the play and executed their revenge in earnest. Then Hieronimo, as a kind of chorus, informs the audience. This sudden transition from illusion to actuality (on the stage) provides a rather sensational stage effect, but it also points to a deeper problem: the nature of dramatic illusion and its bearing on reality.

This problem we find explored in a great many Elizabethan plays. After Kyd, as is well known, the introduction of a play or a masque became a regular feature in revenge tragedies. We find it in Marston's *Antonio's Revenge* (*c.* 1600), in Tourneur's *The Revenger's Tragedy* (*c.* 1606), and, in a rather grotesque way, in Middleton's *Women Beware Women* (*c.* 1621). In Tourneur's play the masque is a particularly appropriate means of carrying out the revenge because the whole tragedy is concerned with the question of disguise and masking. Disguise metaphors are particularly frequent;[11] masques are "treasons licence" (V.i.196), and in them people are "Putting on better faces then their owne" (I.iv.35). Thus the introduction of a masque at the end is in keeping with Tourneur's dramatic style, but the masque is rather too short to be called a play within a play.

In *Women Beware Women,* however, the device is exploited to the full.[12] It is perhaps too ingenious and sensational to be artistically convinc-

10. Cf. the edition by P. Edwards (The Revels Plays [London, 1959]), from which I quote, and my discussion in *The Elizabethan Dumb Show*, pp. 63–71.

11. See especially L. G. Salingar, *"The Revenger's Tragedy* and the Morality Tradition," *Scrutiny*, VI (1937–1938), 402–424; P. Lisca, *"The Revenger's Tragedy:* A Study in Irony," *PQ*, XXXVIII (1959), 242–251; and I-S. Ekeblad, "On the Authorship of *The Revenger's Tragedy," English Studies*, XLI (1960), 225–240. I quote from A. Nicoll's edition (London, 1929).

12. I quote from A. H. Bullen's edition (London, 1885–1886), VI. Cf. also S. Schoenbaum, *Middleton's Tragedies: A Critical Study* (New York, 1955), pp. 130–131.

ing, but it is remarkable for its pointed use of stage properties and dramatic irony and for its ambiguous treatment of dramatic illusion. As in *The Spanish Tragedy,* the spectators are still wondering about the plot of the play when the first "real" murder has already been executed:

> LIVIA (*as Juno*)
> *Now, for a sign of wealth and golden days,*
> *Bright-ey'd prosperity—which all couples love,*
> *Ay, and makes love—take that; our brother Jove*
> *Never denies us of his burning treasure*
> *To express bounty.*
>   [*Isabella falls down and dies.*]
>   DUKE
> She falls down upon't;
> What's the conceit of that?
>   FABRICIO
> As o'erjoy'd belike:
> Too much prosperity o'erjoys us all,
> And she has her lapful, it seems, my lord.
>   DUKE
> This swerves a little from the argument though:
> Look you, my lords.
>   [*Showing paper.*]
>   GUARDIANO
> All's fast: now comes my part to tole him hither;
> Then, with a stamp given, he's despatch'd as cunningly
>   [*Aside.*]
>
>   (V. i. 155–165)

A similar use of masques at the climax of the play is also to be found in some comedies rather akin in structure to the tragedies of revenge. Marston's *The Malcontent* (*c.* 1604) is a good example of this type. Here, too, the unmasking of the villains is achieved by means of a performance at the end of the play, although it does not end in wholesale slaughter as do the revenge tragedies. Middleton's *Your Five Gallants* (*c.* 1605) employs a similar technique. By assuming disguises, the five gallants reveal themselves as what they really are and precipitate their own downfall. The performance here brings out the sharp contrast between appearance and reality, between a person's assumed role and his real character. In all these plays the inserted performances are often no more than a brief masque or dance; but all seem in some measure to be derived from *The Spanish Tragedy,* and all play more or less skillfully on the spectator's awareness of what is actually going on. They all use disguise and acting for purposes of deception and mischief.[13]

It is clear that this motif lends itself particularly well to comic treatment, and it is indeed in comedies that we find the most intriguing use of plays within plays. Middleton seems to have been particularly fond of the device and introduced it with skillful variations into several of his comedies, most ingeniously perhaps in *A Mad World, My Masters* (*c.* 1606), where the play is not only a trick to extort some valuables from the chief spectator (as also happens more crudely in *Hengist, King of Kent*), but where even an "outsider," a constable who threatens to unmask the actors, is unexpectedly dragged into the play and tied fast before the eyes of the spectators, who completely fail to see where the play ends and the practical joke begins. They are vastly amused ("I am deceived, if this prove not a merry comedy and a witty," V.ii.129–130) and even help to confuse the identities: "This is some new player now; they put all their fools to the constable's part still" (V.ii.86–87).[14] Similarly, in *Hengist* (*c.* 1618), Simon insists on being cheated because he wants to take part in the play, while the actor-cheats really mean business and disappear with the properties. Both plays delight in statements which emphasize this ambiguity and leave the listener uncertain as to their true meaning. Thus the Second Cheater warns Simon, who wants to play the clown's part in the comedy: "Good sir tempt me not, my part is soe written that I should cheat your worship: and you were my father."[15] Simon thinks all this refers only to the play and agrees to be cheated.

---

13. There is an interesting scene in the history play *Woodstock* in which King Richard II and some of his men perform a masque before Woodstock immediately before his arrest. Cf. A. P. Rossiter's edition (London, 1946), iv.2. The masque seems to have been introduced mainly for the sake of dramatic contrast.

14. Vol. III of Bullen's edition.

15. Cf. R. C. Bald's edition (New York, 1938), V.i.309 ff; I have lowered superior letters and expanded abbreviations. A similar use of a performance for the purpose of gulling can be found in Robert Tailor's *The Hog Hath Lost His Pearl*. Here, however, the "cheaters" appear in the guise of spirits, not actors.

Similarly, in Middleton and Rowley's *The Spanish Gipsy* (1623) the demarcation line between the play proper and the play within the play is blurred. Here, however, it is the main "actor" (a young gentleman disguised as actor) who has to learn that there is more to the play than he realizes at first. His own father, who sees through the disguise, makes up the plot of a play in which a prodigal son is severely reprimanded by his father. Thus the son (playing the son's part) is prepared by the play for the reception he will meet afterward from his "real" father. A reader of these comedies may sometimes wonder whether the characters are still acting their parts or speaking in person.

This complex use of the play within a play, often resulting in startling shifts of identities and deliberate confusion of the spectators (both on the stage and in the theater), seems to be a distinctly Jacobean feature. In most earlier plays there is a fairly clear-cut division between the two levels of acting, which nevertheless can be just as dramatically effective as the more surprising and novel techniques of later dramatists. For all their ingenuity, Middleton's comedies are no more dramatically coherent and expressive than many earlier plays. There is rarely a deep probing into the problem of reality and illusion in them, but rather a frivolous and lighthearted experimenting with dramatic conventions. They mark, however, a noticeable advance in artistic consciousness and originality of dramatic technique.

This also applies, I would suggest, to the most elaborate example of plays within plays, Massinger's *The Roman Actor* (1626). It is a particularly good specimen of the complex and often contrived structure of many Jacobean plays, but it is a play that for its very adroitness leaves one cold.[16] It could almost be called a scientific exploration of various ways in which plays can be introduced into other plays. The first play is staged (rather like *The Murder of Gonzago*) to exercise a salutary moral effect on some hardened sinner in the audience, but the device fails and the character addressed derives quite a different moral from the play. The second performance illustrates how a play can be mistaken for reality. Domitia

---

16. I am not quite certain whether Brown means more than this when he says, "So skilful a use of the play within a play is, I believe, unparalleled in Elizabethan tragedy" ("Play within a Play," p. 45). Mere elaboration of certain conventions does not always make a good play. I quote from the Gifford edition (London, 1813), II.

betrays her love for Paris by her violent reaction to the performance in which he is about to commit suicide:

PARIS (*as Iphis*)
                              . . . *at your gate,*
As a trophy of your pride and my affliction,
I'll presently hang myself.
              DOMITIA
              Not for the world—
[*Starts from her seat.*]
Restrain him, as you love your lives!
              CÆSAR
              Why are you
Transported thus, Domitia? 'tis a play;
Or, grant it serious, it at no part merits
This passion in you.
              PARIS
              I ne'er purposed, madam,
To do the deed in earnest; though I bow
To your care and tenderness of me.
              DOMITIA
              Let me, sir,
Entreat your pardon; what I saw presented,
Carried me beyond myself.

                                        (III. ii. 387)

This is the opposite technique to that employed in *The Spanish Tragedy* and *Women Beware Women,* in which reality was mistaken for a play. Here the spectator is unmasked by the performance. Illusion serves to bring out reality. By mistaking the play for actuality, the spectator lays bare her deepest emotions. The third play illustrates another technique, the use of a play as a means of revenge, although here the device is not chosen for its efficiency but because it is considered fitting that the famous actor should die in an appropriate and dignified manner, i.e., on stage and in the course of a performance. The play performed partly parallels the action of the "main" play. Both the emperor and the actor seem to play their own lives over again up to the point where play and reality merge into one and the actor is stabbed to death by the jealous emperor. For pure ingenuity this tragedy has no equal among Jacobean plays, but the consistent exploitation of the play motif seems rather too deliberate to be entirely convincing.

There were, however, several other methods of presenting plays within plays. One device found quite frequently was that of "framing" a play and of thus removing it a step further from the audience in the theater. Whereas in all the cases we have considered so far, the "outer" play was the "main" play and the "inner" play only provided an incidental comment on it, usually confined to one or two scenes, the "framed" plays are as a rule far more substantial and extensive than the "frame," which in many cases is very slender. A case in point is Shakespeare's *Taming of the Shrew* (*c*. 1594). Shakespeare introduced some play metaphors into the "Induction" of the comedy and tried to make it more credible, yet he seems to have been so little interested in the frame that he dropped it completely after the first act; whereas *The Taming of a Shrew* has four interruptions by the tinker and is rounded off by his awakening, when he comments on the play and decides to apply its "moral" to his own domestic situation: [17]

> I know now how to tame a shrew,
> I dreamt upon it all this night till now.
>
> (xix. 15–16)

Possibly Shakespeare in fact devised a subtler ending which has been lost, but it might be argued that for him the main purpose of the frame was fulfilled with the Induction: to give the impression that we are not simply watching a play, but a performance, a dream, an illusion. Here, of course, the play is introduced mainly as an entertainment, and the lighthearted plot of the Induction, too, emphasizes the amusing character of the whole performance.

Sometimes, however, and this seems to be a technique developed by the "University Wits," the frame serves to introduce a play that is not so much an entertainment as a dramatic exemplum, a demonstration of some moral. One of the earliest examples of this use of the "framed" play is the anonymous *The Rare Triumphs of Love and Fortune* (1582). Here the frame consists of a formal debate between Venus and Fortune, with

17. Cf. G. Bullough, *Narrative and Dramatic Sources of Shakespeare* (London, 1957), I, for the text of *The Taming of a Shrew* and a discussion of its relation to Shakespeare's play. See also Righter, *Shakespeare and the Idea of the Play*, pp. 104–106, and the very useful article by R. Hosley, "Was There a 'Dramatic Epilogue' to *The Taming of the Shrew?*" *SEL*, I (1961), 17–34, where it is convincingly argued that Shakespeare did *not* write a "dramatic epilogue" to the play.

Jupiter acting as arbiter. As the quarrel cannot be decided by arguments, a
series of historical "shows," i.e., *tableaux vivants,* presenting famous
victims of the power of Love and Fortune, is produced by Mercury. Even
this, however, proves to be inconclusive, whereupon Jupiter suggests that
the two rival goddesses should both try to interfere in the fate of two lovers
to be presented before their eyes. They are in turn favored by Venus and
crossed by Fortune. Each act ends with a "triumph": At first Fortune
seems to carry the day; after another act, Venus has gained the upper hand,
until at last they agree that they are both equal and both subject to
Wisdom.

It is obvious that the play and its frame are very closely interrelated. The
play seems to grow out of the debate between Love and Fortune and
illustrates their conflict. On the other hand, the play gains in depth through
the frame because it is not only an entertaining love story (as it would be
without the frame) but a moral exemplum. The frame constantly reminds
us that the story is not presented for its own sake but for its deeper
significance. The frame also establishes a certain barrier between the
audience in the theater and the play, because we see the two lovers and
their fate only through the eyes of the disputing parties, who are always
present on the stage and watch the performance.

The frame also has a more dramatic function. It creates the illusion that
the fate of the lovers has not yet been decided. Jupiter's request to Venus
and Fortune implies that the story is still in progress and that the outcome
is only to be decided by the conflicting exertions of Love and Fortune. The
brief debates after each act provide a running commentary on the action,
and they also heighten the dramatic tension by vague prophecies, as after
the third act, when Venus seems to triumph and Fortune replies: [18]

> Brag not too much, what thinkst thou I haue doon?
> Nay soft not yet, my sport is not begun.
>
>   (976–977)

There is thus a very effective interplay between the two planes of action,
and the device of the play within a play seems very skillfully adapted to the

---

18. Malone Society Reprints (1930). There is a very similar "frame," a dispute
between Love, Death, and Fortune, in *Soliman and Perseda* (printed in F. S. Boas,
The Works of Thomas Kyd [Oxford, 1901]).

purpose of this dramatic debate. It is interesting to note that technically the frame of Kyd's *The Spanish Tragedy* is very similar, although it serves quite a different dramatic purpose. It shows, however, how closely related some seemingly disparate types of Elizabethan drama are.[19]

Another example of this use of the "framed" play is Greene's *James the Fourth* (*c.* 1590), where again the play is part of an argument between two characters who stand outside and view the performance. Here, too, the argument begins with some "shows," and the play proper only emerges after the first act. It seems, however, to have interested the dramatist more than the frame, because the characters who introduce the shows and the play recede into the background and neither interrupt the performance nor reappear at the end, so that the frame seems more like an induction.[20]

A later and much more elaborate use of the same device is to be found in Fletcher's early play *Four Plays or Moral Representations in One* (*c.* 1612). The title is significant because it makes quite clear that the four short plays, for all their melodramatic qualities and wealth of lively incident, are dramatic exempla; they could almost be described (like *Gorboduc* and some other early Elizabethan plays) as a dramatized "Mirror for Magistrates." The frame presents Emanuel, king of Portugal and Castile, who is about to celebrate his marriage. The four plays performed for him are part of the wedding festivities. The Prologue explicitly, though modestly, draws a parallel between the virtues embodied in the royal couple and those "our weak Scenes can show."[21] After each performance the king draws the appropriate conclusion and thus proves an ideal spectator. His speech after the first play is particularly interesting because it obviously outlines the dramatist's own conception of his art and its moral function:

> What hurt's now in a Play, against which some rail
> So vehemently? thou and I, my love,
> Make excellent use methinks: I learn to be

19. Cf. W. Habicht, "Sénèque et le théâtre populaire pré-shakespearien," *Les Tragédies de Sénèque et le théâtre de la Renaissance,* ed. J. Jacquot (Paris, 1964), pp. 175–187.

20. Cf. E. Welsford, *The Court Masque* (Cambridge, 1927), pp. 279 ff., and Bradbrook, *Themes and Conventions,* p. 45. Peele's *The Old Wives Tale* is also a very interesting example of the use of "framed" plays by the "University Wits."

21. See the edition by A. Glover and A. R. Waller (Cambridge, 1905–1912), X, 287 ff.

A lawful lover void of jealousie,
And thou a constant wife. Sweet Poetry's
A flower, where men, like Bees and Spiders, may
Bear poison, or else sweets and Wax away.
Be venom-drawing Spiders they that will;
I'll be the Bee, and suck the honey still.

(p. 312)

It is thus quite clear that the four plays are primarily didactic and exemplify abstract ideas, as can also be seen from the four "triumphs" following the plays. In these "triumphs" the leading idea of each play is repeated and illustrated by an allegorical pageant, very like some of the "Royal Entries" staged by the populace for their monarchs during the English Renaissance.[22] It seems obvious that Fletcher was greatly influenced by earlier practices and by a conception of the purpose of dramatic art which he does not appear to have followed in his later plays. The use of plays within plays thus proved to be particularly effective when they illustrated the didactic function of drama, because it enabled the dramatist to describe explicitly the lesson he wished the audience to derive from his play.

This use of the "framed" play is, of course, very closely related to some of the more elaborate "inductions" in many Elizabethan and Jacobean plays. A full treatment of these inductions would also have to take into account the various forms of the chorus and the presenter and their origins in classical tragedy as well as in the moralities. It is a fascinating subject which has not, I think, been adequately dealt with yet.[23] I wish only to draw attention to some forms of the chorus and the induction which seem to turn the play about to be performed into a play within a play, or at least to make it quite clear that it is "only" a play by insisting on its artificial character. There seem to be at least two ways of doing this.

22. See, for instance, the collection by J. Nichols, *The Progresses, and Public Processions of Queen Elizabeth* (London, 1788–1821), and, for an excellent survey of pageantry in Elizabethan drama, A. Venezky, *Pageantry on the Shakespearean Stage* (New York, 1951).

23. See, however, the useful survey by C. Leech, "Shakespeare's Prologues and Epilogues," *Studies in Honor of T. W. Baldwin,* ed. D. C. Allen (Urbana, 1958), pp. 150–164, and Sehrt, *Der dramatische Auftakt,* pp. 26–63, for an excellent review of the subject.

One is to present the actors without disguise before the beginning of the actual play, to show the preparations for the performance and thus to stress its illusionary nature. Chettle and Munday's Robin Hood plays, *The Downfall* and *Death of Robert, Earl of Huntingdon* (1598), make very effective use of this device.[24] We watch all the excitement before a dramatic performance, the choice of play, the talk about various technicalities, and the beginning of the play proper, under the supervision of the poet Skelton, who then proceeds to act as chorus and to explain the plot of the play to the audience. The didactic intention is not very obtrusive here. The chief function of the frame is to introduce the actors and to create the atmosphere of a theatrical entertainment. Thus a very close contact is established between the actors and the spectators. The play does not pretend to any "realism," but is frankly presented as a piece of make-believe that can be shortened or drawn out at the audience's pleasure, as becomes clear halfway through the second part when Skelton begins to recite an epilogue but is interrupted by a fellow actor, who requests that Mathilda's story be presented to its end as well.

This dramatic use of the induction later became common in comedies as an effective way of playing with dramatic conventions and of "disillusioning" the audience. In Jonson's comedies, in particular, the actors sometimes pretend to enter into a kind of conspiracy with the spectators against the author or some fellow actors, to draw the audience into their confidence and to comment on the play.[25] This proves that it is misleading to talk of Jacobean drama as becoming more "realistic," as is sometimes done, because these playful inductions suggest that the dramatist's "realism" is often nothing but another artistic device and is not intended to be understood as a true copying of actuality.

Another use of inductions is related to the popular pageants and the earlier interludes: The characters constituting the "frame" of the play are personifications, allegorical figures, or various deities like Venus and Fortune in *The Rare Triumphs of Love and Fortune*. Thus the anonymous *A Warning for Fair Women* (*c.* 1599) begins with a dispute between Tragedy, Comedy, and History. Tragedy carries the argument and begins to introduce the play as a kind of presenter. She also interprets it at regular

24. Tudor Facsimile Texts, ed. J. S. Farmer (1913).
25. E.g., *Cynthia's Revels*.

intervals, pointing the moral and commenting on the action. Again the play is thus distinctly characterized as a play, and the allegorical frame serves to bring out the exemplary meaning of the action, its "message." [26]

A similar introduction is to be found in the anonymous history play *The Valiant Welshman* (*c.* 1612). It begins almost like a masque: [27]

Fortune descends downe from heauen to the Stage, and then shee cals foorth foure Harpers, that by the sound of their Musicke they might awake the ancient Bardh, a kind of Welsh Poet, who long agoe was there intoombed.

FORTUNE

Thus from the high Imperiall Seate of *Ioue,*
Romes awfull Goddesse, Chaunce, descends to view
This Stage and Theater of mortall men,
Whose acts and scenes diuisible by me,
Sometime present a swelling Tragedy
Of discontented men: sometimes againe
My smiles can mould him to a Comicke vayne.

(A 4ʳ)

The bard then explains the history about to be presented and acts as chorus. It is interesting to see how the device of the induction is here combined with the familiar idea of the world as a stage. In the eyes of Fortune, past and present are one. The "Stage and Theater of mortall men" for her has no more reality than the performance on the actual stage. By watching history of the past as a dramatic entertainment, the spectators may learn to practice the same detached attitude toward life and to see themselves within the context of the perennial drama of history. Similar ideas are often implied in plays within plays, and this seems to me to point to the close relationship between the device of the play within a play and the convention of the chorus-induction, not only in a technical sense but in expressing a similar idea of the dramatist's art and its illusionary character.

26. Cf. my *The Elizabethan Dumb Show*, pp. 90–96, for a discussion of this play.
27. Tudor Facsimile Texts, ed. Farmer (1913). Among these forms of introduction might also be counted the frequent appeals to the spectators' imagination (cf. Shakespeare's *Pericles* III.11–14 and many others). They also give the impression that the play to be performed is a play within a play.

There is, finally, another technique which seems to me to bear some relation to the convention of the play within a play. By means of this technique part of the play itself is observed and commented on by some characters from the play as if it were a kind of performance for them. Again *The Spanish Tragedy* provides one of the earliest examples. In Act I, scene ii, Balthazar is led across the stage by Lorenzo and Horatio. The king, together with Hieronimo, watches them and asks for some explanations. Thus Balthazar and Horatio are introduced to the audience by means of a presenter (Hieronimo), and for a short time they appear to us like the characters in an inserted play.

In a similar though much more elaborate manner, Pandarus (as a kind of presenter) introduces the Trojan warriors in Shakespeare's *Troilus and Cressida* (*c.* 1602) by describing them to his niece: [28]

Hector passes

PANDARUS

That's Hector, that, that, look you, that; there's a fellow! Go thy way, Hector! There's a brave man, niece. O brave Hector! Look how he looks. There's a countenance! Is't not a brave man?

(I. ii. 191–194)

Here the audience is given not only a lively portrait of Hector, but one that is comically distorted and reveals more about the commentator than about the person who is thus described. In this respect the scene has much in common with some play scenes. The "audience" is characterized by its reaction to the "play," and the characters in this "play"—Antenor, Hector, Paris, and Troilus—seem to be removed from the actual play, if only for a short moment. They seem to perform a part for the amusement of Pandarus and Cressida, and we see them at first only through the eyes of the busybody. The technique is further developed in the last act where Troilus becomes a spectator and has to watch Cressida's faithlessness without being able to interfere. Diomedes and Cressida, without knowing it, seem to perform a play for Ulysses and Troilus (who in turn are observed by Thersites, who adds his own venomous comments). It is obvious that our own impression of the action is deeply influenced and qualified by

28. I quote from P. Alexander's text (The Tudor Shakespeare) in four volumes (London and Glasgow, 1958), III.

this dramatic technique. Both Cressida's betrayal and the disillusion of Troilus are presented to us at a distance, and we are likely to react to them in a more detached way than we would if they had been presented without any comment and if a simpler dramatic technique had been employed. Our disgust, or pity, for Cressida is softened by the distance between her and us; likewise our compassion for Troilus is qualified by the comments of Thersites, which, although they are by no means "endorsed" by the whole play, yet succeed in making Troilus an object rather than a character with whom we want to identify ourselves.

This technique seems to me to be typical of Jacobean rather than Elizabethan drama. It suggests what has been called an "experimenting with points of view and approaches." [29] In no other play can this technique be better studied than in Webster's two masterpieces. J. R. Brown has drawn attention to Webster's frequent use of commentators on the action.[30] Thus in the first scene of *The Duchess of Malfi* (*c.* 1614), Antonio gives a detailed description of Ferdinand and the cardinal while they are both on stage and engaged in some private dialogue. The audience therefore has had a (not unbiased) account of them before they have had time to reveal themselves by their own speeches and actions. In a later scene (III.iii.48–59) the reaction of the two brothers to the news of their sister's marriage is observed and described by two or three frightened onlookers, and we are made to see it through their eyes. Again the situation is very much like a play within a play. Similarly, the banishment of the duchess is only presented as a dumb show and commented on by two pilgrims who have no other function in the play than to provide this detached commentary on the action. Even more striking is the way in which the murders of Isabella and Camillo in *The White Devil* (*c.* 1612) are "performed" in dumb show like plays within plays, with Brachiano watching and enjoying the success of his own stratagems.

There is perhaps no direct connection between this technique of commented action and indirect plot presentation, on the one hand, and the

29. See W. Sypher, *Four Stages of Renaissance Style: Transformations in Art and Literature 1400–1700* (New York, 1955), p. 156. Sypher's whole chapter on "mannerism" is relevant here (pp. 100–179).

30. See the Revels Plays editions of *The White Devil* and *The Duchess of Malfi* (London, 1960 and 1964). Cf. also I. Glier, *Struktur und Gestaltungsprinzipien in den Dramen John Websters* (Diss., München, 1957), pp. 70–76.

simpler forms of plays within plays, on the other; but the use of these devices often seems to proceed from a similar attitude of the dramatist toward his characters. In *The Duchess of Malfi,* Brown remarks, "the main characters 'live' as if they played on a stage and tried, sometimes consciously, sometimes unconsciously, various disguises" (p. 1).[31] The dramatist does not take sides, but often leaves the spectator to choose between various disguises put on by the play's characters.[32] Webster stresses this actorlike quality of his characters by frequently making them objects for the observation of others, just as in many plays containing plays some of the actors become objects and some spectators. The action seems to take place on several levels simultaneously, and this makes an active cooperation of the audience necessary.

In most of the earlier Elizabethan plays these techniques, if employed at all, serve rather more simple purposes. They either underline the didactic and moral function of the play, as in some plays of the "University Wits," or else they introduce an element of playful experimentation with dramatic conventions. *The Spanish Tragedy* seems a combination of both; it skillfully exploits a great variety of dramatic devices which before had never been used in a single play side by side.

Later dramatists, especially Shakespeare, Webster, and Middleton, introduce plays within plays or similar techniques toward more complex ends. By presenting action on more than one level, the dramatist can imply ambiguous and provocative comments on his characters and their deeds; he can give a detached view of certain dramatic situations and thus leave the audience unsure about their moral bearings. In comedy this can lead to a bewildering confusion of identities and a grotesque distortion of reality. In serious drama it often means a deep probing into the very nature of reality and the validity of certain moral positions.

The play within a play, then, proved to be one of the most versatile and adaptable dramatic conventions. Its development from a fairly straightforward device toward a highly complex and not easily definable dramatic

31. J. Kott's interpretation of *Hamlet* (*Shakespeare Our Contemporary,* pp. 48–61) contains similar ideas. See also the beginning of *The Revenger's Tragedy* and Marston's *Antonio and Mellida* (Act I, the reception of the suitors) for the same technique.

32. Cf. E. Schanzer's definition of Shakespeare's "dramatic coquetry," *The Problem Plays of Shakespeare* (London, 1963), p. 70 and *passim.*

technique is an important aspect of the history of Elizabethan and Jacobean drama, and a fuller investigation—for which this essay can only be a very slight preliminary sketch—would probably reveal many interesting correspondences. Apart from the wider philosophic and aesthetic implications discussed by Fiedler and Nelson, the play within a play seems to me a particularly striking example of the diffuse and experimental character of English Renaissance drama, of its astonishing capacity for assimilating diverse conventions and for creating coherent and unified works of art out of seemingly contradictory elements of style.

The Shakespearean Overplot

Harry Levin

I T IS NOT ARISTOTLE'S FAULT when discussions of plot sound mechanical. The inspirational term he used, when he described it as the soul of tragedy, provided the Greek basis for our word *myth*—a word for whose current connotations the sky is the limit.[1] The Latin synonym, which has given us *fable,* seems constricting and moralistic by contrast. The Gallic equivalent, which is *intrigue,* conveys to us certain overtones of romance and of calculation. As for the Germanic expression, its English cognate is the pedestrian *handling.* Our native monosyllable may well seem even more workmanlike, except that it sometimes introduces a sinister note. A plot originally meant a spot of some kind, and then (merging with *plat* and its associations of flatness) a patch of ground—like the one invaded by the Norwegians in *Hamlet.* Thence it came to mean the ground plan for a building and, by abstraction, the plan or outline of a literary work. Subsequently it has denoted a scheme to be put into action, more and more pejoratively a scheme for nefarious action, roughly synonymous with the French *complot.* It is not for nothing that William Shakespeare was the

---

1. *Poetics,* vi, 14.

contemporary of Guy Fawkes. We know that *plot* was a technical term for a scenario (or, more precisely, a list of scenes) posted backstage in the Elizabethan playhouse. Half a dozen such plots have survived from the repertory of the Henslowe-Alleyn companies.[2] In the producer's account book we also read of a plot (in this case, a sketch for a tragedy) outlined by Ben Jonson and filled in by George Chapman.[3] It was doubtless through such journeywork that Anthony Munday gained the repute, according to Francis Meres, of "our best plotter."[4]

Shakespeare, as a concordance will demonstrate, draws upon most of these meanings and extends them characteristically. "This blessed plot," for John of Gaunt, is England;[5] "this green plot," at the behest of Peter Quince, becomes a stage.[6] "When we mean to build," says Lord Bardolph in *2 Henry IV*, "We first survey the plot, then draw the model," and his explicit speech goes on to underline the metaphorical transference from a plot of ground to a conspiracy.[7] Accordingly it is not uncommon to speak of *laying* a plot. This machination, depending upon the context, could be either an insurrection or a practical joke. Hence, in *1 Henry IV*, Hotspur calls the Percy revolt "a noble plot," while Gadshill tells a thievish accomplice: "Thou layest the plot how."[8] Either situation presupposes the agency of what Shakespeare, referring to Aaron the Moor, designates as a "plotter."[9] Whether the agent is prompted by malice or mischief can spell the difference between a tragic villain and a comic funster. His victim, whether Othello or Parolles, is entitled to cry out with the latter: "Who cannot be crushed by a plot?"[10] Yet in *The Winter's Tale* Leontes suspects plots where there are none, and this is a moot point between the tribunes and Coriolanus.[11] Such characters may be the victims of cir-

---

2. Reproduced in the second volume of W. W. Greg, *Dramatic Documents from the Elizabethan Playhouse* (Oxford, 1931).

3. *Henslowe's Diary*, ed. R. A. Foakes and R. T. Rickert (Cambridge, 1961), pp. 73, 100.

4. In *Elizabethan Critical Essays*, ed. G. Gregory Smith (Oxford, 1904), II, 320.

5. *Richard II*, II.i.50.

6. *A Midsummer Night's Dream*, III.i.3.

7. *2 Henry IV*, I.iii.42–43.

8. *1 Henry IV*, I.iii.279; II.i.56.

9. *Titus Andronicus*, V.iii.122.

10. *All's Well That Ends Well*, IV.iii.360.

11. *The Winter's Tale*, II.i.47; *Coriolanus*, III.i.38, 41.

cumstance or of their own natures, rather than of contrivance. In that event it is the playwright who does the plotting; in fact, it is always he who contrives those patterns which his *dramatis personae* attribute to fate or chance, if not to some human motive. Shakespeare, however, makes no literal mention of *plot* in the theatrical sense. His alternative, borrowed from the vocabulary of rhetoric, is *argument.*

Nonetheless we have frequent occasion to discuss his plots and, since they are complex, to disentangle the principal sequence of events from what is known in eighteenth-century usage as the underplot or, in more recent terminology, as the subplot. *Subplot,* being an etymological bastard, is probably to be preferred by Merriam-Webster stylists; but, since I am timidly feeling my way toward a coinage, I draw back at the prospect of *superplot,* which nothing east of Hollywood could live up to. That the underplot is not a gratuitous episode, but a thematic offshoot of the main plot, has been a gradual realization of Shakespearean criticism. In the Japanese theater the farcical *kyōgen* are not organically related to the solemn *Nō* plays with which they alternate. Zanies and *graciosos,* waggish servants who mimic their stylish masters, have indeed been a standard feature of European comedy. But it is English drama which, to the most elaborate degree, has been characterized by parallel construction, from the ritualized buffooneries of the Wakefield *Second Shepherds' Play* to the baroque derangements of *The Changeling.* And, while such lesser playwrights as Thomas Heywood exploited the license to patch odd pairs together, Shakespeare exerted his genius for harmonizing incongruities. The most suggestive treatment of this subject is William Empson's essay on "Double Plots." This, in turn, is the longest of seven diversified essays which Professor Empson has consolidated by presenting them as variations on the pastoral theme. If his deft presentation gives seven ambiguous twists to the convention of pastoralism, he is not the man to be deterred by ambiguity. Yet his thesis gets in the way of his analysis by insisting that underplots should be pastoral.

So they are, in the callow dramaturgy of Robert Greene which Professor Empson takes as his starting point. With Shakespeare it is much less easy to generalize. A more careful scrutiny of his plots would not stop at the assumption that these are merely double; more often than not they are triple, not to say multiple. Professor Empson's observations are more cogent than his generalizations, and he is justifiably perplexed at applying the twofold formula to *1 Henry IV*. "There are three worlds," he very clearly perceives, "each with its own hero; rebel camp, tavern, and court; chivalric idealism, natural gusto, the cautious politician." [12] To his misgiving that "this makes an unmanageable play," he himself suggests the answer that "the prince belongs to all three parties," consequently managing to meet each of them on its respective ground. Thus Prince Hal effects that intermingling of kings and clowns which, while scandalizing the classicists, established a peculiarly Shakespearean decorum. If his central conflict with Hotspur forms the main plot and his raffish companionship with Falstaff the underplot, surely his strategic relationship with the title character at the most exalted level deserves to be discriminated and named. If the concept of the overplot did not already exist, it would not be difficult to invent, given its analogy with the underplot and the complementary function it could fill. I have found it helpful for understanding the morphology of pre-Shakespearean drama.[13] Consider *The Spanish Tragedy,* by no means the best of models but perhaps the most influential of Elizabethan plays in its time. Here the story of revenge entangled with love is expressly framed by the choric role of the ghost, whose own vendetta foreshadows and goads on the other revenges.

This framework not only initiates the enveloping action but orients the plot toward a wider perspective, the war between Spain and Portugal wherein the ghost lost his life, so that Kyd's title has a collective significance. Few overplots are as formal as this, but most of them occupy a comparable position, looking backward and forward from the highest vantage point over the broadest area, and reaffirming those principles of social and cosmic order which Ulysses enunciates in *Troilus and Cressida.* Insofar as the histories focus on kings, their major business takes place at the elevation of the overplot, while personal matters and lesser personages are brought into the foreground episodically. *Henry V,* an extreme example, maintains the heroic story-line of the epic, with excursions into both the romantic and the realistic. If the king is the animating plotter, he is likely to be a usurper, notoriously so in *Richard III.* When the royal protagonist is plotted against, like Henry VI, he yields the forestage to his

---

12. William Empson, *Some Versions of Pastoral* (Norfolk, Conn., 1960), p. 41.
13. Harry Levin, *The Overreacher: A Study of Christopher Marlowe* (Cambridge, Mass., 1952), pp. 67 ff.

rivals and deputies. Shakespeare's Roman plays can treat political themes with greater flexibility precisely because their protagonists are private individuals. Although Julius Caesar's aspirations to sovereignty accord him a title role, it is Brutus who dominates the dramatic predicament. In his terms, the issue lies between a "personal cause" and "the general"—in other words, the main plot and the overplot—and that formulation holds true for *Coriolanus* and *Antony and Cleopatra*.[14] Against the Alexandrian individualism of the lovers, Shakespeare counterpoises the claims of Roman responsibility; the scale of the sexual involvement is augmented by the imperial forces marshaled against it; the world itself, resounding verbally forty-four times through the play, heightens the stature of the hero.

> The death of Antony
> Is not a single doom; in the name lay
> A moiety of the world.[15]

Later playwrights, giving more weight to feminine roles and erotic motives, might regard the world as well lost. To that extent they slough off the overplot, which is the primary vehicle for the assertion of public duty and higher morality. Shakespeare's tragedies, derived as they are from quasi-historic material, start from and return to the commonweal, both in its foreign and its domestic aspects. Even when they are based on love stories, which were generally considered more congenial to comedy, they never lose sight of the state. At the beginning, the middle, and the end of *Romeo and Juliet,* the Prince of Verona appears in order to remind the feuding families of their civic obligations. Othello's final reminder that he has "done the state some service" consummates an inner struggle which parallels the combats between the Venetians and the Turks.[16] Since *Hamlet* is the most fully elaborated of Shakespeare's works, we are not surprised to find its overplot so highly developed. The time scheme is laid down by the goings and comings of the ambassadors, Danish and English. The national crisis in Denmark is matched by the international tension of its relations with Norway and Norway's with Poland. Hamlet, as a

14. *Julius Caesar*, II.i.11.
15. *Antony and Cleopatra*, V.i.17.
16. *Othello*, V.ii.339.

revenger, has two counterparts: Laertes on the lower plane and Fortinbras on the higher. To omit the Norwegian prince is to devalue the play
by ignoring one of its largest dimensions. Yet Fortinbras was cut out and
his closing speech reassigned to Horatio in the latest production at
Stratford, Connecticut—a fittingly anticlimactic culmination to that ten-
year record of shortsighted bungling and heavy-handed bumbling which
has made the American Shakespeare Festival nothing more than a cultural
embarrassment.

Small wonder, then, if we fail to discern the overplot! Can it be that our
latter-day sense of existence, which discovers its chaotic mirror in the
Theater of the Absurd, has no use for Shakespeare's valedictions with their
reassurances of cosmos? Doubtless it is because the Elizabethans and
Jacobeans were harassed by the uncertain succession to the throne that
their tragedies are so preoccupied with problems of dynastic continuity.
Since a dynasty is both a family and a regime, its internal conflicts may be
envisaged as relating the main plot to the overplot. The division between
Albany and Cornwall, alluded to in the first line of *King Lear* and again in
the first scenes of the second and third acts, is only resolved by the death of
Cornwall in the fourth and the Franco-British battle in the fifth. More
broadly, the "little world of man" is subjected to decay and cruelty in the
macrocosm of outer nature.[17] The condition of the body politic is supernat-
urally challenged when the apparition in *Hamlet* "bodes some strange
eruption to our state."[18] Similarly, but more intensively, *Macbeth* is set in
motion by supernatural machinery. Witches, omens, and oracles sketch a
fatalistic background for the exercise of human will, and document the
play's unique concern with eschatology, with damnation and hell.
Macbeth's three opponents, linked to him by the question of succeeding
progeny, are Macduff, the predestined avenger; Malcolm, the immediate
heir to the crown; and Fleance, the ultimate link between the line of
Banquo and the House of Stuart. The single scene in England, with its
ironic cross-reference to the King's Evil, far from being tangential,
constitutes the vital center of the overplot.

Insofar as the comedies deal with frankly fictitious subject matter and
depend less upon the concerns of statecraft, they are less dependent on

17. *King Lear*, III.i.10.
18. *Hamlet*, I.i.69.

overplots. *The Merry Wives of Windsor* does without one altogether; that may help to explain why it seems comparatively thin; Falstaff can no longer be mock-heroic when he is demobilized from the field of heroics. On the other hand, *The Comedy of Errors,* possibly the most trifling piece in the canon, is reinforced by the suspense of Aegeon's condemnation. Tragic elements play a minor part in comedy with Shakespeare, just as comic elements do in tragedy. Menaces averted by happy endings tend to produce those Polonian hybrids which we have retrospectively agreed to classify as romances. An Italianate overplot is no match for the British plot of *Cymbeline,* especially when aided by a Welsh underplot. The antagonisms of *The Winter's Tale,* shifting from marital jealousy to parental dudgeon with the generations, move from Sicilia to Bohemia and back again for a tragicomic resolution. Here the geographical displacement makes room for a pastoral retreat, as it elsewhere does when courtiers withdraw into the forest. Typically, in *As You Like It,* the exiled duke ends by returning to court along with the suitably mated lovers, relinquishing the Forest of Arden to its bucolic denizens. The structure of *The Tempest* is diagrammatic, not simply in its perfected unity or in its symbolic pattern of withdrawal and return, but in its three analogous conspiracies: Sebastian's for the kingdom of Naples, Antonio's for the dukedom of Milan, and Caliban's for the rule of the island. Prospero, through his magical control of spirits, attains an overview which sees all and thwarts cross-purposes.

Comparably, in *Measure for Measure,* the duke is a retiring *deus ex machina;* his unworthy regent, Angelo, is tested and discredited by being temporarily elevated to the overplot. *All's Well That Ends Well* allows its decisions to hinge on the King of France, as the god in a much more loosely plotted machine. Yet it is not supernal authority so much as men's wits—or, more commonly, women's—which intervene to counterplot against trickery. *The Merchant of Venice* conflates two traditional motifs, the pound of flesh and the choice of caskets, when Portia crosses over to Venice from Belmont and tempers legalism with love. There are times, however, when such countermeasures are less effective than mere contingencies. "Our indiscretion sometime serves us well," so Hamlet puts it, "When our deep plots do pall." [19] In *Much Ado About Nothing* the witless constabu-

19. *Ibid.,* V.ii.9.

lary blunders into the exposure of a wile which has deceived the more serious characters. "What your wisdoms could not discover," they are admonished, "these shallow fools have brought to light." [20] Folly, in the person of the fool, sheds more light than self-complacent wisdom; but greatness is not thrust upon the lowly, as Malvolio painfully learns in *Twelfth Night,* where he remains the lowest of four aspirants seeking Olivia's hand at four different levels of society and of the plot. The social and amorous hierarchy of *A Midsummer Night's Dream* is at least as extensive. Above the two interchangeable pairs of Athenian lovers stand two sets of presiding figures, Oberon and Titania mutually suspecting one another of interrelationships with Hippolyta and Theseus, while Bottom momentarily ascends from his nethermost status to bask in the favors of the Fairy Queen.

This chain of courtship reaches its sublimated height when Oberon pays his compliments to the "fair Vestal," Queen Elizabeth.[21] Royal command may well have created something of an additional overplot in the very pageantry of the initial performance. The play within the play reflects those circumstances while burlesquing the theme of lovers' frustrations. The myth it dramatizes, Pyramus and Thisbe, is seriously paralleled by *Romeo and Juliet.* It is among the various mythological precedents evoked by the third happy couple of *The Merchant of Venice,* Jessica and Lorenzo in Portia's garden: "In such a night as this . . ." [22] Shakespeare's characters learn to know themselves by projecting archetypes from Greco-Roman mythology or, with deeper resonance, from Judeo-Christian scripture. Richard II goes through his deposition scene as if he were reenacting a passion play. Cardinal Wolsey recognizes, at the opposite pole, that when the king's favorite falls, "he falls like Lucifer, / Never to hope again." [23] All tragedy, of course, could be traced to that original fall; it was the overplot that adumbrated all subsequent plots. It had been Lucifer, re-arising from hell as Satan, who unrolled the mystery cycles. When Marlowe's Faustus inquires about devils, Mephistophilis informs him that they are

20. *Much Ado About Nothing,* V.i.239.
21. *A Midsummer Night's Dream,* II.i.158.
22. *The Merchant of Venice,* V.i.1 ff.
23. *Henry VIII,* III.ii.371.

> Unhappy spirits that fell with Lucifer,
> Conspir'd against our God with Lucifer,
> And are forever damn'd with Lucifer.[24]

Just as the conjurations of Dr. Faustus are parodied by the antics of clowns, so his destiny is prefigured by that of the Eternal Adversary. And just as the relation of the underplot to the main plot is parodic, so the relation of the overplot to the main plot is figural—a glimpse exemplifying some grander design, an indication that the play at hand is but an interlude from a universal drama performed in the great *theatrum mundi*. Curiously enough, the same Marlovian cadence reechoes when the Percies conspire against Henry IV. Their bone of contention is Edmund Mortimer, probably a more legitimate claimant to the kingship than the more active contenders, whose absent claim becomes vocal as Hotspur fills the stage with his name:

> He said he would not ransom Mortimer,
> Forbade my tongue to speak of Mortimer,
> But I will find him when he lies asleep,
> And in his ear I'll holloa "Mortimer." [25]

With *1 Henry IV* we come back to our organizing principle, with the hope of having illustrated some of its possible uses, since that showpiece embodies the three Shakespearean genres within its structural equilibrium: the comedy of Falstaff as the underplot, the tragedy of Hotspur as the main plot, and the history of Henry IV as the overplot.

24. Christopher Marlowe, *The Tragical History of Doctor Faustus,* ed. F. S Boas (London, 1932), I.iii.73–75.
25. *1 Henry IV*, I.iii.119–122.

The Wit-Interludes and the Form of Pre-Shakespearean "Romantic Comedy"

Werner Habicht

I

PRE-SHAKESPEAREAN "romantic comedy" is no less difficult to define as a dramatic genre than, say, the early English history play. Robert Greene has been credited with the "discovery" of "the type known as Romantic Comedy"; [1] but an analysis of the formal elements that go to make up Greene's plays, as well as of the thematic patterns that give them their unity, might well show their indebtedness to the conventions of the Tudor interlude, only some of which stem from romance. There would be more justification in describing Greene's plays, especially *Friar Bacon and Friar Bungay* and *James IV*, as a climax in the development of the interlude than as prototypes of a "new" kind of drama. If we turn back to earlier English dramatizations of romantic material, we must in fact realize that in them the dramatic structure is not, or not primarily, constituted by the conventions of romance action. Medwall's *Fulgens and Lucrece* (*c.* 1497), for example, derives its dramatic qualities, for all its wooing elements, from the juxtaposition of serious and parodistic debate. The author of

---

1. W. Thorp, *The Triumph of Realism in Elizabethan Drama 1558–1612* (Princeton, 1928), p. 51; similarly, C. F. T. Brooke, *The Tudor Drama* (Boston, 1911), p. 263: "Greene may be safely reckoned as the founder of this type of drama."

73

Calisto and Melibea (*c.* 1527) shaped the romantic plot, taken out of Acts I and IV of the Spanish *Celestina,* so as to produce a dramatic exemplum of Melibea's temptation and repentance. Plays like *Common Conditions,* dating from the fifteen-seventies, which actually are dramatized romances, nevertheless owe much of their dramatic structure to popular stage conventions foreign to their narrative sources—to the ubiquitous part of the Vice, who arranges and links the episodes, to the mechanism of alternation between serious and comic scenes, etc.[2] Nor could the literary form of English romantic drama be fully explained if extant texts allowed us to relate its origin to the miracle play. In the pieces in the Digby manuscript, on which our knowledge of the English saints' play must largely be based, are not the legends themselves shaped into drama by conventions of unrelated origin? [3]

If, then, we judge from extant dramatic texts and refrain from wondering what the numerous lost plays with "romantic" titles might have been like,[4] it seems that there is, in the early Tudor period, no clue to such a thing as romantic drama as an autonomous form. Where narrative romance was to be presented as drama, its content and form were subjected to, and combined with, current dramatic modes and patterns. Pre-Shakespearean plays that are often very vaguely described as romantic comedies [5]

2. H. Medwall's *Fulgens and Lucrece,* ed. F. S. Boas and A. W. Reed (London, 1926); for a recent discussion of debate and parody as structural elements, see G. K. Hunter, *John Lyly: The Humanist as Courtier* (London, 1962), Chap. III. *Calisto and Melibea* (by J. Rastell?), Malone Society Reprints (Oxford, 1908); cf. W. Fehse, *Christof Wirsungs deutsche Celestinaübersetzungen* (Diss., Halle, 1902), p. 68. *Common Conditions* (anon.), ed. Brooke, Elizabethan Club Reprints (New Haven, 1915); for a discussion of the traditional elements of the play's structure, see D. M. Bevington, *From* Mankind *to* Marlowe (Cambridge, Mass., 1962), pp. 191–194.

3. Cf. J. M. Manly, "The Miracle Play in Mediaeval England," *Essays by Divers Hands,* N. S., VII (1927), 133–153; see also F. D. Hoeniger, introd. to *Pericles,* [New] Arden Shakespeare (London, 1963), p. lxxxviii.

4. See the entries in A. Harbage's *Annals of English Drama 975–1700,* rev. S. Schoenbaum (London, 1964), pp. 40 ff.; and cf. C. R. Baskerville, "Some Evidence for Early English Romantic Plays in England," *MP,* XIV (1916 / 17), 229–251, 467–512; A. W. Reed, *The Beginnings of the English Secular and Romantic Drama,* Shakespeare Association Lecture (London, 1922); L. M. Ellison, *The Early Romantic Drama at the English Court* (Chicago, 1917).

5. The critical value of the term "romantic" in this context (not to speak of its

can in fact be best assessed if we are ready to consider them as experiments in combining divers formal elements.

It is this mixture of formal elements, so essential to the development of Elizabethan drama, which needs further elucidation; and one approach—a historical one—is an examination of its crude beginnings in the Tudor interludes.[6] The mongrel or hybrid nature of these plays, far from merely being the result of the obvious combining of allegory and literal plot, of the abstract and the concrete (so often pointed out), is due to fusions of a whole range of conventions of native and classical, homiletic and romantic, dramatic and nondramatic origin. Features of the morality, of homily, satire, and *exemplum,* of romance, and of Roman drama (as interpreted by the humanists)—all these, in however simplified a state, play their part in shaping the interludes and in expressing their moral themes.

It is true that mixed genres may also be found in nondramatic, in homiletic and didactic literature of the period, even in the sources of moralities and interludes themselves. And yet to produce effective drama fresh combinations had to be made. The rise of "the type known as Romantic Comedy" is only one part of this development, which I should merely like to illustrate here by discussing the structure of the *Wit*-interludes. (Its more general aspects I treat at length elsewhere.) If in doing so I concentrate on the literary nature of the plays, this should not minimize the importance of acting and staging conditions for their dramatic structure, which has, indeed, been aptly demonstrated in recent studies.[7]

application to a period) has suffered from the diversity of its definitions and undefined uses. For want of a better word, I use it here as an adjective derived from "romance" to imply the general characteristics and traditions of Greek, medieval, or Italian narrative romance, as described, for example, by S. L. Wolff, *The Greek Romances in Elizabethan Prose Fiction* (New York, 1912), B. E. C. Davis, *Edmund Spenser* (London, 1933), pp. 78–99, or E. C. Pettet, *Shakespeare and the Romance Tradition* (London, 1949).

6. This aspect has been neglected in M. Doran's monumental work on the subject (*Endeavors of Art: A Study of Form in Elizabethan Drama* [Madison, 1954]).

7. See especially E. Lauf, *Die Bühnenanweisungen in den englischen Moralitäten und Interludien bis 1570* (Diss., Münster, 1932); T. W. Craik, *The Tudor Interlude* (Leicester, 1958); G. Wickham, *Early English Stages* (London, 1959), I, 229–253; Bevington, *From* Mankind *to Marlowe.*

The *Wit*-interludes—Redford's *Wit and Science* (*c.*1539), its later adaptation, *The Marriage of Wit and Science* (*c.* 1568), and *The Marriage
between Wit and Wisdom* (*c.* 1579) [8]—interdependent for their matter as
they obviously are, have been compared more than once, with critical
results as divergent as the standards applied and the viewpoints adopted.
Older literary historians, identifying progress with either increased classicism or increased realism, tended to deplore the abstractness and didactic
qualities of Redford's *Wit and Science* and to praise somewhat lavishly the
two later pieces. *The Marriage of Wit and Science,* for example, called
forth J. P. Collier's commendation for its classical division into acts and
scenes,[9] which, however, as T. W. Baldwin has since pointed out, is quite
external and loose.[10] *The Marriage between Wit and Wisdom* emerged (in
C. M. Gayley's words) as "the highest mark" in the class of pedagogical
interludes [11]—mainly because of its scenes of farce and "realism," however
digressive these may be. The standards underlying such judgments need
no renewed refutation; they failed to do justice to the peculiar dramatic
mode of the interludes and to look for their unity of theme. On the other
hand, more recent critics, who have considered the *Wit*-plays as moralities
from the point of view of allegory, have tended to turn the earlier
evaluations upside down and to disqualify the two later plays precisely for
their lack of abstract, allegorical coherence. *The Marriage between Wit
and Wisdom* is dismissed by Bernard Spivack as "an example of allegorical
drama on its last legs," [12] and excused by David Bevington as being the
result of an adaptation of the originally academic theme to the coarser
acting conventions of the popular stage.[13] But surely the *Wit*-plays are

---

8. I use the following editions here: *Wit and Science,* Malone Society Reprints,
ed. A. Brown (Oxford, 1951); *The Marriage of Wit and Science,* ed. Brown,
Malone Society Reprints (Oxford, 1960); *The Marriage between Wit and Wisdom,*
ed. J. O. Halliwell, Shakespeare Society (London, 1864). I have modernized the
spelling of the characters' names, expanded abbreviations, and substituted *th* for
the thorn.

9. See the introduction in Hazlitt's *Dodsley,* II, 322.

10. *Shakspere's Five-Act Structure* (Urbana, 1947), pp. 426–428.

11. *Representative English Comedies,* ed. C. M. Gayley (New York, 1903–1914),
I, lxxi, lxxiv. For a similar view, see Brooke, *Tudor Drama,* p. 78.

12. *Shakespeare and the Allegory of Evil* (New York and London, 1958), p. 333.

13. *From* Mankind *to* Marlowe, pp. 22–25.

neither moralities nor realistic (or romantic) drama as such. To regard them as either is to neglect part of their dramatic life. They are mixtures of morality and romance, and a literary evaluation should try to determine the degree with which an interpenetration of the two results in dramatic effectiveness.

The morality element of the *Wit*-interludes resides not merely in their allegory but, more notably, in their thematic pattern—in the typical English morality sequence of temptation, fall, sin, penance, and regeneration.[14] The essential turning points of the moral play are temptation and repentance, whether or not there is, in addition to the personified inner and outer forces of good and evil, a "mankind hero" to experience them on the stage, and whether the thematic interest is focused theologically on the spiritual *imago* of man or, secularized, on man political or on man in the state of education (as in the *Wit*-interludes). In these crucial moral situations man—the stage protagonist as well as the audience—is confronted with personified outer forces, with tempter and savior, and man's inner conflict provoked by such confrontation is externalized in the struggle of his personified inner qualities. Some sixteenth-century moral interludes tend to humanize this drama. As early as in Medwall's *Nature* (*c.* 1495) personified outer forces (Nature, World) play a minimal part, and that only at the outset of the play. The actual moral drama explores man's psychological conflicts (externalized in the debate between Reason and Sensuality) as well as his vices and virtues. Thus man is driven into repentance not by Death or some formidable messenger of God but by Reason regaining supremacy.[15] The same is true of Redford's *Wit and Science,* in which even the protagonist Wit himself, although his part corresponds formally to the role of the old "Mankind hero," is no longer (as were Humanum Genus, Anima, or Mankind) a comprehensive symbol existing beside the personifications of his inner self. For allegorically Wit is only one part of the human soul which is unfolded by the whole configuration of the play's personifications. The allegory is reduced

14. See R. L. Ramsay's analysis in his introduction to Skelton's *Magnyfycence,* EETS, E. S., XCVIII (1906), which is still fundamental.

15. Medwall's *Nature,* ed. A. Brandl, in *Quellen des englischen Dramas vor Shakespeare,* Quellen und Forschungen, LXXX (Strassburg, 1898), ll. 1214 ff. Cf. W. Farnham, *The Medieval Heritage of Elizabethan Tragedy* (Berkeley, 1936), pp. 199–201.

to a coherent, indeed human, level, and this facilitates its transposition into the dramatic metaphor of a coherent—romantic—action.

Romantic imagery, on the other hand, was of course already connected with the allegory of earlier moralities.[16] In those, however, love metaphors had little function in the dramatic structure. Farcical or lyrically romantic scenes of love were (and were to continue in sixteenth-century moralities) manifestations of evil, of the folly into which man is tempted. Occasionally, it is true, the stage image of sinful lust is confronted with the image of godly love. In *The Trial of Treasure* (*c.* 1567) [17] there are not only love scenes showing the perversion of Bad Man (called Lust) in his erotic union with Lady Treasure; there is also a spiritual marriage of Good Man (Just) with Lady Trust. But only the scenes presenting the sinful union are adorned with romantic, as well as farcical, material, of which the virtuous union is quite free. In spite of the antithetical thematic structure of the play, its moral contrasts are not projected into expressive contrasts between love and lust. Even where, in plays as early as *Mankind* or *Wisdom* (fifteenth century),[18] the mystical imagery of the sources accounts for the actual presence of such metaphorical contrast, it is not borne out dramatically. In *Mankind,* for example, Mercy winds up the opening sermon with a kiss ("Kysse me now, my dere darlyng"; l. 300), while Newguise, one of the worldly tempters, relates an erotic farce; but this remains a momentary image without relevance for the play's over-all structure.

It is in the *Wit*-plays that moral contrasts and contrasts of love are really superimposed, that the moral conflict of man (or, more precisely, of the young scholar) is projected into metaphorical conflicts of true love and foolish lust,[19] and that the stereotyped sequence of the moral situations is

16. See Spivack, *Allegory of Evil*, p. 218 f.
17. In Hazlitt's *Dodsley*, III.
18. *The Macro Plays*, EETS, E. S., XCIV (1904).
19. The point is in fact made in *The Marriage of Wit and Science:*
    Not fanteses force, not vayne and Idle toyes of loue,
    Not hope of that whych commenlye doth suiters moue,
    But fixed fast good wyll that neuer shall relent,
    And vertues force that shines in you bade him geue this attempte.
                                                                   (ll. 448–451)
    Cf. also Philip's *Patient Grissill*, Malone Society Reprints (Oxford, 1909), ll. 660–665.

interlinked with an up-and-down movement oscillating between dangers and rescues which is so typical of romantic story. The idea of such a combination of pedagogical moral allegory and romantic image stems, of course, from works like Martianus Capella's *De Nuptiae* and Stephen Hawes's *The Pastime of Pleasure.* But whereas these earlier authors had used the allegory of love as a pretext for encyclopedic displays of learning, there is no such intention in the *Wit*-plays, whose drama is centered around the crucial situations of the moral play—temptation, degeneration, repentance, regeneration—however deprived of their original theological content, however humanized these situations may now be.

II

In Redford's *Wit and Science* these basic situations are dramatized in forms of expression archtypical of the morality. The opening, which is lost, may have been (if we can judge from the adaptation in *The Marriage of Wit and Science*) an exhortation of the protagonist by Nature. Further exhortation is then actually furnished by Instruction (ll. 72 ff.) : This corresponds to the traditional sermon opening of many moralities. It is contrasted by the isolated self-introductory solo appearance of Evil (Tediousness) (ll. 145 ff.), comparable with the equally isolated first speeches of World, Devil, and Flesh at the beginning of *The Castle of Perseverance.* The contrast is enhanced by contrasting language, meter, and gesture, as was the opening contrast between Mercy and the trio of worldly seducers in *Mankind.* Then there are the morality forms for temptation and fall: the protagonist's repeated dismissals of instruction; his subjection by Tediousness; the debate of opposing principles (Honest Recreation and Idleness), which, like the debate between the opposing two angels in *Perseverance* or that between Reason and Sensuality in *Nature,* externalizes man's initial inner dualism; and the momentous exit of the good partner which ends the debate and which marks the beginning of man's depravation. Again, morality conventions are behind the formal elements that demonstrate degeneration and folly. Wit is duped and lulled into sleep by Idleness, like Mankind by the devil. His perversion, like that of many morality sinners, is symbolized in physical disfiguration: His face is blackened, and he now wears the foolish garb of Ignorance. The following scenes are loaded with the effects of burlesque, which in the morality tradition shows degeneration as a grotesque and comical perversion of values. Wit, by his fall turned into "a nawgty vycious foole" (l. 808), is henceforth a parody of his better self, contrasting with Lady Science's noble resistance against her tempters, who represent the World (ll. 641 ff.). World, as a personification or as a concept, had been the main contriver of man's temptation in homiletic plays.

Even more rigid morality forms serve to express repentance and regeneration. The repentance is brought about by Wit's glance into the mirror, which shows him his distorted appearance and which symbolizes his recognition of folly. The analogous situation in *Wisdom,* for example, had been presented as a spectacular confrontation of the degenerated powers of the soul (Mind, Will, and Understanding) with Anima, their own perverted self, who appeared "in the most horrybul wyse, fowlere than a fende" (l. 905). Later, Wager too was to evoke the mirror symbol in his *Mary Magdalene,* when Knowledge of Sin comes to join the sinful heroine.[20] In both *Mary Magdalene* and *Wit and Science* the mirror also draws the audience into the play. To Mary Magdalene the glass shows that "all men" are damned for sin, and Wit literally holds up the glass which shows him his folly for the audience to look into (l. 833).[21] Recognition leads to a moment of despair, conventionally uttered in the *taedium vitae* formula ("Alas / alas / that ever I was borne"; l. 849). Despair is overcome by what can be recognized as the typical morality dramatization of the allegory of penance: There are Wit's contrite lamentation, his confession, and his whipping by Shame (corresponding to the three parts of penance). Finally, pardon and regeneration are conventionally symbolized by new clothes, and the concluding dialogue, like the concluding scenes of *Mankind* or *Wisdom,* contains the play's *applicatio.*

But the morality pattern of the play is presented through the image of the wooing of Lady Science by Wit, the chivalrous youth, that is to say in a romantic plot, which introduces another completely different dramatic movement. Therefore, although traditional formal conventions serve to express their moral content, temptation and repentance are not concentrated in single reversals but dispersed to form a series of changes in

20. *The Life and Repentance of Mary Magdalene,* ed. F. I. Carpenter (Chicago, 1902), l. 1058.

21. For the mirror as a symbol in the interludes, see Craik, *Tudor Interlude,* p. 25.

fortune. Temptation is a string of obstacles which beset the wooing, of dangers alternating with rescues.

At the point where the extant text starts, a typically romantic obstacle—the disparity in social status—has just been smoothed away by the Lady's father, Reason (ll. 13 ff.). Then Wit has to fight against Tediousness, the club-swinging wild man, as a test of love. Wit's recklessness in not waiting for a token from his lady ("wherebye / hope of her favor may spryng"; l. 95 f.) gets him into danger, and a blow from Tediousness' club smashes him to the ground. But—again a typical romantic reversal—Wit only appears to be dead: Honest Recreation and the chorus of her attendants awaken him with their healing music and give him new strength. Then comes a new danger, because Wit, in a surfeit of pleasure, forgets about his destined bride, which results in angry departures—first of father Reason, then of Honest Recreation—so that Idleness, in whose lap Wit falls asleep, can exchange the hero's clothes for those of Ignorance, the fool. This symbolizes Wit's moral corruption conventionally enough, and yet it is at the same time a perversion of his love: At the sight of his Lady Science he behaves as a burlesque lover, as a *vilain,* and he greets her with obscenities and bold kisses—with lust, not love. The contrast provided by Science's temptation is also stated in romantic terms. Her worldly tempters are suitors whose wooing homage jeopardizes the love of the pair intended for each other. Science, however, resists them out of loving faithfulness to her knight.

Repentance and regeneration are, like temptation and fall, expanded into a sequence of romantic reversals. Not only is Wit saved from despair, not only is his punishment broken off, not only is he presented with "new aparell" (l. 903), but Wit has to enter danger and battle again (as the Red Cross Knight is to do later after his escape from Despair). He has to overcome Tediousness and—symbol is here linked with allegory—to attain Mount Parnassus. But the action is romantic. The fight with the monster in the wilderness offstage is crowned by Wit's triumphant entry with the monster's severed head at the top of his lance. Once again Wit receives a new garment (the "gowne of knoledge"; l. 1016). The end is the marriage of Wit and Science; formally, it is a marriage of a romantic happy ending with the didactic *applicatio* in the concluding dialogue.

The structure of *Wit and Science* is shaped by the moral meaning and its allegorical dramatization as much as it is by the themes and movements of the metaphorical romance of love and adventure. The crucial morality situations, conveyed as they are in traditional forms of expression, are overlaid by a wealth of incident without loss to the thematic structure and didactic unity of the play. The merit of *Wit and Science* is, therefore, to be judged not merely by the fact that the love story itself forms a coherent plot,[22] but by the success with which morality and romance are fused.

III

In the two later *Wit*-interludes the romantic story is even more obtrusively present than the allegory it stands for, yet this does not necessarily improve their dramatic quality. In *The Marriage of Wit and Science* the theme, plot, and main characters of Redford's play have been taken over, but the author appears to be more concerned with the romantic image than with the play's pattern of ideas, which in some places he loses sight of altogether, thus breaking up the allegorical coherence.[23]

This is mainly because the morality forms of expression, which were clearly identifiable in Redford's *Wit and Science,* have now largely been abandoned. In *The Marriage of Wit and Science* the moral arguments of Instruction's admonitory speech, to which Wit pays no heed, have faded away. Tediousness' grotesque self-introductory monologue (the self-assertion of evil) is lacking, and so is the dualistic debate between Idleness and Honest Recreation. The burlesque that demonstrated Wit's fall and folly is toned down; Science's contrasting temptation is omitted. Only for the presentation of repentance and regeneration are the morality conventions still made use of, but even here a number of thematic significances have dropped out. The site of the last battle is no longer Mount Parnassus but the tournament lists, and there is no direct *applicatio* at the end.

22. The coherence of the metaphorical plot has been demonstrated, and somewhat overemphasized, by A. Lombardi, *Il dramma pre-Shakespeareano* (Venice, 1957), pp. 161–168, who regrettably does not consider the two later *Wit*-plays.

23. This has already been pointed out by W. R. Mackenzie, *The English Moralities from the Point of View of Allegory* (Boston, 1914). A certain confusion in the romantic plot itself has been cleared up by the most recent editor of the play, who has noticed a transposition of two sections of the text in the early edition; see Brown's introduction to the Malone Society reprint, pp. vii–ix.

Instead, the romantic metaphor serves, to a larger extent than in *Wit and Science,* to motivate and develop the action. Wit, like Man in Medwall's *Nature,* is sent on his way by the goddess Nature, yet what sets the play going is not the ideas contained in the latter's sermon (as in *Nature*), but the declaration of Wit's intention as a suitor. And Will, the newly created figure, is only introduced as a page where he is needed for the courting expedition. What wins Science's heart is a eulogy on Wit's outward appearance delivered by Will. Above all, the love test is now more played up than the idea it stands for. When Science sets her suitor the task of conquering the jealous monster Tediousness, there are few allegorical undertones:

> Here out my tale, I haue a mortall foe:
> That lurketh in the woode, hearby as you come and goe,
> This monstrous Giant, beares a grudge to me and mine,
> And wyll attempt to kepe thee backe, from this desier of thine.
>
> (ll. 889–892)

In fact, Tediousness is not really (as he had been in *Wit and Science*) Evil that stands threateningly in the path of a Mankind hero. Instead the hero, like a knight of romance, challenges him to battle:

> Come forth thou monster fell, in drowsy darknes hydde;
> For here is *Witte* Dame Natures sonne, that doth thee battaile bid.
>
> (ll. 940 f.)

To bring about Wit's regeneration, the love of his lady is now also more important than it had been in *Wit and Science.* The forgiveness he receives is the result of Science's loving intercession with her severe father, Reason (l. 1368). And in the second fight, which is a tournament scene, Wit is spurred to victory by the encouraging looks of his lady, who has promised him,

> Here in this Closet our selfe, will sette and see,
> Your manly feates, and your successe in fyght:
> Strike home couragiously, for you and mee,
>
> (ll. 1415–1417)

while Instruction gives tactical advice for the battle rather than moral admonition. There is no other ending to the play than the happy wedding.

In short, the allegorical idea is not efficiently brought home to the audience because the play lacks the forms of expression suitable for its dramatic statement. The metaphorical romantic highlights—the lover's tasks and emotions, the spectacular quality of the battles—force themselves on the attention of the audience. Much of the moral impact of the play's situations and their significant sequence is lost. Instead the structure of *The Marriage of Wit and Science* is largely determined by the vicissitudes of fortune, by the alternation of joyful and sad events. These are accentuated by speeches of lamentation and of triumph. The laments, which are on the whole more elaborate than in *Wit and Science,* do not so much express moral perception as bemoan the inconstancy of fortune. When defeated by Tediousness, Wit (not Will, as the old edition has it) complains without self-knowledge:

> Ah my mishap my desperate mishap,
> In whom ill fortune poureth downe, all mishap at a clappe,
> What shall become of me, where shal I hyde my head?
> . . . .
> Causles I perishe here, and cause to curse I haue.
>
> (ll. 1017–1023)

The lament provoked by the look into the mirror (of Reason) is amplified with stereotyped formulae of grief:

> O woofull wretch to whom shall I complaine,
> What salue may serue to salue my sore, or to redresse my payne . . .
>
> (ll. 1346 f.)

Happy moments are, on the other hand, rhetorically emphasized with speeches of love and triumph. There is a string of amorous oxymora in Wit's rhapsody when he for the first time approaches Science's house (ll. 799 ff.); he triumphs when the bethrothal is accomplished (ll. 932 ff.); his entrance with the monster's severed head, unaccompanied by moral comment, celebrates his final victory; praise of good fortune crowns the wedding:

> My payne is paste, my gladnes to beginne,
> My taske is done, my hart is set at rest,
> My foe subdued, my Ladyes loue possest.
>
> (ll. 1542–1544)

The clearest symptom, however, of the author's predominating interest in the romantic possibilities of the play is the way he handles the part of Will, Wit's page, for whom there is no model in Redford's *Wit and Science.* An allegorical pairing of Wit and Will would be in full accordance with psychological theory of the time, and yet the figures Wit and Will do not function as complementary allegories here. Will is mainly a dramatic type, a *servus currens* with some of the characteristics of the Vice of other interludes. But, unlike the morality Vice, he is not primarily the hero's seducer, nor does his involvement with the hero externalize the latter's moral perversity. He is the contriver of reversals of the action. As a messenger of love he not only replaces the colorless personification Diligence of *Wit and Science,* but he also continually helps, parodies, and harms Wit in his amorous expedition. He wins favor for the suitor in Science's house, but he also threatens to thwart Wit's plans ("I will marre your mariage if you do clitter"; l. 276). His bold recommendation brings about the betrothal, but his participation in Wit's reckless first fight with Tediousness makes the outcome of it doubtful, so that Instruction warns Wit: "Good sir be ruled and leaue this peuish elfe" (l. 707). Will's part is in fact akin to that of the Vice in dramatized romances, a role that is to be further developed in figures like Common Conditions (*Common Conditions*) and Subtle Shift (*Clyomon and Clamydes*).

Thus the author of *The Marriage of Wit and Science* has gone beyond Redford in the dramatization of romance. But the romantic spectacle and the rudimentary love poetry have now outgrown the moral content, to the detriment of the play's thematic structure. Further experiments were to be necessary before a new synthesis of romantic and moral drama could be found.

IV

Written a decade later, *The Marriage between Wit and Wisdom* is a fresh move in such a direction, but in spite of his more original approach to his material, the anonymous author has only managed to smother the moral structure even more with romantic incident. Many of the differences between this play and the two earlier ones must be set down to the different conditions of production, as Bevington has pointed out. Yet the use of popular acting conventions does not provide the play with a thematic structure; it helps instead to cram as many reversals as possible into the action. The love and adventure plot, the metaphor of the moral allegory, is no longer organized by the morality pattern (as in fact is the comparable succession of episodes in *Cambyses*). It is split up into episodic adventures and interspersed with farcical scenes; and each of the adventure episodes contains romantic reversals from happiness to unhappiness and back to happiness which are contrived by the Vice and by other personifications.

In this play there is a conventional Vice, Idleness; but his part, which is expanded into a star role, mainly helps to provide a romantic pattern. In one episode he uses his customary trick of substituting names in order to bring about Wit's slumber in the lap of Wantonness (a harlot from the stock of prodigal plays). It is significant that she is here called Wantonness, the erotic thus being no longer a metaphor for idleness as in the two earlier *Wit*-plays, but a more direct expression of love perverted into lust; it is also presented more obscenely. But soon Good Nurture comes to Wit's rescue. The fight against the monster (here called Irksomeness), indeed both fights against him, the shameful and the victorious, are included in a further episode (pp. 35–38) in which again the Vice, by means of another substitution of names, provides danger for the hero, leading the utterly unsuspecting Wit into an ambush in which the monster's club strikes him to the ground. And again rescue follows immediately. Wit is lovingly nursed to health by none other than Lady Wisdom, so that, inspired by the evidence of her favor, he can win the second battle. In *Wit and Science* the two fights marked the principal turning points of the whole play, thus emphasizing the crucial moral situations, temptation and regeneration. Here they are included in a single scene, and a very short one at that, in which consequently a breathtaking sequence of radical reversals of fortune takes place. And there is more to come. "Anne aduenture this I seek, not hauing runne my race," says Wit, and in another adventure episode a romantic motif no less typical than the others is exploited: Wit, led into a trap by Fancy, lands in a dungeon, from which he is posthaste freed by Good Nurture. The wedding at the end crowns the adventures.

Even the farcical scenes in which the Vice gets involved with all kinds of low types—Ruffians, Cook, Mother Bee, Beadle—and the way they are inserted between the "romantic" episodes, seem to be dictated by the pattern of changes of fortune. They do not reflect the theme of the play in their burlesque and satire as they do to a certain extent in *Cambyses.* In the "romantic" Wit episodes the Vice triumphs with his arts of seduction; in the ensuing farcical scenes he himself falls into traps, is unmasked, beaten, or arrested. "This," says the Vice, pronouncing as it were the motto of the play, "is a world to see how fortune chaungeth" (p. 49).

V

The two later *Wit*-interludes clearly fall short of Redford's *Wit and Science.* The emphasis on romantic incident and romantic reversals of the action and the introduction of farcical episodes are not enough in themselves to make effective and thematically coherent drama. The decadence of the tradition of the morality play has something to do with this failure, but it is not the essential reason. The failure is the result of a disintegration of moral theme and romantic theme, of the morality structure and the movement of romance. The forms expressive of moral situations which were developed in the moral play have been abandoned, and no new forms have yet been found to state dramatically a moral theme through romance or to explore the inner values of romance itself. The development of pre-Shakespearean romantic comedy is a search for new methods to achieve this aim.

Already in Philip's interlude *Patient and Meek Grissill* (*c.* 1559), for example, the structure is focused on crucial moral situations, temptation and regeneration, by the manipulation of the literal plot just as much as by the use of residual morality conventions. At the same time, however, these situations are extended into the oscillating movement of romance whose reversals are motivated by the faithful love of the heroine and the jealousy of her prince, and heightened by speeches of lament and happiness, some of them independent of the play's source. The dramatic methods which in *Patient Grissill* appear in a crude state are then further developed and controlled in more elaborate plays like Whetstone's *Promos and Cassandra* (1578) or indeed Greene's *James IV.* As for dramatized romances, a comparison between *Common Conditions* and *Clyomon and Clamydes* could show, too, that in the latter (and later) play more effort is made than in the former to present the plot in such a way as to demonstrate the thematic values inherent in it. Honor is dramatically opposed to cowardice, love to lust, and a principle of justice and equity is represented by King Alexander, who, like Jupiter in *The Rare Triumphs of Love and Fortune,* appears in the center of stately and dominating scenes. The dramatic use of magic in plays like Munday's *John a Kent and John a Cumber* or Greene's *Friar Bacon and Friar Bungay* is another contribution to this development of a form of romantic comedy which went on before Shakespeare achieved a unity of moral theme and romantic spectacle in the poetry of his plays.[24]

24. The points hinted at in the last paragraph will be discussed in full in a forthcoming monograph, the manuscript of which is completed. Of the plays mentioned, *Promos and Cassandra* is conveniently accessible in G. Bullough's *Narrative and Dramatic Sources of Shakespeare* (London, 1958), II; the others are in Malone Society Reprints.

Ironies of Justice
in The Spanish Tragedy

G. K. Hunter

T HE ASSUMPTION that *The Spanish Tragedy* is usefully categorized as a "revenge play" and that this categorization gives us a means of differentiating what is essential in the text from what is peripheral—this has governed most that has been said about Kyd's play. And this is a pity, because the play when looked at in these terms shows up as rather a botched piece of work.

It is no doubt an inevitable part of the tendency of literary historians that they should look everywhere for indications of historical progress. Certainly this has caused them to search among the "amorphous" (i.e., nonmodern) dramatic forms of the Elizabethans for signs and portents of the coming of Scribe and the "well-made" play. The revenge motif, in particular, has been seen as important because (to quote Moody Prior) it

had the advantage of imposing a fairly strict pattern on the play. It thus assisted in discouraging multiple narratives and irrelevant episodes, and, in general, acted as a check on the tendency toward diffuseness and digression which was a common defect of popular Elizabethan drama.[1]

1. Moody E. Prior, *The Language of Tragedy* (New York, 1947), p. 47.

Percy Simpson, in the same general terms, sees the revenge motif as imposing on Elizabethan dramaturgy the Aristotelian virtues of beginning, middle, and end: "The beginning is effectively supplied by the murder; the end should be effectively supplied by the vengeance. The problem for the working dramatist was skilfully to bridge the gap between the two." [2]

Unfortunately this pattern of progress shows the actual products it seeks to explain as rather unsatisfactory parts of the very progression which is adduced to explain them. Prior finds *The Spanish Tragedy* to be ensnared in the very "multiple narratives and irrelevant episodes" that the revenge motif was supposed to discourage. He speaks of "the disproportionate amount of preliminary preparation necessary before Hieronimo is introduced as the avenging agent," [3] and also of "the introduction of the story of the treacherous noble in the Portuguese Court, which has no bearing on the main action." [4] Fredson Bowers tells us that "the ghost has no real concern with the play" and that "the fundamental motive for the tragic action . . . is not conceived until midway in the play." [5] Simpson has much the same attitude. After the passage quoted above, he goes on to apply it to Kyd:

Now Kyd, who had a keen eye for dramatic situation and, in his happy moments, a powerful style, does at critical points fumble the action. His main theme, as the early title-page announces, is "the lamentable end of Don Horatio," avenged at the cost of his own life by his aged father Hieronimo. But the induction brings in the ghost of Horatio's friend, Don Andrea, and the personified figure of Revenge. [6]

Later Simpson speaks more unequivocally of

the disconnectedness, the waste of opportunity, and the dramatic unevenness of much of the writing. [7]

2. Percy Simpson, "The Theme of Revenge in Elizabethan Tragedy," British Academy Shakespeare Lecture for 1935, p. 9.

3. Prior, pp. 46 f.

4. *Ibid.*, p. 46.

5. F. T. Bowers, *Elizabethan Revenge Tragedy* (Princeton, 1940, 1959), p. 71.

6. Simpson, pp. 9 ff.

7. *Ibid.*, p. 14.

This attitude toward the revenge play in general and *The Spanish Tragedy* in particular has persisted in criticism. Philip Edwards' recent and excellent edition of the play (1959) speaks of the "prolix early scenes" and tells us that "it is very hard to justify the sub-plot . . . the relevance of theme is very slight" (p. liii). But at the same time as these attitudes persist, their historical foundations are disappearing. The assumption that the Elizabethan play inherited from the Tudor interlude a diffuse form which reflects mere incompetence—this becomes increasingly difficult to sustain in the light of recent studies of the interlude by Craik,[8] Spivack,[9] Bevington,[10] and Habicht.[11] These, in their different ways, present the interlude as a serious form, in which flat characterization, repetitiveness, and dependence on a multiplicity of short episodes are not defects, but rather means perfectly adapted to express that age's moral and religious (rather than psychological or social) view of human destiny. Persons are seen to be less important than theme; they exist to illustrate rather than represent; and narrative line gives way to the illustration of doctrine. I may quote Bevington's remarks on the late morality, Lupton's *All for Money* (*c.* 1577):

The unity of *All for Money,* as in so many popular "episodic" plays, is the single-ness of theme (man's greed) manifested in a variety of episodes. This theme becomes more important than the fate of individuals. Characters are drawn to illustrate a single motif of human behavior, and are given no more depth than is necessary to make a point. The full course of their lives has no relevance here. It is the course of the moral formula that is all-important: the genealogy of sin, the analysis of its origins, motivations, and processes, the depiction of its worldly success and ultimate downfall—all seen in the perspective of moral up-rightness, the beginning and end of virtuous living. The parts succeed each other as *exempla* to a homily, written for an audience that perceived a rich totality in matters of faith. The success of the play lies in varied illustration, in "multiple unity" and gathering of impact, not in the crisis of the individual moment.[12]

8. T. W. Craik, *The Tudor Interlude* (Leicester, 1958).

9. Bernard Spivack, *Shakespeare and the Allegory of Evil* (New York, 1958).

10. D. M. Bevington, *From* Mankind *to* Marlowe (Cambridge, Mass., 1962).

11. Werner Habicht, "Sénèque et le théâtre pré-Shakespearien," in *Sénèque et le théâtre de la Renaissance,* ed. Jacquot (Paris, 1964). Dr. Habicht's book *Studien zur Dramenform vor Shakespeare* is due to appear (Winter Verlag, Heidelberg) in 1966.

12. Bevington, p. 166.

If *The Spanish Tragedy* is seen not so much as the harbinger of *Hamlet* (not to mention Scribe), but more as the inheritor of a complex and rich tradition of moralizing dramaturgy, the actual structure of the play begins to make more sense, and the traditional strictures that Prior and Simpson re-echo lose much of their relevance. The text of the play does not appear to give its complete attention to the enactment of revenge. True. But this may be because the play is not centrally concerned with the enactment of revenge. Much more obsessive is the question of justice. Indeed we may hazard an initial statement that if revenge provides the plot line of the play (i.e., play structure as seen from Scribe's point of view), justice provides the thematic center of the play (i.e., play structure as seen from the point of view of the Tudor interlude).

The centrality of the concept of justice serves to explain much of the so-called "preliminary preparation" of the first two acts. The play opens with Don Andrea, who has been slain in the late war between Spain and Portugal. Don Andrea's journey after death is through an infernal landscape devoted to working out justice. He is set before Minos, Rhadamanthus, and Aeacus, the judges of the classical afterlife; they are unable to resolve his legal status and refer him to a higher authority—to the monarchs of the underworld, Pluto and Proserpine. On his way to their court he passes through the enactments of Hell's precisely organized justice —horribly poetic justice indeed:

> Where bloudie furies shakes their whips of steele,
> And poore *Ixion* turnes an endles wheele;
> Where vsurers are choakt with melting golde,
> And wantons are imbraste with ouglie Snakes,
> And murderers grone with neuer killing wounds,
> And periurde wightes scalded in boyling lead,
> And all foule sinnes with torments ouerwhelmd.
>
> (I.i.65–71)[13]

But Don Andrea is not allowed to complete his search for justice amid the palpable abstractions of Hell. What the higher court orders is that he should be sent back to earth to observe how the gods operate *there,* and for this purpose he is given Revenge as his companion and guide:

13. The text of quotations from *The Spanish Tragedy* is that of F. S. Boas (Oxford, 1901, 1955).

Forthwith, *Revenge,* she rounded thee in th' eare,
And bad thee lead me through the gates of Horn,
Where dreames haue passage in the silent night.
No sooner had she spoke, but we were heere,
I wot not how, in twinkling of an eye.

REVENGE

Then know, *Andrea,* that thou art ariu'd
Where thou shalt see the author of thy death,

. . . .

Depriu'd of life by *Bel-imperia.*

(I.i.81–87, 89)

Revenge here seems to bear the same relation to justice as Talus (in Book V of *The Faerie Queene*) does to Artegall—that is, he is the emotionless and terrifyingly nonhuman executive arm of the legality that is being demonstrated. But Revenge, unlike Talus, does not act in his own person; his presence guarantees that the human action will work out justly, but he is not seen to make it do so. The departure of Andrea and Revenge through the gates of horn, Virgil's *porta*—

Cornea, qua veris facilis datur exitus umbris—

and their arrival at the Spanish court, can indeed be seen as dramatic equivalents to the introductory sequences of medieval dream allegory. The play may be viewed in this sense as what Andrea dreams, as an allegory of perfect justice: "The gods are indeed just; and now you shall see how their justice works out." We are promised a mathematical perfection of total recompense, where justice and revenge are identical. From this point of view the human beings who appear in Andrea's dream—the characters of the play, scheming, complaining, and hoping—are not to be taken by the audience as the independent and self-willed individuals they suppose themselves to be, but in fact only as the puppets of a predetermined and omnicompetent justice that they (the characters) cannot see and never really understand. But *we* (watching the whole stage) must never lose sight of this piece of knowledge.

The concern with justice in the opening scenes establishes an ironic set of responses for the audience and an ironic mode of construction for the play. The structure, indeed, may remind us of a Ptolemaic model of the universe, one level of awareness outside another level of awareness and, outside the whole, the unsleeping eye of God.

The disjunction between what the audience knows and what is known in the Spanish court is established straightaway when the "play proper" starts. The Spaniards congratulate themselves on the late victory and stress the unimportance of the losses:

> All wel, my soueraigne Liege, except some few
> That are deceast by fortune of the warre.
>
> (I.ii.2–3)

And again: "Victorie, my Liege, and that with little losse." *We,* seeing Andrea sitting on the stage, know that the "little losse" can be too easily discounted and that the "some few" may yet blemish the complacency of the court and the overconfident assumption that justice is already achieved:

> Then blest be heauen, and guider of the heauens,
> From whose faire influence such iustice flowes.
>
> (I.ii.10–11)

We now see assembled before us the characters who are to be involved in the final demonstration of justice, centrally Don Balthazar, who is to die (we have been told) by the hand of Bel-imperia. But what we see in the opening scenes is no movement that can be understood as leading toward the death of Balthazar. What happens involves Balthazar with a variety of different kinds of justice, but the play is obviously more interested in exploring thematic comprehensiveness than in moving toward any narrative consequence.

The problem of deciding justly between competing claims to truth, which has appeared already in the dispute between Aeacus and Rhadamanthus, recurs in the contest between Lorenzo and Horatio, who dispute which of them, in law, has Balthazar as prisoner; and the king shows a Solomon-like wisdom in making a just decision:

> Then by my iudgement thus your strife shall end:
> You both deserue, and both shall haue reward.
> Nephew, thou tookst his weapon and his horse:
> His weapons and his horse are thy reward.

> *Horatio,* thou didst force him first to yeeld:
> His ransome therefore is thy valours fee; [etc.].

(I.ii.178–183)

Expectation is tuned into a competency of human justice that *we* know cannot finally be sustained against the meddling of divine justice in this human scene.

The next scene introduces the Portuguese episode so famous for its irrelevance to the main action. The first scene of the "play proper" showed the Spaniards rejoicing over their victory and absorbing Balthazar into their court life. What the second (Portuguese) scene does is to show us the other side of the coin—the Portingales bewailing their defeat. And actually the Portuguese scenes serve as a continuous counterpoint against the earlier stages of *The Spanish Tragedy,* not only setting Portuguese sorrow against the Spanish mirth of the first scene, but later inverting the counterpoint and setting the viceroy's joy at his son's recovery against Hieronimo's cry of sorrow and demand for vengeance. Moreover, the long aria of grief put into the viceroy's mouth in I.iii gives the first statement of what is to become the central theme of *The Spanish Tragedy,* certainly the central and most famous impulse in its rhetoric—that frantic poetry of loss and sense of universal injustice which was to give Hieronimo his fame. We can see that, in spatial terms, the viceroy prepares the way for Hieronimo by living through the same class of experience—the loss of a son. Hieronimo makes this point quite explicitly when he says at the end of the play:

> Speake, Portaguise, whose losse resembles mine:
> If thou canst weepe vpon thy *Balthazar,*
> Tis like I wailde for my *Horatio.*

(IV.iv.114–116)

The viceroy does not weep at this point, when Balthazar is really dead, but the opening scenes and the speeches in which he bewails his supposed death sustain our sense of what Hieronimo is referring to. Moreover, the connection between national sin and individual sorrow which seems to be implied in the main story of Hieronimo and Horatio is quite explicit in the Portuguese episode:

> My late ambition hath distaind my faith;
> My breach of faith occasiond bloudie warres;

Those bloudie warres haue spent my treasure;
And with my treasure my peoples blood;
And with their blood, my ioy and best beloued,
My best beloued, my sweete and onely Sonne.

(I.iii.33–38)

But this scene of sorrow does more than prepare for the second and central lost son, Don Horatio; it establishes an ironic countercurrent inside the framework of the general information that has been given us by Andrea and Revenge. Not only is it deeply ironic to see the viceroy bewailing the death of a son, who is at that moment involved in the murder of another son, Horatio, and the bereavement of another father (and we should note that this second bereavement is one which cannot, this time, be avoided as if by a miracle [see III.xiv.34]). But more, the general framework of the play tells us that it is ironic even when the viceroy changes from lamentation to rejoicing; for *we* know that the relationship with Bel-imperia which looks so auspicious from inside the play will be the actual cause of his death.

The short fable of human fallibility and divine concern which supplies the narrative (as against the thematic) substance of the Portuguese episode —this feeds into the main plot an expectation that ". . . murder cannot be hid: / Time is the author both of truth and right, / And time will bring this trecherie to light" (II.v.58–60); it strengthens the expectation which Revenge and Andrea arouse by their very presence—that wrong must soon, and inevitably, be followed by retribution. It is no accident that places the second Portuguese scene (III.i)—which shows Alexandro rescued from death, as if by miracle, at the very last moment—immediately after the death of Horatio and the first sounds of Hieronimo's passion: "What out-cries pluck me from my naked bed, [etc.]" (II.v.1) The discovery of Horatio is the center of the main plot, being the reenactment in real life of the death which began the action of the play; for Don Horatio is, as it were, the living surrogate for the ghost Andrea. As he was friend and revenger to Andrea on the battlefield, so he has taken on the role of lover to Bel-imperia, and so too he falls victim to Balthazar (and his confederates). And this is the point in the play where the sense of just gods directing a revenge on Balthazar is at its lowest ebb. As Andrea understandably exclaims to Revenge:

> Broughtst thou me hether to encrease my paine?
> I lookt that *Balthazar* should haue beene slaine:
> But tis my freend *Horatio* that is slaine,
> And they abuse fair *Bel-imperia,*
> On whom I doted more then all the world,
> Because she lou'd me more then all the world.
>
> (II.vi.1–6)

The reinforcement of the justice theme at this point is, therefore, particularly useful. Even if the Portuguese episode had no other function, this one would seem to justify it.

Andrea was returned to earth by the just gods, to witness a parable of perfect recompense, a parable which would reenact the story of his life, but cleared of the ambiguities and uncertainties that had surrounded him. The death of Horatio re-presents the death of Andrea, but presents it as a definite crime (as the death of Andrea was not) and makes Balthazar into a definite criminal (as in the battle he was not). More important, the death of Horatio raises up an agent of recompense who has the best claim to justification in his action—the father of the victim and a man renowned for state service, the chief judicial functionary of the court. Kyd goes out of his way to show Hieronimo in this function and to make the first citizen tell us that

> . . . for learning and for law,
> There is not any Aduocate in Spaine
> That can preuaile, or will take halfe the paine
> That he will in pursuit of equitie.
>
> (III.xiii.51–54)

Hieronimo is justly at the center of *The Spanish Tragedy* because he is constructed to embody perfectly the central question about justice that the play poses: the question, "How can a human being pursue the path of justice?" Hieronimo is constructed to suggest both complete justification of motive (his outraged fatherhood) and the strongest advantages in social position. And as such he is groomed to be the perfect victim of a justice machine that uses up and destroys even this paragon. Herein lies the truly cathartic quality of *The Spanish Tragedy:* If this man, Kyd seems to be saying, fails to find any secure way of justice on earth, how will it fare with

you and me? For Hieronimo, for all his devotion to the cause of justice, is
as much a puppet of the play's divine system of recompense as are the other
characters in the action. He is stuck on the ironic pin of his ignorance; we
watch his struggles to keep the action at a legal and human level with
involvement, with sympathy, but with assurance of their predestinate
failure:

> Thus must we toyle in other mens extreames,
> That know not how to remedie our owne;
> And doe them iustice, when uniustly we,
> For all our wrongs, can compasse no redresse.
> But shall I neuer liue to see the day,
> That I may come (by iustice of the heauens)
> To know the cause that may my cares allay?
> This toyles my body, this consumeth age,
> That onely I to all men iust must be,
> And neither Gods nor men be iust to me.
>   DEPUTY
> Worthy *Hieronimo,* your office askes
> A care to punish such as doe transgresse.
>   HIERONIMO
> So ist my duety to regarde his death,
> Who, when he liued, deserued my dearest blood.
>   (III.vi.1–14)

He calls on heavenly justice; what he cannot know is that his agony and
frustration are part of the process of heavenly justice. As his madness takes
him nearer and nearer the nightmare world of Revenge and Andrea, this
mode of irony is reinforced. Hieronimo tells us:

> Though on this earth iustice will not be found,
> Ile downe to hell, and in this passion
> Knock at the dismall gates of *Plutos* Court,
>
> . . . .
>
> Till we do gaine that *Proserpine* may grant
> Reuenge on them that murd<e>red my Sonne.
>   (III.xiii.108–110,120–121)

What he cannot know is that this is precisely what Don Andrea has
already done—indeed the explanation of the whole action of the play up to
this point. Again and again he calls on the justices of Hell:

Goe backe, my sonne, complaine to *Eacus,*
For heeres no iustice; gentle boy, be gone,
For iustice is exiled from the earth:
Hieronimo will beare thee company.
Thy mother cries on righteous *Radamant*
For iust reuenge against the murderers.

(III.xiii.137–142)

. . . thou then a furie art,
Sent from the emptie Kingdome of blacke night,
To sommon me to make appearance
Before grim *Mynos* and iust *Radamant,*
To plague *Hieronimo* that is remisse,
And seekes not vengeance for *Horatioes* death.

(III.xiii.152–157)

But these infernal judges have already acted. All that Hieronimo can see is that he, the justice, the magistrate, the proponent of civil order, is living in a world where justice is impossible, where

. . . neither pietie nor pittie mooues
The King to iustice or compasion,

(IV.ii.2–3)

and where heavenly justice does not seem to be filling in the lacuna left by the failure of civil justice:

O sacred heauens, if this vnhallowed deed,
If this inhumane and barberous attempt,
If this incomparable murder thus
Of mine, but now no more my sonne,
Shall vnreueald and vnreuenged passe,
How should we tearme your dealings to be iust,
If you vniustly deale with those, that in your iustice trust?

(III.ii.5–11)

The heavens are not asleep, in fact, but their wakefulness has a different aspect from that which mortals expect. Hieronimo knows the orthodox Christian doctrine of Romans XII.19, which tells us ("Vindicta mihi, ego retribuam, dicit Dominus") to leave revenge to God:

Vindicta mihi.
I, heauen will be reuenged of euery ill;
Nor will they suffer murder vnrepaide.
Then stay, *Hieronimo,* attend their will:
For mortall men may not appoint their time.

(III.xiii.1–5)

But no more than Andrea can he apply this knowledge or relate it to what
is happening to himself and to those around him. Andrea feels that
everything is going the wrong way:

I lookt that *Balthazar* should haue beene slaine:
But tis my freend *Horatio* that is slaine.

(II.vi.2 ff.)

And when (in the next act) he finds that Revenge has actually been
sleeping while the wicked continued their triumph, Heaven's conspiracy
with injustice seems to be complete. But Revenge is coldly contemptuous
of these passionate human outcries:

Thus worldlings ground, what they haue dreamd, vpon.
Content thy selfe, *Andrea;* though I sleepe,
Yet is my mood soliciting their soules.
. . . .
Nor dies *Reuenge,* although he sleepe awhile;
For in vnquiet quietnes is faind,
And slumbring is a common worldly wile.
Beholde, *Andrea,* for an instance, how
Reuenge hath slept, and then imagine thou
What tis to be subiect to destinie.
    [*Enter a dumme shew.*]

(III.xv.17–19,22–27)

The menace and even horror of Revenge's outlook, for those who are
"subject to destiny," needs to be stressed. The presence of a justice machine
in this play is no more cozily reassuring than in Kafka's *Strafkolonie.* For
the irony of its operation works against Andrea and Hieronimo no less
than against Lorenzo and Balthazar.

All in *The Spanish Tragedy* are caught in the toils of their ignorance
and incomprehension, each with his own sense of knowledge and power
preserved intact, and blindly confident of his own (baseless) under-

standing, even down to the level of the boy with the box (III.v). This episode—the only clearly comic piece of business in *The Spanish Tragedy* —catches the basic irony of the play in its simplest form. The boy's preliminary explanation of the trap set up, and his key sentence, "Ist not a scuruie iest that a man should iest himselfe to death?" establishes the usual Kydian disjunction in the levels of comprehension. Throughout the following trial scene (III.vi) the boy stands pointing to the empty box, like a cynical emblem of man's hope for justice; and yet the irony has also (as is usual in the play) further levels of complexity. For Lorenzo, the organizer of the ironic show which seals Pedringano's lips even while it betrays his body to the hangman, is himself a victim, not only in the larger irony of Revenge's scrutiny but also in the minor irony that it is his very cleverness that betrays him: It is Pedringano's letter that confirms Hieronimo's knowledge of the murderers of Horatio. Lorenzo, indeed, as Hieronimo remarks, "marcht in a net and thought himselfe unseen" even at the time he was entrapping others.

Hieronimo prides himself on his devotion to justice and his thoroughness as a judge, but he serves divine justice by ceasing to be just at all in any human sense. The feeling of incomprehension, of not knowing where he is, in terms of the standards by which he has ordered his life—this drives him mad; but even here he reinforces the play's constant concern with justice by his mad fantasies of journeys into the hellish landscape of infernal justice.

> *Hieronimo,* tis time for thee to trudge:
> Downe by the dale that flowes with purple gore,
> Standeth a firie Tower; there sits a iudge
> Vpon a seat of steele and molten brasse, [etc.]
>
> (III.xii.6–9)

His incomprehension is inescapable because it is a function of his humanity. His madness is a direct result of the collision of his human sense of justice with the quite different processes of divine justice; for it is a fearful thing to fall into the hands of a just God. The absorption of the human into the divine justice machine is the destruction of the human, and Hieronimo becomes the instrument of Revenge by becoming inhuman. He becomes part of the hellish landscape of his imagination. In the play of Soliman and Perseda that he organizes we have yet another reenactment of the situation that began with Don Andrea. Bel-imperia (certainly resolute even if not certainly chaste) plays the part of "Perseda chaste and resolute." Balthazar, the princely lover who hoped to win Bel-imperia from her common lovers (Andrea, Horatio), plays the Emperor Soliman, who hopes to win Perseda from her common love. The crimes and killings in the play are organized by the Bashaw or Pasha, and this is the part to be played by Hieronimo himself. When asked, "But which of us is to performe that parte?" he replies:

> O, that will I, my Lords, make no doubt of it:
> Ile play the murderer, I warrant you,
> For I already haue conceited that.
>
> (IV.i.130–133)

The Spanish Tragedy as a whole has continuously set the marionette-like action of the man whose destiny is predetermined against the sense of choice or willpower in the passionate and self-confident individual. Continuously we have had actors watching actors but being watched themselves by still other actors (watched by the audience). *We* watch Revenge and Andrea watching Lorenzo watching Horatio and Bel-imperia; we watch Revenge and Andrea watching Hieronimo watching Pedringano watching the boy with the box; and at each point in this chain what seems free will to the individual seems only a predetermined *act* to the onlookers.

In the play within the play, in Hieronimo's playlet of Soliman and Perseda, this interest reaches its climax. The illusion of free will is suspended. The four central characters are absorbed into an action which acts out their just relationships *for them*. The net has closed, character has become role, speech has changed to ritual; the end is now totally predetermined. The play itself is a flat puppet-like action with a total absence of personal involvement; but as the characters intone their flat, liturgical responses to one another there is an enormous *frisson* of irony or disparity between what they say and what *we* know to be meant.

Hieronimo himself has become *instrument* rather than agent. *He* knows that his life has been absorbed into the ritual and that he cannot escape back into humanity, and he accepts this Hegelian kind of freedom (freedom as the knowledge of necessity) with a resolution at once noble and inhuman. At the end of his play he comes forward to speak his own epilogue:

> Heere breake we off our sundrie languages,
>
> . . . .
>
> And, Princes, now beholde *Hieronimo,*
> Author and actor in this Tragedie,
> Bearing his latest fortune in his fist;
> And will as resolute conclude his parte
> As any of the Actors gone before.
> And, Gentles, thus I end my play.
>
> (IV.iv.74,146–151)

Commentators on the denouement of *The Spanish Tragedy* usually concentrate on the human *mess* which follows Hieronimo's failure to complete his life in ritual, noticing the break in the pattern rather than the pattern itself. But I think that the nature of the final actions is only kept in focus if we see them as measuring the gap between the dream of justice and the haphazard and inefficient human actions that so often must embody it. This is a recurrent interest of a writer like Seneca. When he describes the suicide of Cato Uticensis, his greatest hero, he is not content to relate his fortitude in doing the deed; he stresses the horror of Cato's failure to finish himself off in one clean blow. What he is concerned to show is the persistence of Cato's will to die, in spite of his own inefficiency. And I think a similar concern to contrast the will to martyrdom with the *mess* of actual martyrdom can be seen at the end of *The Spanish Tragedy.*

A martyr is rather exceptional if his suffering is not prolonged and humanly degrading; a martyr whose soul had been antiseptically abstracted from his body would be rather unlike those whose histories thronged the Elizabethan imagination, whether from *The Golden Legend* or from its local equivalent, Foxe's *Acts and Monuments.* We should remember that it was not simply Zeno who anticipated Hieronimo by biting out his own tongue, but St. Christina as well. Much ink has been spilled in sympathy for Castile, who is struck down at the end of the play, simply because he stands too close to the protagonist. But Castile is, of course, identified with the tormenters who seek to interrupt the ritual and prevent it from completing itself. It is Castile who suggests that torture is still of use, to compel Hieronimo to *write* the names of his confederates. And the death of Castile confers another dramatic advantage: It transfers mourning to the highest personage on the stage. The king of Spain has hitherto been concerned with the miseries of existence only at second hand. Now, at the end of the play, he himself becomes a principal mourner, as is indicated well enough in the final stage direction:

The Trumpets sound a dead march, the King of Spaine *mourning after his brothers body, and the* King of Portingale *bearing the body of his sonne.*

In the final episode we return to the justice of Hell, where the characters of the play now supply the classical examples of sin and wickedness with which the play began ("Place *Don Lorenzo* on *Ixions* Wheele," [IV.v.33]). A last judgment places everyone where he morally belongs (as in the *Last Judgment* play at the end of the mystery cycles), but we would do less than justice to the complexity of this play if we did not notice that humanity has been sacrificed so that justice can be fulfilled. Revenge has been completed; we have seen what Fulke Greville describes as the mode of modern tragedy: "God's revenging aspect upon every particular sin to the despair and confusion of mortality."

Theme, Imagery, and Unity
in A Chaste Maid in Cheapside

Ruby Chatterji

RICHARD LEVIN'S RECENT ARTICLE on the interrelations of the four plots of *A Chaste Maid in Cheapside* does justice to the highly complex structure of this fascinating comedy and covers an area of Middleton criticism so far practically neglected.[1] While admiring the details of Professor Levin's elaborate and meticulous analysis, I feel, nevertheless, that the ground plan of the play is still missing. What fundamental design did Middleton have in mind when mustering with such splendid skill his own architectonic abilities? Why did he select the particular episodes that he did? In other words, what exactly brings together and unifies the various plots of the play, not excluding the Touchwood Senior episode? The answer, I believe, has to be sought not merely at the level of plot (causal or analogical), but at yet another level, at which Middleton has ultimately integrated his work and with which the level of plot is correlated. *A Chaste Maid in Cheapside* is a fine achievement of the Elizabethan multiple unity, since, as has been recognized, the distinction of the play lies in its range and inclusiveness, the forging into coherent artistic pattern of material apparently heterogeneous, an ingenious reconciliation of dis-

1. Richard Levin, "The Four Plots of *A Chaste Maid in Cheapside*," *R. E. S.*, XVI (1965), 14–24.

cordants into a well-integrated comic whole. Middleton was dramatist enough to make a virtue of a necessity, even to glory in it. Among other modes of dramatic unification conventionally resorted to in the Elizabethan period, particularly when an unwieldy number of episodes or subplots were concerned, the most potent, though not always the most obvious, was the thematic. *A Chaste Maid in Cheapside* not only subscribes to this thematic unity, but, belonging as the play does to the genre of poetic drama, its language—particularly its imagery—also contributes significantly to the integration of the different dramatic components, endorsing the author's unified comic vision. A consideration of the play's principal theme and of its image technique can therefore, I believe, provide the necessary clue to its organization.

I

Middleton's favorite perspective, that of looking at life in terms of the family, has received critical comment.[2] It is this viewpoint that attains final comic shape in *A Chaste Maid in Cheapside,* as it awaits tragic shape in *Women Beware Women* and *The Changeling.* In fact the family is the nexus of the play's various complications, the basis of its thematic as well as structural unity. The progress of the action admittedly depends on intrigue and counterintrigue, and they get delightfully complicated in the play's course. Yet, critically speaking, the initial comic situations, together with the problems they pose, become far more relevant to the understanding of the play than the intrigues. The latter exist not for themselves (as they do in *A Mad World, My Masters*) but for the comic solutions they provide, even if not originally intended to do so, as answers to these problems. The characters are intimately related to the situations and actions because the situations are either created by the characters or depend on them, while the intrigues are motivated by the characters in their conflict and interaction. Whereas in an early play like *The Phoenix* Middleton tries to link up fortuitously diverse satiric units through family relationships, by the time he writes *A Chaste Maid in Cheapside* not only are family ties used to

2. S. Schoenbaum, "*A Chaste Maid in Cheapside* and Middleton's City Comedy," *Studies in the English Renaissance Drama in Memory of Karl Julius Holzknecht,* ed. Josephine W. Bennett *et al.* (New York, 1959), pp. 292–293.

establish "causal connexions among the different plots," but the family itself as a functional dramatic unit becomes the focus of his comedy.

The family, as theme, is a subject of perennial human interest, with its appeal to fundamental instincts, but in this play it gains considerable local value by being rooted to a particular, Jacobean, social setting. In *A Chaste Maid in Cheapside* the concept of the family is comically explored in almost all conceivable detail, but primarily in relation to begetting and birth, the necessary corollaries of the social institution of marriage. The rearing and upbringing of children, from the time of birth till the time they are well settled in life to start families of their own, also naturally constitute the comic concern of this play. The family, in all its implications, receives more systematic comic attention here than in any other play of Middleton or for that matter, perhaps, in any other Jacobean comedy. Therefore, to look at the play is to look at its various family units (out of which situation, character, action, mood, all emerge) and to study the problems in which each has become involved as a family. All the different plots are comic variations on this family theme.

We are introduced first to the Yellowhammer household, a typically bourgeois goldsmith family, which engenders both the Moll and Tim plots. Since the children in this family are already grown up, the prime concern of the parents is their proper education and marriage, and these are well under way in the very first scene. As representative citizen parents, the Yellowhammers share Quomodo's attitude of the social climber and seek to gain status by finding rich upper-class matches for both daughter and son. Maudlin Yellowhammer, the mistress of the house, is a proud descendant of Noah's wife in the miracle plays, her energies as scold being directed not to her husband but to her daughter. She is introduced loudly upbraiding her daughter for not responding sufficiently to her music and dancing lessons. Her frank contrast of her own youth, "I was lightsome and quick two years before I was married" (I.i.10–11),[3] with her daughter's, whom she depreciates as fit to be a plumber's daughter and not a goldsmith's, is rich in ironic implications, both moral and professional. In her ardor to recommend the knight to her daughter, it appears that she herself would like to have him, if only she could. Middleton's irony consciously plays upon the mother-daughter relationship, and one is

3. Thomas Middleton, *Works,* ed. A. H. Bullen (London, 1885–1886), used as the reference text.

obliquely reminded of Lethe's theory regarding Thomasine's affections (in *Michaelmas Term*), as in other respects Thomasine is an obvious contrast to Mistress Yellowhammer. Finding her daughter's responses to the knight so cold, Maudlin also uses Falso's language of tender grievance (over his niece)[4] and tries to goad her into a distasteful match. On her daughter's escape from the house, the virago is reported to have been seen in her full physical violence, hotly chasing her runaway daughter in a smelt boat and tugging her back by the hair. Though she is depicted as a cruel mother to Moll, here the action is farcical, the exaggeration and incongruity of her behavior making her role comic. Maudlin is the typical shrew. Still tugging Moll's hair, she wishes to make her own daughter "an example / For all the neighbours' daughters" (IV.iii.48), and triumphantly presents her to her father: "I've brought your jewel by the hair" (IV.iii.51).

Maudlin's husband, though overshadowed, represents the reverse of the same coin. He shares his wife's citizen aspirations and takes care to lock up his daughter safely, like his gold. Informed of his would-be son-in-law's moral depravity, he merely refers to his none-too-spotless youth and decides in favor of the match; after all, "The knight is rich" (IV.i.258). Marriage to him, then, is but an act of social convenience, though his own daughter is involved. Even her presumed death does not deter him from manipulating for the "rich Brecknock gentlewoman" (V.ii.98) as a good match for his son, to which his wife echoes assent. Lastly, when neither marriage turns out to his satisfaction he can still appease his citizen instincts for thrift by economizing on a joint wedding feast. A stock comic idea in Middleton, the single feast for a double purpose (compare *A Mad World, My Masters, A Trick to Catch the Old One*), is here given a satiric point.

Maudlin's relations with her son also occasion much comic business. Tim is solicitously being provided a Cambridge education, silver spoon included, so that he may turn out a bachelor of art "and that's half a knight" (I.i.153). Like mother, like son. If Tim has the foolish pedantry to send a Latin letter, Maudlin has the presumption to interpret it, claiming,

---

4. FALSO. A foolish coy bashful thing it is; she's afraid to lie with her own uncle.
                                                              (*The Phoenix*, II.iii.32–33)
   Cf. MAUDLIN. . . . Faith, the baggage [is]
A bashful girl, sir; these young things are shamefac'd.   (I.i.115–116)

"I was wont to understand him" (I.i.65–66). But the irony is that she can neither read Latin nor understand him as a mother (her social inferior, Hobson's porter, is at least shrewd enough to misconstrue the Latin to his own advantage), and Middleton makes the most of a dramatic situation by linking up the verbal comedy to traits of character. Maudlin sends for Tim from Cambridge because "There's a great marriage / Towards for him. . . . A huge heir in Wales at least to nineteen mountains / Besides her goods and cattle" (III.ii.107–110). She tries to embolden him for wooing by calling him up among the female company of gossips at the Allwit christening, and characteristically offers him six sugarplums, which even her fool of a son resents. She also presumes to discuss her son's academic progress with his tutor. Trusting to the direct method of wooing, she locks the door on her son and the "Brecknock gentlewoman," but her plans are nearly frustrated by the fool's Latin pretensions. Tim's sole occupation in the play seems to be a fool's delight in parading his folly. The logical disputes of Tim and his tutor (IV.i) follow upon the irrational quarrel of the Kixes (III.iii), and both would appear on the stage as equally devoid of reason and farcically exaggerated, though on different planes.

The Welsh courtesan, as bait, combines the traditions of a rich heiress (as in *A Trick to Catch the Old One*) and a pure virgin (as in *A Mad World, My Masters*), but is rather basely drawn, with none of the redeeming virtues of her predecessors. Dramatically she is a perfect match for Tim: a prize for his own stupidity and a retribution for his parents' covetousness, since the professed heiress is found to possess nothing at all, not even her maidenhead.

Moll is the only chaste person in this highly dubious household, as, apparently, in all Cheapside. In her single-minded devotion to her lover and her frantic efforts to be united with him, she is a romantic comedy heroine, complete with swan song. Yet Middleton seems to have used dramatic shorthand in delineating her character. Shorn of the pathetic sentiment surrounding a Rose (in Dekker's *The Shoemakers' Holiday*) or a Luce (in *The Knight of the Burning Pestle*), Moll is depicted as the active partner in intrigue, escaping through unromantic holes and gutters. Even when she calls upon death (IV.iii), the context must dispel all pathos: Her parents scold in characteristic language, and her fatuous brother conceives the bright idea of keeping watch over her in armor (an obvious burlesque). Later when she appears to be dying (V.ii), her parents still wrangle in mutual faultfinding while Tim and his tutor vie with each other to compose epitaphs in what they regard as a fight against time. To ask a Jacobean public theater audience to restrain laughter at such provocation would be asking the impossible. Surely Middleton knew what he was doing. One suspects the spirit of Littlewit's Hero and Leander puppet show to have entered surreptitiously in the handling of Moll and her affairs by the dramatist.

Touchwood Junior is drawn in the tradition of witty intriguer heroes like Middleton's own Follywit and Witgood. He wins a wit combat with Yellowhammer all in "good mirth," the father-in-law realizing too late that the posy on the ring is a joke at his own expense. The emphasis is again on parental relationship. Just as Yellowhammer puts himself on guard—"we cannot be too wary in our children" (I.i.169)—Touchwood Junior aims at "blinding parents' eyes," at the same time comically justifying his action: "Rather than the gain should fall to a stranger, / 'Twas honesty in me t'enrich my father" (I.i.164–165). As in the case of all intriguer heroes, he has a standby, his brother, who thus also has a family link to him.

That the Moll and Tim sequences are related as opposites has been observed by Professor Levin, but it needs to be stressed that the contrast is clinched by both characters belonging to the same household and involving the same set of parents, who play no negligible, if opposed, parts in the two plots. In fact the contrast lies fundamentally in the children's relation to their parents and the parents' respective attitudes. Moll is the rebellious daughter, making her own choice of a husband and resisting their imposition of Sir Walter, much to their annoyance. Tim is the docile son, gloating in his Cambridge learning, appreciated and shown off by his mother, smacking his lips over an arranged match, acquiescent in his parents' values, even siding with them in their harassment of his sister. By the time their two stories end, the parents too, we hope, have learned their lesson of parental folly. In respect to mood, while a general farcical tone unites the Yellowhammers with affairs of both daughter and son, yet the solid realism of the goldsmith's house (unrivaled even in *Eastward Ho*), with its harsh mercenariness, sets off the romantic plot, on the one hand, and the low farce, on the other, both equally removed imaginatively.

If the Yellowhammer family is taken up with problems of grown-up children, the problems of the other three families of the play concern the begetting and birth of children and also their maintenance. In fact, the relation of "riches" to "children," a favorite comic idea of Middleton (compare *Michaelmas Term*), is fully elaborated in this play: "Some only can get riches and no children; / We only can get children and no riches" (II.i.11–12). The two contrasted situations sum up the predicament of the Kixes and the Touchwoods. The Allwits glory in someone else's wealth and have to put up with someone else's children. The Yellowhammers, possessing both children and riches, value riches above their children. All pose problems for the comedy.

From the point of view of the family, the Allwit household represents the most outrageous comic situation that Middleton ever contrived. Though he may have taken hints from literary sources,[5] the comic technique of inflation-plus-inversion is a mode congenial to Middleton that attains final expression here. (It is, in fact, present as early as *The Phoenix*, in the treatment of the captain who envies his friend's being kept by a courtesan and who in his turn unhesitatingly sells his wife.) The stock figure of the jealous husband who unintentionally helps his wife to cuckold him (like Harebrain) is reversed in the contented cuckold, Allwit. The comedy is savagely grotesque. Allwit's soliloquy cataloguing point by point the blessings of a cuckold's life (I.ii.11–56) is a *reductio ad absurdum* which appalls and shocks by its Swiftian irony of logical rigor. The comic apogee is reached with the complete inversion of roles between husband and cuckolder. Sir Walter is made to smart under the stings of jealousy while Allwit falls a-singing of dildoes. To the servants he is no longer the master but the mistress' husband.

The family theme is emphasized by the inclusion of children. Nick and Wat innocently (but ironically) refer to Allwit as their father while he curses them under his breath as bastards. Their education and future are often referred to, and it is significant that even Sir Walter wishes to prevent his bastards from mingling with the legitimate children he hopes to get in marriage. Mistress Allwit is conspicuous in the state of expecting her seventh bastard; the baby is born and christened. The family position is dramatically explored in what are regarded as the best scenes of the play, those connected with the christening of the bastard. By the very nature of the situation, this christening is a flagrant violation of all that the

5. Schoenbaum, p. 294.

traditional ritual stands for—divine blessing, intimate family ties, social harmony—though the form is rigidly maintained. Allwit limits his task to inviting the gossips. Sir Walter not only supervises everything but sacrilegiously offers himself as the godfather to his own begotten child, in order to deceive the world. With appropriate symbolic significance Allwit gets into one of Sir Walter's suits on the morning of the busy day. The situation provokes numerous *double entendres*. Properly enough, at the christening most of the conversation dwells on the topics of begetting and birth and the correct upbringing of children, so that these scenes not only appeal by their realism but also underline the major theme of the play.

The comic corollary of the explosive Allwit situation is the fantastic action of the wittol, who does his best to subvert the marriage prospects of the cuckolder in fear of losing his own source of income. His poor relation, Davy, having a similar ax to grind, incites him to this attempt. The ensuing scene (IV.i), in which Allwit describes himself most truthfully in highly derogatory terms, under the guise of a well-wisher and a relative to the Yellowhammers, is supreme in Middleton's concentric irony. Allwit's pose as a moral guardian is as ridiculous as his imposture of being a relation is false. And even so, what is the true nature of the benefit that he is supposed to reap for himself by this devious stratagem? But, of course, Yellowhammer can be trusted to get over his momentary moral compunctions as soon as Allwit's back is turned, and Allwit's purpose is defeated without his even realizing it.

Sir Walter's wound comes like the announcement of doomsday to the Allwit family. Mistress Allwit falls in a faint, while Allwit is ready to depart from this world with Sir Walter. This unnatural parasitic relationship (contrasted with that of the natural parasite, Davy) is amusingly shocking. Sir Walter's penitence and realization of sin are at first regarded as "raving," and the whore and her bastards are employed to restore him to his senses. That the children should be made to appeal to Sir Walter as the last resort of the Allwits again ironically points up the family theme. But since this only provokes the "will" of curses, the incorrigible Allwit family take their revenge by forsaking Sir Walter altogether in his hour of need. Husband and wife now become amicably reconciled, and their depravity is absolute as they brazenly plan to set up lodgings in the Strand with the very stock of Sir Walter's leftover goods.

Since a family is the thematic and structural unit of the play, Sir Walter

Whorehound is to be regarded as the villain of the piece in his active role of
the disrupter of families. His final rejection by the Allwits is in the ironic
parting-shot tradition of Middleton (compare Proditor's turning on the
captain in *The Phoenix*). A close parallel to Penitent Brothel in his
repentance, Sir Walter is, however, steeped so far in sin that it is impossible
for him to save himself or reform others. His futile penitence and the lack
of salvation become almost a tragic theme at this point (echoing *Dr.
Faustus* and *Macbeth*) and look forward to Middleton's own tragedies:

> Her pleasing pleasures now hath poison'd me,
> Which I exchang'd my soul for.
>
> (V.i.80–81)

A comic villain may have appropriate comic retribution, and so long as
serious sentiment is kept at bay one makes no objection; but the introduction of penitence, its poetic intensity combined with its ineffectuality, tends
to disrupt the comic tone. After all, the comic (and cynical) question posed
so far has been: As between equals, Allwit and Sir Walter, who reaps the
greater advantage? Evidently Middleton's purpose is to alienate audience
sympathy from the Allwits, for although Sir Walter is the dramatic villain,
Allwit is made the principal satiric target at this point.

Touchwood Senior's family life offers an allied dramatic theme. Husband and wife might have lived happily had not the husband's fertility
proved so disastrous. "You do but touch and take" (II.i.69), ruefully
observes the Country Girl, who appears with his bastard and gives him a
piece of her mind before she can be bribed off. A farcical episode is made
out of the clever disposal of the bastard. The discovery of a child for a
lamb's head in the time of Lent recalls the Mak episode of the Towneley
Second Shepherds' Play, in reverse. Middleton shows his dramatic skill by
making a topical digression into a derivative comic incident. Sandwiched
between scenes of the Allwit christening, its thematic link is the social
accommodation of bastards. While Allwit has apparently resigned his
family duties out of perversity, Touchwood has been forced to do so by
sheer necessity; the comic smugness and complacency of one stands out
against the comic uneasiness and reluctance of the other. Touchwood's
hyperbolic eulogies on his wife's perfection may be contrasted with
Allwit's sneering grotesqueries about his. The two wives, too, are well
balanced: Mistress Touchwood and Mistress Allwit are both fertile, but

while Mistress Touchwood is fully prepared to contain her desires and live away from her husband, Mistress Allwit cuckolds her husband by indulging them, though living under the same roof.

In exact contrast to the Touchwoods stand the Kixes, whose marriage has proved equally unhappy for lack of children. But while the Touchwoods are patiently submissive to fate and decide upon living separately, the Kixes refuse to accept their situation calmly. They "fall out like giants, and fall in like children" (III.iii.48) and are seen alternately scolding and kissing in bold, farcical manner. They quarrel aggressively on the constant theme of begetting and birth, charging each other with infertility. "O that e'er I was begot, or bred, or born!" (II.i.117) Lady Kix laments, her language subconsciously expressing her own desires as well as reiterating the play's theme. Kix's bargain with Touchwood Senior—the payment by results and the even distribution of the reward over different stages in the actual process of having a child—has the typical Middleton touch:

> One hundred pound now in hand.
> . . . .
> Another hundred when my wife is quick;
> The third when she's brought a-bed; and the last hundred
> When the child cries, for if't should be still-born,
> It doth no good, sir.
>
> (III.iii.127–131)

Not only is it supposed to be a neat and careful business deal, but once more the comic theme of begetting and birth is closely explored. The Kixes' excess of joy when the medicine takes (as it must) farcically matches their previous wrangling.

The Kixes and the Touchwoods are an immediately contrasted pair of problem families. They have the affinity of belonging to the same type of genial farce, and neatly dovetail into each other when they team up to maintain and perpetuate their respective families, the lighthearted spirit of the solution almost anticipating Restoration comedy. The Allwit family, on the other hand, sets off both of these by its sordidly mercenary character. A kind of comic ratio may then be established if we compare the atmosphere of the Yellowhammer household in relation to the Moll and Tim sequences with that of the Allwit household in relation to the Touchwood and Kix plots, while taking into account at the same time the fact that the Yellowhammers and Allwits, as citizens of Cheapside, share a common scale of values.

The denouement, as befitting a comedy, is meant to bring about a happy ending all round, and it actually succeeds in preserving the various family units intact. Master and Mistress Yellowhammer continue their joint citizen life and have the (somewhat equivocal) satisfaction of seeing their children married and thus starting new families. Moll and Touchwood Junior undergo a comic resurrection from death and are married, presumably to live happily ever after. Even Tim's wife announces she will turn honest, if not by logic then by marriage. The Allwits are unexpectedly, if reluctantly, rescued from their abnormal situation and plan to live together as best they may. The family troubles of both the Touchwoods and the Kixes are blissfully over. Sir Walter, however, has no family. He courts Moll more for her dowry than for anything else, and tries to pass off his courtesan as a virgin. He undermines the very concept of marriage in a citizen household, and also seeks to thrive on the barrenness of another couple. Therefore he alone is punished. His real punishment is the disinheritance, which ties up neatly with the rest of the play, but Middleton lays it on heavily by confining him to prison for debt. As a consequence, "Reverend and honourable Matrimony" (". . . thou that mak'st the bed / Both pleasant and legitimately fruitful!" [*The Phoenix*, II.ii.166–167]) can now feel safe.

The supreme irony of the play is, of course, that the methods of solution are often as questionable as the problematic situations themselves, so that, though surface respectability is ensured, it is a patched-up one. In the course of the play each family is proved to have violated the basic assumptions of marriage. If Maudlin has been "light" with her dancing master, Yellowhammer has a bastard now grown up. Tim is married to a courtesan. Mistress Allwit has seven bastards including the one that is born, while Touchwood Senior may have had any number. Sir Oliver threatens to keep a whore and shares with Allwit the dishonor of becoming a contented cuckold, though presumably an unconscious one. Lady Kix claims she was other than barren in court, and readily accepts the kind of help that Touchwood Senior has to offer. Even Touchwood Junior is consciously responsible for his brother's dubious intrigue. Moll, the chaste maid of the title, alone is impeccable.

Yet as in the case of Wycherley's *The Country Wife,* the exuberance proves quite amusing; "we stop judging and start counting" (to borrow a phrase), as I have done. What has been remarked of Horner's stratagems may be equally applicable to the stratagems in the present play: "They are morally preposterous and factually incredible," demanding "a setting of outrageous farce." [6] Touchwood's device to cure the Kixes is both ironical and fantastic, resembling the china episode in *The Country Wife*. The monstrosity of the Allwit household may be compared to the Horner situation; in both the assumptions go unquestioned, the comedy lying in what follows given such premises and in the extent of the absurdity to which conclusions can be pursued without the play's going up *in fumo*. Middleton and Wycherley share this highly explosive comic quality in their best plays, though their social values may differ considerably.

II

The language of *A Chaste Maid in Cheapside* reflects its dramatic maturity, and is completely adapted to its stylistic requirements. The play's imaginative conception demanded a verse medium, and while Middleton transfers the suppleness and flexibility of his prose to verse, at the same time the verse remains capable of lending itself to the necessary stylization. Transitions from prose to verse are made imperceptibly, unlike the rigid, sealed-off divisions of his early plays. In effect, the highly dramatic quality of his medium in the mature tragedies is already anticipated. Speech is carefully governed by the local necessities of character and mood, of realism and comic inflation: Citizen colloquialism, indecent grotesquery, parody of Latin and scholastic logic, Puritan Old-Testament idiom, Welsh dialect—all find their place in this linguistic medley and contribute toward the total comic effect. Though Middleton's use of imagery is remarkably sparing, compared with that of his contemporaries, an over-all poetic organization has been achieved by a significant pattern of images and key words related to the play's comic themes and attitudes.

The play's main theme being the family, the word "house" is repeatedly used with particular appropriateness and almost symbolic significance. A tension is set up among the subtly variant meanings of the term—dwelling,

6. T. W. Craik, "Aspects of Satire in Wycherley's Plays," *English Studies*, XLI (1960).

home, family, lineage—often with ironic intention. Allwit effusively expresses his gratitude to Sir Walter:

> I thank him, has maintain'd my house this ten years;
> Not only keeps my wife, but 'a keeps me
> And all my family.
>
> (I.ii.15–17)

Sir Walter has maintained his house simply in the financial sense, as also ironically in begetting his family, and the abnormality of the Allwit situation is adequately defined. On the news of Sir Walter's wound, Mistress Allwit laments, "A misery of a house" (V.i.1), and Allwit echoes her: ". . . here's like to be / A good house kept, when we're all together down" (V.i.9–10). Again there is the interplay of meanings to which dramatic irony is added, since the kind of "house" kept so far has meant a total inversion of both house and housekeeping. When Allwit again takes up the word—"Cannot our house be private to ourselves" (V.i.137), "You have been somewhat bolder in my house / Than I could well like of" (V.i.143–144)—and finally drives Sir Walter literally out of his house (place of refuge), all his previous usages of the term and its different meanings are ironically brought to bear on his action.

Conversely, the Kixes presumably take the Touchwood Seniors within their house—"I've purse, and bed, and board for you" (V.iv.73)—in their unconsciously ironical mutual-benefit arrangement. Touchwood Senior refuses to keep his own bastard, on the ground "I've no dwelling; / I brake up house but this morning" (II.i.90–91), which factually describes his plight while serving as an excellent excuse for his reluctance. When the exasperated Sir Oliver threatens "to give up house" and keep a "fruitful whore" (III.iii.59), Touchwood Senior in his turn tries to pacify him by promising means "To get and multiply within your house" (III.iii.64), where the double meaning is again ironically obvious. The Kixes' situation is chorically summed up by their maid: ". . . weeping or railing, / That's our house-harmony" (II.i.166–167). Her irony underlines the problem that it is in fact "house-harmony" which has been violently jarred into discord in the various family units that come within the play's comic scope. The future continuity of happy family life is also hinted at in the same terms when Touchwood Senior banteringly refers to Moll's marriage: "Now you keep house, sister" (V.iv.49).

Language imagery, both literal (e.g., references, descriptions) and figurative (simile, metaphor, analogy), is coordinated with stage imagery (e.g., action, stage property) to give the effect of unified comic vision. The Cheapside goldsmiths speak with their broad citizen accent while their vulgarity and debased scale of values are reflected in their language. Their class and professional biases are never forgotten: Their imagery is characteristically drawn from their wealth. Maudlin's contemptuous admonition of her daughter in the opening scene establishes her identity: "You fit for a knight's bed! drowsy-browed, dull-eyed, drossy-spirited!" (I.i.11–12); or

> You dance like a plumber's daughter, and deserve
> Two thousand-pound in lead to your marriage,
> And not in goldsmith's ware.
>
> (I.i.20–22)

Not only does the virago have her choice of vigorous epithets (comically pointed by alliteration), as does her husband when sufficiently roused, but the goldsmith's wife's pride of profession is revealed in the sharply contrasted pairs of images: dross / lead against gold, plumber against goldsmith. Middleton's irony is of course at Maudlin's expense, and the traditional moralistic undertone of the intrinsic value of lead over gold (as symbolized by Portia's caskets) is given an interesting comic twist.

Gold imagery is a composite part of the play's pattern. Realistically correct in the context of a goldsmith's family trade (one must remember such stage business as the weighing of a customer's gold chain in I.i and the ironic ring-making episode), this image is made to carry poetic significance by being related to the play's themes of greed and commercialism.

> I bring thee up to turn thee into gold, wench,
> And make thy fortune shine like your bright trade;
> A goldsmith's shop sets out a city maid. —
>
> (I.i.103–105)

says Sir Walter to his Welsh whore. (Notice the comic emphasis by the use of a concluding couplet and a sawlike generalization.) Here turning into gold has the connotations of both exchange and alchemy, while "shine" and "bright," normally applied to gold, are given ironic turns by being linked euphemistically to a dubious profession; "setting out" carries *double entendre* and multiple shades of meaning: "to embellish, adorn, deck out," "to display for sale," with perhaps the additional suggestion of "precious stone set in gold" (*O.E.D.*). Allwit also uses the gold image to describe literally and figuratively what he considers his unique situation: "I have the name, and in his gold I shine" (I.ii.40). Yellowhammer's concern to keep Moll in safe custody is expressed in the conventional language of a miser hoarding gold (compare *A Staple of News,* IV.i).

> In the meantime I will lock up this baggage
> As carefully as my gold; she shall see
> As little sun, if a close room or so
> Can keep her from the light on't.
>
> (III.i.40–43)

Maudlin, echoing her husband sarcastically, uses a related image: "I've brought your jewel by the hair" (IV.iii.51). Even Tim cannot forbear using the family imagery: "Chang'd? gold into white money was ne'er so chang'd / As is my sister's colour into paleness" (V.ii.16–17).

Literal references to wealth and riches reinforce the figurative imagery in evoking a world of commercialized values:

> I shall receive two thousand pound in gold,
> And a sweet maidenhead worth forty.
>
> (IV.iii.77–78)

Sir Walter anticipates his good fortune purely in financial terms. "O how miraculously did my father's plate 'scape! . . . Besides three chains of pearl and a box of coral" (IV.ii.2, 4), comments Tim thankfully at his sister's disappearance. (One is reminded of Shylock's dual sorrow for his daughter and his ducats.) A mother thus expresses concern for her dying daughter:

> The doctor's making a most sovereign drink for thee,
> The worst ingredience dissolv'd pearl and amber;
> We spare no cost, girl.
>
> (V.ii.24–26)

> Thou shalt have all the wishes of thy heart
> That wealth can purchase!
>
> (V.ii.82–83)

Yellowhammer couples "riches" with love: "You overwhelm me, sir, with love and riches" (I.i.132)—where the comic juxtaposition also contains dramatic irony by unwittingly referring to a penniless whore.

Touchwood Junior's attitude defines the dramatic norm from which others have departed: "How strangely busy is the devil and riches" (I.i.159), and the two implied equations are meant to counterbalance each other. When Touchwood Junior himself uses gold imagery, it is in conjunction with a vegetative image, "And shake the golden fruit into her lap" (III.iii.12), where the implications are not primarily commercial, though the suggestion of Kix's getting both child and property is subtly present.

Food imagery, particularly of flesh, is pervasively used in the play, since most of the *dramatis personae* are perpetually being driven by some kind of appetite: for food, for sex, for money. Stage imagery is correlated with language imagery, and an intricate texture results. Maudlin's recommendation of a husband—"had not such a piece of flesh been ordained, what had us wives been good for? to make salads, or else cried up and down for samphire" (I.i.6–9)—is typical; to her, food and sex are almost interchangeable concepts, and the pursuit of the image to include the fine distinction between flesh and vegetable is ludicrously comic. Allwit's wife "longs" for nothing "but pickled cucumbers" (I.ii.7) and Sir Walter's coming: Food and sex, governed by the same verb, are brought together, resulting in a comic grossness of attitude, particularly in its dramatic context. Allwit aptly likens his position to that of a man "Finding a table furnish'd to his hand" (I.ii.12) and in his turn refuses to "feed the wife plump for another's veins" (I.ii.47); he also resists "being eaten with jealousy to the inmost bone."

Combined with the food-eating imagery, anatomical references reinforce the sense of physical grossness. The latter is further exemplified in such phrases as "rip my belly up to the throat" (III.ii.194), "With one that's scarce th' hinder quarter of a man" (III.iii.83), "what cares colon here for Lent?" (II.ii.79). Literal references to food, whether in speech or action, often acquire an unhealthy savor by their sensual associations and rankness of context. Such are the references to sweetmeats and the action of their distribution and pocketing, with Allwit's pungent asides, in the christening scene (III.ii), where poor Tim finds his sugarplums so insipid; or Allwit's enumeration of his wife's delicacies (I.ii.37). The list of aphrodisiacs (III.iii.17–19) on which Touchwood Senior is made to dine brings food and sex together on a farcical level. Even Touchwood Junior speaks of himself in terms of eating: "Or else pick a' famine" (I.i.140), "it but whets my stomach, which is too sharp-set already" (I.i.145).

Middleton's comic use of the flesh image seems to be popularly inspired. "Mutton" was a contemporary cant term for a prostitute, and the *double entendre* whenever flesh is mentioned must have been quite transparent to the popular audience. This is easily perceived when Touchwood Junior refers to Sir Walter's Welsh whore—". . . and brought up his ewe-mutton to find / A ram at London" (I.i.138–139)—where the idea of the coupling of animals is fused into it (compare *Othello,* I.i.88–89). Touchwood Senior takes up the same image: "I keep of purpose two or three gulls in pickle / To eat such mutton with" (II.i.80–81); and he defines his ideal of marriage in similar terms: "The feast of marriage is not lust, but love" (II.i.50), while its opposite is to "suck out others'."

In the scene of the disposal of the bastard by the Country Girl (II.ii), stage imagery spills over into language imagery, and a complex of interrelations between associated images is established, contributing significantly to the play's comic unification. "Flesh" is made to apply to both human beings and animals, comically obscuring the differentia; and "flesh" also suggests food and sex, as it does elsewhere. Live animal, dead animal, animal flesh, human flesh, live human being—these concepts are variously juxtaposed, fused or disjuncted, combined and recombined to maintain a taut irony. Touchwood Senior refers to his bastard as "this half yard of flesh, in which, I think, / It wants a nail or two" (II.i.83–84), and expresses his anxious concern about its disposal: "What shift she'll make now with this piece of flesh / In this strict time of Lent, I cannot imagine; / Flesh dare not peep abroad now" (II.i.105–107). The identifica-tion between human being and animal flesh is complete. Figurative interchanging of a human being with an animal is translated into stage action in the ruse practiced by the Country Girl on the promoters. As a general background of the play, Lent with its "carnal strictness" (the phrase itself is telling) serves to emphasize the irony of all the different types of appetite depicted; but locally the concentration is on the desire for flesh (meat) as the passion of the season. Touchwood Senior comments on Lady Kix's behavior:

> I hold my life she's in deep passion
> For the imprisonment of veal and mutton
> Now kept in garrets; weeps for some calf's head now:
> Methinks her husband's head might serve with bacon.
>
> (II.i.119–122)

The Lenten scene (II.ii) ironically proliferates with figurative and literal references to food, particularly meat: "This Lent will fat the whoresons up with sweetbreads, / And lard their whores with lambstones" (II.ii.64–65). "A bird" (II.ii.74), though primarily a term derived from snaring, is also food by implication, followed by references to veal, green-sauce, green goose. Meat is contrasted with fish, which symbolizes the strictness of Lent. Allwit's "scornful stomach" will admit no fish; a man caught by promoters must do with "herrings and milk pottage" in lieu of meat, while the promoters gloat over their seized veal. Guesses about the bastard, with "rump uncovered" and disguised under "a good fat loin of mutton," range over "a quarter of lamb," "a shoulder of mutton," "loin of veal," and a "lamb's head." The victims of the imposture see their folly in terms of expense for food: "Half our gettings / Must run in sugar-sops," since they have been figuratively made "calves' heads," and they exasperatedly leave the stage to "roast their loin of mutton." It appears that Lent might turn into a veritable banquet of flesh on the street outside, while inside Allwit's house comfits and wine are served at an ironical christening. One type of social corruption reinforces another analogically, and both are partially expressed in terms of an inordinate desire for food.

Animal imagery is the peculiar prerogative of Allwit in keeping with his character, though it is Whorehound who is named after an animal by the vice of his nature. While Yellowhammer refers to Moll as "minx" (III.i.48) and Lady Kix dubs her husband "grub" (III.iii.98) in the heat of passion, Allwit quite dispassionately regards his wife as a pig: "My wife's as great as she can wallow" (I.ii.6); "As now she's even upon the point of grunting" (I.ii.30). He describes the promoters as hungry dogs, "sheep-biting mongrels" (II.ii.94). Connotations of animal and human being coalesce in his comic conceits:

> Ha, how now? what are these that stand so close
> At the street-corner, pricking up their ears
> And snuffing up their noses, like rich men's dogs

> When the first course goes in? . . .
>
> .   .   .   .
> T'arrest the dead corps of poor calves and sheep.
>
> (II.ii.54–57, 59)

Various bodily processes referred to or depicted on the stage—eating, drinking, kissing, copulating, begetting, wetting—stress the physical aspect of human beings and bring them closer to the animal kingdom, not only in Allwit's speeches, where they predominate, but practically throughout the play.

Apart from the major images considered, minor images may also be shown to link up with the major imagery by association. Even when independently used, such images nonetheless perform a functional role by being intimately connected with theme and characterization. The term "fat" is often applied in association with the animal-cum-human imagery, perhaps implying that human beings fattening on the flesh of animals imbibe their subhuman qualities. Such is Sir Walter's characterization of the promoters' bawds:

> The bawds will be so fat with what they earn,
> Their chins will hang like udders by Easter-eve,
> And, being stroak'd, will give the milk of witches—
>
> (II.ii.67–69)

where supernatural associations are also added, the inflated and deliberate grotesquery being an intrinsic quality of his language throughout the play. Allwit's analogies for the wittol's household dovetail the different implications of "flesh" with a commercial image appropriate in the play's bourgeois background:

> As other trades thrive, butchers by selling flesh,
> Poulters by vending conies . . . .
>
> (IV.i.226–227)

Imagery of poison, though not outstanding in the play's scheme, is connected with the food/meat imagery, on the one hand, and animal imagery, on the other, since the opposite of food is poison and it is also the property of certain animals to exude poison. The promoters, as the chief targets of topical satire, are the subjects of the most direct animal imagery, characteristically addressed by Allwit as dogs (already quoted) and reptiles:

> And other poisonous officers, that infect
> And with a venomous breath taint every goodness.
>
> (II.i.115–116)

The most poignant expression of the poison image is in Sir Walter's repentance:

> My taste grows bitter; the round world all gall now;
> Her pleasing pleasures now hath poison'd me,
> Which I exchang'd my soul for.
>
> (V.i.79–81)

His meat has turned into poison, which now sickens him (the alliteration fixes the paradox), and the commercial metaphor in a religious context underlines the profanity of his action. The fish-flesh opposition, set up naturally in its Lenten context, is taken up with a difference in the incident of Moll's escape by water. Maudlin takes a smelt boat, which leads Tim to comment that she goes "afishing" for Moll, to which Yellowhammer concludes: "She'll catch a goodly dish of gudgeons now, / Will serve us all to supper" (IV.iii.44–45). When Moll is dragged back half-drowned, Tim describes the scene:

> She hath brought her from the water like a mermaid;
> She's but half my sister now, as far as the flesh goes,
> The rest may be sold to fishwives.
>
> (IV.iii.53–55)

But here fish and mermaid carry sexual *double entendres*. As representative of the bourgeoisie, the Yellowhammers' stock of imagery also includes other forms of merchandise (apart from their family—gold / jewel—images) or financial transactions:

> As there's no woman made without a flaw;
> Your purest lawns have frays, and cambrics bracks.
> But 'tis a husband solders up all cracks.
>
> (I.i.34–36)

E'en plain, sufficient subsidy-words serves us, sir.

(I.i.128)

The concepts of dry and wet are counters playfully tossed about in the play's scheme. Kix, as his name implies, is barren and therefore dry; " 'Tis our dry barrenness puffs up Sir Walter" (II.i.153), Lady Kix complains. Wetness applies to fertility, and Touchwood Senior is supposed to get "Nine children by one water that he useth" (II.i.174); his sallies are also referred to as "drinkings abroad." But wetness also implies urine. The gossips refer to a girl too wet to be married; Allwit comments on fingers washed in urine, and suspiciously looks for wet under the stools. Tim is nauseated by the wet kisses of a gossip. In a serious context, dryness is lack of grace; Sir Walter bequeaths the Allwits:

> All barrenness of joy, a drouth of virtue,
> And dearth of all repentance.

(V.i.103–104)

Such examples illustrate Middleton's way with language, the effort of the conscious artist to wring different meanings out of the same word, adapting a similar method to comic or tragic issues. This mode of work becomes most systematized in his greatest play, *The Changeling*.

Middleton was no mean artist, and particularly when writing his major comedy he appears to have completely mastered the art of unity in variety. Therefore, the first impression of a bewildering medley, rich but crazy, turns out on closer inspection (and the play demands such scrutiny) to be a vitality and exuberance well within the dramatist's control. A wide range and variety of situations, characters, actions, moods, language are integrated within the play's scheme. The comic tone ranges from hilarious farce to the grimly grotesque, and all shadings from the light to the sombre are present in this chiaroscuro effect. The realism of Middleton has been repeatedly noticed, and *A Chaste Maid in Cheapside* is obviously rooted in the everyday realities of the Jacobean social world: its class conflict, citizen behavior, puritan hypocrisy. Localization in space—London of Cheapside —is balanced by localization in time: Lent with its strict laws and their violations. But what is artistically more significant is the play's stylization, the comic distortion and violent coloring that the characters, almost caricatures, receive through the audacious poetic technique that Middleton adopts as the final phase of his comic development. It is as though the realism of Middleton's social comedies—*The Phoenix, Your Five Gallants, Michaelmas Term*—combines with the fancifulness of his domestic-intrigue comedies—*A Mad World, My Masters, A Trick to Catch the Old One*—and both together acquire a new direction, testifying to a rare synthesis of poetic sensibility and intellectual energy in the play's comic organization. Perhaps only the peculiarly sophisticated yet accommodating nature of the Jacobean public stage could do full justice to this distinctive play, yet one would like to see *A Chaste Maid in Cheapside* revived today.

Bartholomew Fair *as Blasphemy*

Jackson I. Cope

. . . my lord of Winton told me, he told him, he was (in his long retyrement and sicknes, when he saw him, which was often) much aflickted, that hee had profain'd the scripture, in his playes; and lamented it with horror. . . .
Izaak Walton to John Aubrey
(*Jonson,* ed. Herford and Simpson, I, 181–182)

I

IN THE MACILENTE of *Every Man Out of His Humour,* who shares enough characteristics to be identified as a *persona* for the author Asper and for the author Jonson, the creative imagination controlling a dramatic world is embodied as a madman. The creator's poem is the satiric image of his own vileness, but once projected upon this stage of fools, that vileness is purified, the madness runs its course, and the whole is reduced to play, to the wispy breath of a theatrical impromptu, when Macilente sighs, "I could wish / They might turn wise upon it, and be sav'd now, / So heav'n were pleasd: but let them vanish, vapours" (V.xi.63–65).

I make the point in order to sharpen our focus through contrast, for in *Bartholomew Fair* the created comes into independent life (as does the embedded analogue of the wooden puppet who converts the living puritan), refusing to relinquish its autonomy into the hands of a hapless authority the ways of whose world are as mad as those of Macilente's. There is sufficient ethical questioning here to have evoked Professor Heffner's conclusion to one of the most careful examinations of the play: "All search for warrant seems as absurd as Troubleall's. . . . Whim, animal appetite, and sordid greed have complete sway over men's actions without as well as within the fair; the fair merely provides the heightened

conditions under which their disguises fall off and the elemental motivations become manifest." [1] But there is more than ethical questioning in
Bartholomew Fair: It probes the wellsprings of religious consciousness to
discover absurdity in the fullest sense of the word in both conscience and
providence, in works and in grace—indeed, in all varieties of view which
focus in the implicit axiom that there obtains some teleological relation
between creator and creation, between God and the world. So much is this
true that we might define Jonson's work as an anti-morality play.

II

"Enormities," cries Adam Overdo, justice of the court of Pie-powders
and hence immediate authority over the economies of the play, "Many are
the yearly enormities of this Fair." [2] He is right, the word and the thing

1. Ray L. Heffner, Jr., "Unifying Symbols in the Comedy of Ben Jonson," in
English Stage Comedy: English Institute Essays, 1954 (New York, 1955), p. 96.
That *Bartholomew Fair* was contemporarily recognized as a study in arbitrary
authority as the cause of both puritan and profane social revolts is demonstrated by
Richard Brome's *Covent-Garden Weeded* (1632–1633). Here the "weeder" is a
justice of the peace who invokes "my Reverend Ancestor *Justice Adam Overdoe*"
for precedent in hunting out all the "enormities" (*Dramatic Works of Richard
Brome* [London, 1873], II, 2–3). These enormities turn out to be hypocritical
puritanism in a young man whose motive was to cross the will of an uncontrollably
dominating, whimsical father, and wild carousing on the part of other sons allegedly
studying . . . law. There is a hubbub of patented "protestations" among the
members of the Philoblathicus roaring club (II, 39–41) which corresponds closely to
the "vapouring" contest of *Bartholomew Fair,* and there is the eventual discovery by
the twin authorities, Crosswill and Cockbrain, that their efforts not only have
caused, but cannot control, revolt by their progeny. While Brome's play lacks the
symbolic structure which broadens Jonson's scope, it nonetheless has been closely
studied by one critic who concludes justifiably that "a cautious correlation can be
made between the terms of this play and the circumstances of Caroline England.
. . . Brome here approaches in humorous terms the fact that . . . an inflexible and
unintelligently restrictive policy on the part of the paternal state can induce a
desperate and equally inflexible reaction" (R. J. Kaufmann, *Richard Brome,
Caroline Playwright* [New York, 1961], pp. 86–87; cf. 67–87).
2. II.i.42. All citations are from the Revels Plays edition of *Bartholomew Fair,*
ed. E. A. Horsman (London, 1960). It is pertinent to notice that the justice fails in
his duty and holds no Pie-powders Court at all on this notable day; see IV.vi.64–69.

threading through the course of his disguised observation of a hubbub emanating from thieves, whores, pimps, and pudding stuffers. And there is fast approaching that fullness of time which he has awaited, the judgment day: "this is the special day for detection of those foresaid enormities" (II.i.44-45). It is the day because he has come among the children of the fair in the guise of a fool to record the scenes of sin: "Here is my black book for the purpose, this [disguise] the cloud that hides me" (II.i.46-47). Immediately his discoveries begin, as sharp practitioners enter threatening to betray one another in the name of the Pie-powder justice. "I am glad," observes Overdo, "to hear my name is their terror, yet" (II.ii.27). It is a refrain which he repeats to the fright of Knockem, the horse courser, later: "is not my name your terror?" (V.vi.11). But the justice is not yet ready to flood the revels of iniquity with the storm of his terror: "neither is the hour of my severity yet come, to reveal myself, wherein, cloud-like, I will break out in rain and hail, lightning and thunder, upon the head of enormity" (V.ii.3-6). As he once observes, ripeness is all: "I will not discover who I am till my due time; and yet still all shall be, as I said ever, in Justice' name" (III.iii.39-40).

"And it came to pass on the third day in the morning, that there were thunders and lightnings, and a thick cloud upon the mount . . . so that all the people that was in the camp trembled" (Exodus XIX.16). Thus begins the description of the coming of the commandments that Moses relates in the detailed reading of "the book of this law," which, replete with reminiscences of the fiery cloud of concealment, constitutes the "Fifth Book of Moses, called Deuteronomy." As the course of human history is fulfilled in the Apocalypse of the New Testament, the imagery once more gathers into familiar conjunctions—properly, for he who here "cometh in clouds" is "Alpha and Omega, the beginning and the ending" (Revelation I.7-8). From the cloud issues the vision of the sealed book of judgment, "For the great day of his wrath is come" (VI.17) when "hail and fire mingled with blood, and they were cast upon the earth" (VIII.7). Clearly Justice Overdo formulates his mission of raining judgment upon Bartholomew Fair in the imagery of Jehovah's judgments, such as that which came upon Tyre, Old Testament archetype of corrupting riches: "The merchants of Sheba and Raamah, they were thy merchants: they occupied in thy fairs with chief of all spices, and with all precious stones, and gold. . . . Thy riches, and thy fairs, thy merchandise . . . in the midst of

thee, shall fall into the midst of the seas in the day of thy ruin. . . . Thou
hast defiled thy sanctuaries by the multitude of thine iniquities, by the
iniquity of thy traffic; therefore will I bring forth a fire from the midst of
thee. . . . All they that know thee among the people shall be astonished at
thee: thou shalt be a terror, and never shalt thou be any more" (Ezekiel
XXVII, XXVIII *passim*). This was the type of judgment held up by Jesus
before those "like unto children sitting in the markets" when he promised:
"I say unto you, it shall be more tolerable for Tyre and Sidon at the day of
judgment, than for you" (Matthew XI.22).

The bent for thinking in scriptural imagery constitutes a superficially
improbable similarity between what one reader has tagged "the conscientious Anglican judge Overdo and the fanatical Puritan preacher Busy," [3]
for Zeal-of-the-Land too turns instinctively to Old Testament types for his
justification in pulling down the gingerbread stall:

I was mov'd in spirit, to be here, this day, in this Fair, this wicked, and foul
Fair . . . to protest against the abuses of it, the foul abuses of it, in regard of
the afflicted saints, that are troubled, very much troubled, exceedingly troubled,
with the opening of the merchandise of Babylon again. . . .

(III.vi.82–87)

Neither puritanical zeal nor Scripture was reserved for those outside the
Establishment in 1614, [4] and it might be agreed that Overdo's near-
blasphemous self-references converge with the milieu of the Purecraft-
Littlewit household merely to enlarge the anti-puritan satire and remind
that zeal is as accessible to the ignorant as to the hypocritical. It might be
agreed, that is, did not the others of the fair acquiesce in Adam Overdo's
consciousness of a Jehovan authority, did not the action thoroughly
support Troubleall's assertion that "If you have Justice Overdo's warrant,
'tis well: you are safe; that is the warrant of warrants" (IV.i.18–19). And
this last absolute seal of power is woven by echo as well as implication into

3. Henry W. Wells, *Elizabethan and Jacobean Playwrights* (New York, 1939),
p. 205.

4. For a fascinating Anglican case history one can turn to that of Henry Burton,
preacher at St. Matthew's in London, who from his pulpit stimulated his notorious
parishioner John Bastwick; see William Haller, *The Rise of Puritanism* (New York,
1938), pp. 250–259. Cf. the general survey in William P. Holden, *Anti-Puritan
Satire, 1572–1642* (New Haven, 1954), pp. 137–141, 151–152.

the imagistic apotheosis of the justice when Troubleall cries out: "I mark
no name, but Adam Overdo; that is the name of names; he only is the
sufficient magistrate; and that name I reverence" (IV.vi.145–147; cf.
Ephesians I.21, Philippians II.9).

His name *does* strike terror among the stalls, as his own minions the
watchmen assert in language appropriate only for the anger of a god:

BRISTLE

He will sit upright o' the bench, an' you mark him, as a candle i' the socket, and
give light to the whole court in every business.

HAGGIS

But he will burn blue, and swell like a boil (God bless us) an' he be angry.

BRISTLE

Aye, and he will be angry too, when he list, that's more: and when he is angry,
be it right or wrong, he has the law on's side, ever. I mark that too.

(IV.i.69–76)

Bristle's last remark embeds whimsy pretty deeply into the thunderer's
nature, beyond furnishing a pointed Shakespearean allusion. It will be
remembered that in the *Discoveries* Jonson observed of Shakespeare that

Many times he fell into those things, could not escape laughter: As when hee
said in the person of *Caesar*, one speaking to him; *Caesar, thou dost me wrong.*
Hee replyed: *Caesar did never wrong, but with just cause:* and such like; which
were ridiculous.[5]

The passage on a law as ridiculous as it is absolute so fascinated Jonson that
he tossed it to his audience as a mere tag again in the Induction to *The
Staple of News,* and its appearance as allusion in *Bartholomew Fair* leads
us back to its own Induction, for there, too, Shakespeare had appeared in a
motley supplied by his friend's satiric gibes.

The book-holder's articles of agreement with the audience not only serve
to fuse their world with that of Jonson's fair, as Professor Horsman has
demonstrated,[6] but also to initiate the movement of three themes which

5. *Ben Jonson,* ed. C. H. Herford and P. and E. Simpson (Oxford, 1925–1952),
VIII, 584. For the fullest discussion see J. Dover Wilson, "Ben Jonson and *Julius
Caesar,*" *Shakespeare Survey* 2, ed. Allardyce Nicoll (Cambridge, 1949), pp. 38–42.

6. "Introduction," ed. cit., pp. xiv–xix.

will eventually converge: (1) antiquated judgments, (2) legalism, and (3) puritanism—the last through the inevitable ambiguity of the repeated term "covenant." [7] It is in relation to the first of these themes that the book-holder gives an ambivalent judgment upon those wits whose "virtuous and staid ignorance" shows in their constancy, from which they "will swear *Jeronimo* or *Andronicus* are the best plays yet" (Induction, 98–113). These are, of course, revenge plays in the old tradition of poetic justice rough-hewn—the justice of "eye for eye, tooth for tooth, hand for hand," the justice of the old law. *The Spanish Tragedy* was Jonson's (and everyone's) inevitable target for ridicule from *Every Man in His Humour* onward, but *Titus Andronicus* is mentioned nowhere else in his works. The reason for its appearance here is, I believe, to bridge by association the leap from the book-holder's catalogue of antiquated types to the sudden attack on Shakespeare's more recent romances:

If there be never a servant-monster i' the Fair, who can help it? he says; nor a nest of antics? He is loth to make Nature afraid in his plays, like those that beget *Tales, Tempests,* and such like drolleries.

(128–132)

The point is that if *Titus Andronicus* is a play of just revenge, *The Winter's Tale* and *The Tempest* had closed Shakespeare's career in an aura of mercy providentially triumphant, with man's divine nature shining through his disguising passions, as Perdita shone through her peasant's weeds. From the time that Edgar told Gloucester, "Thy life's a miracle," the theme echoed, and it has become a commonplace to observe Prospero's insistence. "How came we ashore?" inquires Miranda at the opening. "By Providence divine," responds her father. And at the close Ferdinand assures all that Miranda is mortal, not goddess, "But by immortal Providence she's mine." Such cries of wonder are the proper chords with which to harmonize the ironic counterpoint of Busy's cry, "We are delivered by

7. For the modern audience, this legal word's religious aspect might coalesce with the other Old Testament language only in retrospect. But in Jonson's early-century London, the puritans' specialized adaptation of "covenant" certainly dominated over the secular sense; see Champlin Burrage, *The Early English Dissenters . . . 1550–1641* (Cambridge, 1912), I, 68 ff., esp. 75 n, 76–77.

miracle" (IV.vi.160) when Troubleall frees the victims of the stocks in the course of his own providential wanderings.[8] These cries are more than expressions of pious confidence in the gods that be, however, in plays which center upon men whose magic embodies the power of deity; for the late Shakespeare they are the symbolic tropes which broaden the implications of his plot into a restatement of the universal validity in the Christian design of man's divine comedy. Jonson alludes to these very recent plays, then, to orient our attention to the symbolic mode of his own drama of God and man and Providence, but the pattern is of a very different design in a world wherein the staff of quasi-omnipotence is carried by Overdo rather than by Prospero.

Moreover, even in ironically warning his audience not to be "so solemnly ridiculous as to search out who was meant by the Ginger-bread-woman . . . what Mirror of Magistrates is meant by the Justice" (136–149), Jonson concludes with a clue for the true "grounded judgments and understandings" as to the direction in which such allegorical spying might naturally lead. Let no one, warns the book-holder, charge "profaneness because a madman cries, 'God quit you,' or 'bless you'" (153–154).[9]

But the profanity is explicit, and persistent, throughout the last two acts, threaded as they are by Troubleall's crazed course through the mazes of the fair's intrigues. He has scarcely entered, seeking authority, when he departs with his fixed phrase: "I do only hope you have warrant, for what

8. It is interesting to notice that G. C. Thayer, *Ben Jonson: Studies in the Plays* (Norman, 1963), pp. 224–225 reads *The New Inn* as an approach toward the regeneration patterns of *The Winter's Tale* and *The Tempest*.

9. Overdo's topical identification has been much discussed. But for our context, it is worth recalling two points: (1) that "mirror" cannot here be used in the sense of a warning glass and (2) that the word sometimes means "paragon" in the seventeenth century, an ambiguity which allows it to function simultaneously by warning against allegorical reading and by inviting one to read the symbolic identity of Overdo and his Jehovan prototype. See the alternative discussions in *Jonson*, X, 177, and in Horsman, pp. xx–xxi, 12 n. My argument below makes apparent on internal rather than historical grounds that Herford and Simpson have implied an incorrect solution to the rhetorical question they raise concerning "profaneness": "Throughout the play Troubleall invariably says 'quit you,' 'multiply you,' 'save you,' 'bless you,'. . . . He never prefixes 'God.' Has this prefix been omitted from the text because of the statute against profaning God's name in plays?" (*Jonson*, X, 177–178).

you do, and so, quit you, and so, multiply you" (IV.i.13–15).[10] The
watchmen, Dame Purecraft, Grace, Winwife, Quarlous—all who meet
him are given the benediction, "quit you, and multiply you," innocuous
enough until it suddenly echoes with the blasphemous turn which reinforces Overdo's own self-epithets and identifies him as the drama's deity.
Frustrated, Cokes cries after a departing Troubleall, "you are a very
coxcomb, do you hear?" And Troubleall returns the terrible reply:

I think I am; if Justice Overdo sign to it, I am, and so we are all; he'll quit us
all, multiply us all.

(IV.ii.107–109)

It may yet be objected with Jonson to such a politic picklock of the scene
as I have played to this point that the profanity has been poured from the
vessel of a madman; but to turn now to an exploration of the action as a
whole will be to justify Dame Purecraft's observation: "Mad, do they call
him! The world is mad in error, but he is mad in truth" (IV.vi.163–164).

III

Nowhere is the revolutionary dispensation of the New Testament in
relation to that of the Old Testament anatomized with more ringing
clarity than in Paul's Epistle to the Romans. "But now we are delivered
from the law . . . that we should serve in newness of spirit, and not in the
oldness of the letter" (Romans VII.6). Here are intertwined two of the
dominant themes which control the action of *Bartholomew Fair*: legalism
and an antiquated severity of judgment.[11] The Induction immediately and

10. *Jonson*, X, 178, glosses from Isaac's blessing to Jacob: "God Almighty bless
thee, and make thee fruitful, and multiply thee" (Genesis XXVIII.3). In any case,
"multiply" is the most ubiquitous of Old Testament blessings, and its progenitive
quality enters into the sexual aspect of *Bartholomew Fair,* which is concerned so
largely with fruitfulness vs. sterility, as discussed below. "Quit" is also emphatically
pointed at the basic quality of the symbolic action, I believe. This word, like
"covenant," bridges the legal and religious vocabularies, and in each offers that
forgiveness (or "mercy") which balances strict justice.

11. A conflicting view, i.e., that "denial of the value of antiquity and learning
seems to be associated with infertility," has been argued by Thayer, *Ben Jonson,*
pp. 139–140 *et passim*.

insistently associates antiquated views with precisely the passing of judgment. The stage-keeper comes in clucking at the perverse author who would not listen to his seasoned advice: "for the whole play, will you ha' the truth on't? . . . it is like to be a very conceited scurvy one, in plain English. . . . I kept the stage in Master Tarlton's time, I thank my stars. Ho! an' that man had liv'd to have play'd in *Bartholomew Fair. . . .*" Chasing this carping nostalgist from the stage, the book-holder is ambiguously satiric at the expense of one we have earlier noticed, "he that will swear *Jeronimo* or *Andronicus* are the best plays yet . . . whose judgement . . . hath stood still, these five and twenty, or thirty years." Such judgments in favor of the old plays of vengeful retribution (contrasted, we recall, with the providentially merciful romances) dovetail intrinsically, of course, into the legalistic Old Testament attitudes and language of Justice Overdo. And it is perhaps appropriate at this point to notice that where he imagines his fullness of "due time" only as "the hour of my severity," he is inverting the province of another Pauline concept and phrase, one which leads us back to the implications of Romans: "When the fulness of the time was come, God sent forth his Son, made of a woman, made under the law, to redeem them that were under the law" (Galatians IV.4–5; cf. Ephesians I.10).

The insistence upon old, superseded standards provides only a set from which attention is directed toward the ultimate implications of legalism in both secular and theological contexts. And it is in these respects that we are invited to contrast the justice, externally disguised as fool and madman, with the hypocritical puritan Busy, whose disguise is his mimicry of Overdo's genuine Old Testament conscientiousness before the "law." Quarlous' description of the Banbury brother is instructive:

A notable hypocritical vermin it is. . . . One that stands upon his face more than his faith, at all times. . . . of a most lunatic conscience. . . . by his profession, he will ever be i' the state of innocence, though, and childhood; derides all antiquity; defies any other learning than inspiration. . . .

(I.iii.133–143)

A casuist who derides antiquity (and for all of his Old Testament imagery, he would justify the eating of roast pig "to profess our hate and loathing of Judaism" [I.vi.94–95]) is a law unto himself; he claims both the authority of Overdo over the consciences of men and the innocence of Cokes. "Childhood," like the "law," is a face [12] which, looked beneath, reveals his kinship with the "children of the Fair," "sons and daughters of Smithfield" (II.vi.61–64). Essence or exterior, however, legalism pursued to its issue in action succeeds in yoking Overdo for a moment of truth with his mimic Busy in the stocks, that trap which blind justice constructs as a retributive symbol for its self-defeat and immobility in a world of the flesh.[13] In *Volpone* the law personified in the ambiguous justice of the *avvocatori* might seem to triumph at least over the disguises of more cunning hypocrisy; in *The Alchemist* the law of the land is bilked precisely by "Face." But in *Bartholomew Fair* neither the law nor Busy's "face" can master the seething chaos of a fair filled with fighting and beating and shouting which defies the very principle of order, even that order of self-interest imposed from beneath the disguises which served so well in Jonson's earlier comedies.

But let us now widen our focus to follow the history and value of two converging legal props: Coke's license and Overdo's warrant,[14] for it is just these symbols which will lead us through a demonstration that law has been corrupted into the letter (false warrant), as in Shylock's bond, and that Grace is for sale because the quality of mercy is unknown in a world blinded by conscience and mad with literal authority.

"Buy any pears, pears, fine, very fine pears," shouts the costermonger, to Joan Trash's chorus of "Buy any ginger-bread, gilt ginger-bread," counterpointed by Nightingale's "Buy any ballads; new ballads?" (II.ii.32 ff.). This is our first introduction to Bartholomew Fair—like those of Tyre, a

---

12. For Busy, casuistry is the manufacture of masks. As he explains to the Littlewits on the subject of eating pig, it "hath a face of offence with the weak, a great face, a foul face, but that face may have a veil put over it, and be shadowed as it were" (I.vi.66–69). This "veil" is a hypocrite's counterpart, of course, to Overdo's "cloud" and Wasp's "vapours"; see below, pp. 141–142.

13. The symbolic stocks are a traditional device borrowed from the morality plays; see T. W. Craik, *The Tudor Interlude* (Leicester, 1962), pp. 92–96.

14. Littlewit, dispenser of the license, and Overdo, dispenser of the warrant, agree in accepting classification under the rubric of "fool." Overdo makes love to the term by adopting the disguise: "They may have seen many a fool in the habit of a Justice; but never till now, a Justice in the habit of a fool" (II.i.7–9); Littlewit is delighted with Win's epithet: "A fool-John she calls me. . . . Pretty littlewit of velvet! A fool-John!" (I.iii.52–53; cf. I.i.27–29).

type of commercialism.[15] The tinkle of trinkets and coins provides background music which culminates in Cokes's insistence upon buying all: ". . . shut up shop presently, friend. I'll buy both it and thee too, to carry down with me, and her hamper, beside. . . . What's the price, at a word, o' thy whole shop" (III.iv.138–143). But innocent silliness deepens into sin when the citizens' wives are persuaded to whore in the interest of the pig booth,[16] and then commercialism goes yet deeper, to the very bases of order, when Littlewit the proctor buys the justice of the stocks for Busy in order to rid himself of the puritan's warnings, happily crying out as his opponent is dragged off: "Was not this shilling well ventur'd, Win, for our liberty?" (III.vi.109). Here is justice doubly corrupted, as the legal representative has to buy true justice for the wrong reasons. But even yet the power of money has not been exhausted; it will go to the very source of authority and responsibility itself. For Overdo, the godlike magistrate of the fair, is corrupted with his world's disease. His ward is Grace, that one freest of God's gifts to man, but "he bought me, sir," Grace explains; "and now he will marry me to his wife's brother . . . or else I must pay value o' my land" (III.v.275–278).

Possession is more than nine parts of the law when Grace can be had by barter through Overdo's warrant, a point even more pressingly urged by the string of thefts and forgeries which thread the play. These begin, like the huckstering, in Edgworth's almost venial removal of Cokes's superfluous purse under the glass eyes of Overdo himself. But they soon center upon license and warrant, those dead letters of the law written, respectively, by a "Littlewit" giving Grace to a "Cokes" and an overdoer giving carte blanche to a madman. The absolute power and emptiness of the license is emphasized at once when Wasp, coming to claim it, refuses even to look at the contents: "nay, never open, or read it to me, . . . I am no clerk, I scorn to be sav'd by my book, i' faith . . . fold it up o' your word and gi'it me; what must you ha' for't?" (I.iv.5–8). The sacredness of the Word is parodied as the unread document is conveyed to Wasp in the

---

15. For a detailed history of the commercial origins and emphasis of the fair through Jonson's time, see Henry Morley, *Memoirs of Bartholomew Fair* (London, 1880), pp. 13–141.

16. IV.v. Alice, beating Mistress Overdo, complains against amateurism: "The poor common whores can ha' no traffic, for the privy rich ones; your caps and hoods of velvet call away our customers, and lick the fat from us" (68–70).

ark of a "black box" wherein the Word can be possessed without being known, and it is only the box itself that Wasp haggles over: "you must have a mark for your thing here, and eightpence for the box; I could ha' sav'd twopence i' that, an' I had bought it myself" (I.iv.21–23). When Cokes joins his guardian, the emphasis upon the sheer physical nature of the letter is reiterated as his appeals to see the license are rebuffed by Wasp's reminder that "there's nothing in't but hard words: and what would you see't for?" and Cokes replies, "I would see the length and the breadth on't, that's all." [17] Wasp refuses, and Cokes, too, settles for the ark rather than the Word: "Then I'll see't at home, and I'll look upo' the case here" (I.v.30–40). Such innocent trust in possession is easy prey for the predators of the fair, however, and when Quarlous employs Edgworth to steal the license from Wasp, the cutpurse further develops the earlier confusion of values concerning insides and outsides:

Would you ha' the box and all, sir? or only that, that is in't? I'll get you that, and leave him the box to play with still (which will be the harder o' the two).
(III.v.254–256)

Yet the cutpurse is only a tool, ironically similar to Cokes and Wasp themselves in assessing ark and law alike as mere things. Quarlous knows better the power of the letter and insists more unscrupulously upon real possession, and it is he who ultimately manages the largest theft by forging the license which has meant so little to those with a merely exterior understanding of its authority:

It is money that I want; why should I not marry the money, when 'tis offer'd me? I have a licence and all, it is but razing out one name, and putting in another.
(V.ii.80–83)

It is Quarlous, too, disguised as Troubleall, who acquires Overdo's "warrant." Overdo, at last trying to show his mercy toward the man made mad by his unbending justice, instead gives infinite power (the warrant bearing only his signature on a page to be filled in at the possessor's will) to the thief who thus steals Grace from his very hands. In the discovery scene

17. "And they shall make an ark of shittim wood: two cubits and a half shall be the length thereof, and a cubit and a half the breadth thereof" (Exodus XXV.10).

at the close, it is his possession of these two documents of the law which gives Quarlous absolute authority, and humbles Overdo to mere "Adam, flesh and Blood." But perhaps the cruelest irony and severest comment on the world of the fair comes earlier, when Quarlous' theft of Troubleall's clothing in the interest of disguise not only gains him the warrant, but forces the madly conscientious victim himself into the vicious circle in which he too becomes a hunted thief who "has stol'n Gammer Urs'la's pan" to cover his nakedness (V.vi.52 ff.).[18]

Commercialism, then, readily passes into theft and corrodes all within its ambience.[19] But what the entangled motifs of money and theft demonstrate is that authority resides in possession, a power as arbitrary as that of the Old Testament Jehovah whose whimsical qualities echo so dangerously in Justice Overdo.

We can view the arbitrariness from its other side if we consider the state of the innocent rather than of the corrupt actors. Overdo's unscrupulous employment of his power of disposition over Grace drives his ward into exposing herself to the lottery of a blind destiny when she agrees to marry the man whose chance word "but of two, or three syllables at most" is chosen by the next passerby. Not only does this scroll of fortune ring one more change upon the terrible power of the literal word emptied of spirit, but it also compounds that horror when the arbitrator of her future turns out to be that "fine ragged prophet," the madman Troubleall (IV.iii). Grace is fully conscious of the absurdity of her marital lottery, yet sees an absurd choice as the only suitable mode of coping with an absurd world, arguing that it would be "levity" to pretend to choose rationally between men on a two hours' acquaintance in the fair. Cokes, on the other hand, like Overdo, is in fact what Busy pretends to be: "he will ever be i' the state of innocence . . . and childhood." His toyshop enjoyment of the fair as of the world draws children into his orbit everywhere. "We walk'd London," Wasp explains, and Cokes "would name you all the signs over, as he went, aloud: and where he spied a parrot, or a monkey, there he was pitch'd,

---

18. An episode parallel in its comment to those in which Overdo, attempting to save Edgworth from bad companions, is first beaten and then stocked, being mistaken for the very thief he is unwittingly attempting to aid (II.vi and III.v).

19. It is proper to recall at this point L. C. Knights' classic account of piracy and high finance among the Jacobeans in *Drama and Society in the Age of Jonson* (London, 1937).

with all the little-long-coats about him" (I.iv.102–114), a scene reenacted when he is surrounded by children before the puppet booth. As even the pimp Whit can discern, "He is a child i' faith, la" (V.iv.218–219).[20] But Wasp, sharing Overdo's wrath and blindness, is no more able than the justice to protect his ward from the theft and cheating of the fair.

These are the two extremes, the fully perspicacious innocence of Grace and the childish innocence of Cokes, but they meet in the third victim, Troubleall. Once a minion of the law, "an officer in the court of Pie-powders," he was ". . . put out on his place by Justice Overdo. . . . Upon which he took an idle conceit, and's run mad upon't. So that, ever since, he will do nothing but by Justice Overdo's warrant" (IV.i.49–54). Justice has made Troubleall over from judge to innocent, as ignorant as Cokes and, like him, seeking no longer the substance of the law but the mere letter of the warrant. Willy-nilly the innocent—Grace with her word lottery, Cokes with his "length and breadth" conception of the license, Troubleall with his blind confidence in warrant—have been absorbed by the sterile, literal legalism of Overdo's world.

IV

Let us now perceive in more detail how action and language coalesce to make this law-maddened Troubleall into a figure of destiny at its most capricious, the very fact of whose madness makes his agency in the affairs of Grace, Cokes, Purecraft, Winwife, and Quarlous determining.

Even the indirect preparation for Troubleall's role in Dame Purecraft's life is couched in terms which make him the specter of an ambiguously conceived destiny, since the fortune-tellers have advised that good lady (perhaps in a cheat but perhaps by diabolic oracle, for as Littlewit says, "the devil can equivocate, as well as a shopkeeper"), "she shall never have happy hour, unless she marry within this sen'night, and when it is, it must be a madman, they say" (I.ii.30 ff.). And so the idea of a providential destiny enters, to be associated with the peregrinating Troubleall through-out the drama. When Grace invents her lottery, it is because "destiny has a high hand in business of this nature" (IV.iii.51–52), and when the "fine

20. Cf. the interaction of this image of Cokes as a child in the fair with the New Testament warning to "children sitting in the markets" cited p. 130 above.

ragged prophet, dropp'd down i' the nick" arrives the next moment, crying
"Heaven quit you, gentlemen," Quarlous comments, "a fortune-teller we
ha' made him" (75 ff.). Winwife, later admitting that he has won Grace
by "the benefit of [her] fortune," reassures her that it may have seemed a
blind action but that eventualities will "make you rather to think that, in
this choice, she [Fortune] had both her eyes" (V.ii.33–34). Quarlous, too,
senses something divine in Troubleall, "my tatter'd soothsayer . . . who
was my judge . . . [to decide] whose word he has damn'd or sav'd" by
awarding the gift of Grace (IV.vi.42–44). They all would seem to echo in
their reactions Busy's own ejaculation when Troubleall inadvertently frees
the prisoners from the stocks: "We are delivered by miracle . . . this
madness was of the spirit" (IV.vi.160–161).

Troubleall, the omnipresent destiny of *Bartholomew Fair,* has been
made mad by the omnipotent Overdo because this latter Jehovah-like
figure refused him mercy in the name of justice, thus exaggerating his
agent's conscience beyond the limits of reason.[21] There is logic in the
unreason because conscience *must* be an irrational concept when it depends
upon arbitrary, blind authority: A blind God must create a blind destiny,
call it Providence though men may. And Overdo's own gropings toward a
realization have approached this discovery when he admits that he begins
"to think that, by a spice of collateral justice, Adam Overdo deserv'd this
beating; for I, the said Adam, was one cause (a by-cause) why the purse
was lost" (III.iii.2–6). It is an attitude reinforced by Nightingale's ballad,
which begs all to remember that if purses are stolen from his audience, they
have been taken as well in Westminster Hall, demanding hence, *"why
should the judges be free from this curse, / More than my poor self, for
cutting the purse?"* (III.v.79 ff.). From this vantage point we can see the
fair's corruption as both emanating from and encroaching upon the actions
of its controlling authority.

V

It is here necessary to recall that blindness is not an imported metaphor
for this world's disorder, but one implanted at important junctures in the
very texture of *Bartholomew Fair.* We have already noticed two versions

21. Cf. the comments upon Busy and puritanism, pp. 135–136 above.

of this image of ignorance, one in Winwife's promise that Troubleall's choice has been made through a fortune with "both her eyes," and the other in Overdo's "cloud that hides me" (p. 129 above). This latter, we may remember, takes literal form as the guise of "a certain middling thing, between a fool and a madman" (II.ii.147–148), more tightly binding the persons and qualities of Overdo and Troubleall. Overdo hopes that this disguise will serve to prevent others from seeing into his identity, because public officials can only "see with other men's eyes; a foolish constable, or a sleepy watchman . . . ourselves thought little better, if not arrant fools, for believing 'em. I, Adam Overdo, am resolv'd therefore to spare spy-money hereafter, and make mine own discoveries" (II.i.29–42). It is soon apparent, though, that the cloud effectively prevents Overdo from seeing out as well, since he immediately mistakes Knockem for a cutpurse (II.iii) and then, blind to thefts performed before his very eyes, mistakes the cutpurse Edgworth for an innocent (II.iv). In this Overdo is like the minor guardian, Wasp, who will not read the license and who loses it in the course of an angry outburst of "vapouring" as arbitrary as Overdo's own when he cries, "I have no reason, nor will I hear of no reason, nor will I look for no reason, and he is an ass that either knows any, or looks for't from me . . . I am not i' the right, nor never was i' the right, nor never will be i' the right, while I am in my right mind" (IV.iv.37–40, 60–68).

And Wasp's vision clouded in the vapours brings us to that center within the center of the fair, Ursula's pig booth. It is here that we must seek the governing metaphors, for the vapors rise from the heat of this diabolic furnace, to provide infernal counterpart to Overdo's own cloud of unknowing.

Ursula characterizes her booth and occupation by swearing that "Hell's a kind of cold cellar to't" (II.ii.44), a point affirmed by the shocked Overdo, who, upon hearing unnoticed the enumeration of her cheats, cries: "This is the very womb and bed of enormity" (II.ii.107). The lurid heat continues to arise, and if Busy sees that "the wares are the wares of devils. And the whole Fair is the shop of Satan," he focuses his intuition upon Ursula directly in scriptural phrasing:

. . . the fleshy woman (which you call Urs'la) is above all to be avoided, having the marks upon her, of the three enemies of man: the world, as being in the Fair; the devil, as being in the fire; and the flesh, as being herself.

                                                                    (III.vi.32–36)

For once Busy is justified, for it is the pig booth and its mistress from which the vapors, both in the physical sense of smoke and heat and in the metaphorical sense of the quarreling game, arise. And Ursula is not only an angry woman, but the very champion of discord, of the lust, theft, fighting, and litigation which dominate a legalistic world gone berserk. There is a strange scene near the opening which in relation to the plot appears an elaborately pointless excrescence, but in fact is richly symbolic in its iconographic details. And following closely upon Overdo's first extended characterization of himself and his role in Old Testament imagery, it serves as counterpointing commentary upon his blindly self-righteous legalism and justice.

Winwife and Quarlous, entering the fair, are immediately hailed by Knockem, the pimp, who, hoping to strike up an opportunity for game, invites them to drink and take tobacco at the pig booth.[22] Quarlous soon produces trouble with Knockem, and Ursula's tapster tries to prevent the fast-developing conflict, pleading "for the honour of our booth, none o' your vapours here," only to be unexpectedly scolded by Ursula, who emerges waving a firebrand, angrily defending anger itself:

Why, you thin lean polecat you, an' they have a mind to be i' their vapours, must you hinder 'em? . . . Must you be drawing the air of pacification here, while I am tormented, within, i' the fire, you weasel?

(II.v.57–61)

Amused, the city wits taunt her upon her anger, with Knockem keeping up a wary chorus of encouragement, until Ursula rushes in shouting, "Gi' me my pig-pan hither a little. I'll scald you hence, an' you will not go" (II.v.132–133). In the general confusion she drops the grease upon herself, crying out; "Curse of hell . . . I ha' scalded my leg, my leg, my leg, my leg" (151–152). This is sufficient to send Winwife and Quarlous off, and they are forgotten as the fair folk gather about, pull down Ursula's hose,

---

22. The invitation to the pleasures of Ursula's booth should be recalled when one hears Busy's remark immediately preceding his identification of Ursula as world, flesh, and devil: "bottle ale is a drink of Satan's . . . devised to puff us up and make us swell in this latter age of vanity, as the smoke of tobacco to keep us in mist and error" (III.vi.29–32). Overdo elaborately expands the attack on "froth" and tobacco, claiming that the latter makes "the brain smok'd like the backside of the pigwoman's booth" (II.vi.40–41).

and treat her leg, while observing upon it in Knockem's equine vocabulary: "body o' me, she has the mallanders, the scratches, the crown scab,
and the quitter bone, i' the tother leg" (167–168). The scene seems pointless
because it is without further consequences: The gentlemen escape un-
touched, and when we next see Ursula she angrily shrugs off her injury as
insignificant and rushes about as energetically as before. Its importance
emerges, however, if we open the mythographic compendiums with which
Jonson so proudly annotated the masques. For these encyclopedias reveal
that the details of this action have been selected to transmute Ursula from a
mere exemplum of the angry woman into a symbol. The increasingly
pointed scriptural images, I have argued, eventually permit us to see in
Overdo not just another shallow justice, but the very fount of Old
Testament legalism. This scene of the scalding allows us to identify the pig
woman as *Ate, Discordia* herself.[23]

In Ripa's account, *Discordia* is depicted as carrying a firebrand in one
hand, legal papers in the other, and with her feet encircled by clouds, since
she is not only the patroness of fiery passions (and hence metaphorical
blindness), but especially of litigiousness. Cartari presents the same account
in detail, and has a woodcut illustrating the vapors which surround her
legs, adding the further observation that she always "ha le gambe torte." [24]
In such accounts we can see the source of that tableau-like presentation we
have just reviewed: Ursula emerging from her smoking kitchen holding
high a firebrand, goading on the quarrels, scalding her own "gambe torte"

---

23. In the *Masque of Queens* (1609) Jonson employs *Ate,* or *Mischief,* as Dame
of the witches, and in this masque she imprecates: "Exhale Earth's rott'nest vapors; /
And strike a blindnesse, through these blazing tapers / . . . see euery foote be
bare" at the height of her attempt to bring hubbub on for the "roaring boys"
(*Jonson,* VII, 296, 299–300). Cf. Jonson's long note "n" (pp. 286–287) discussing
the iconography and sources of *"Ate,* or *mischeife* (for so I interpret it),"* which
indicates a different but historically related tradition of development, even while
Jonson retains the central images of misty vapors and blindness.

24. Cesare Ripa, *Iconologia* (Padova, 1625), p. 178; Vicenzo Cartari, *Imagini
delli dei de gl'antichi* (Venetia, 1674), pp. 197–198. Spenser, splitting *Discordia*
into the mother-son combination of Occasion and Furor, adopts the emphatic
detail of Jonson's Ursula scene as well as the flaming torch: "Her other leg was
lame, that she no'te walke" (*Faerie Queene,* II.iv.4). Cf. *Works of Edmund Spenser,*
ed. E. Greenlaw *et al.* (Baltimore, 1932), II, 226–227 (McManaway) on other
emblem sources for the legs and speculations on cross-fertilization of iconography.

—a proper mistress for Overdo's world of blind, angry justice which Haggis and Bristle center for us in their description of Overdo: "he will burn blue . . . an' he be angry. . . . and when he is angry, be it right or wrong, he has the law on's side."

Ursula, of course, has her other role as the pig woman, and while the first layer of sensuality and gluttony is apparent without apparatus, it should be noticed that the pig has other, and perhaps more precisely relevant, emblematic significances. Valeriano is most apposite in making the pig symbol of "Taverna, o luogo publico disonesto," that very pig booth of the play whence all the corruption emanates as well as gathers, reaching its climax with the whoring adventures of the cits' wives. But Valeriano adds a further note to his discussion which ties such a public place closely into the *Discordia* tradition, when he shows in elaborate fashion how the Egyptians treated the pig as a symbol of blindness and therefore chaos.[25]

25. Giovanni Piero Valeriano, *I ieroglifici* (Venetia, 1625), pp. 111, 114. There is a further interweaving of these symbolic traditions when Winwife denominates Ursula "Mother o' the Furies, I think, by her firebrand" (II.v.71). The mother of the Furies was variously identified as Night or Darkness, and Boccaccio's explanation is the metaphoric blindness of unreasoning passion:

Le chiamano figliuole d'Acheronte; & della Notte, non per altra ragione (à me pare) che per questa. Quando non succedono secondo il disio i voleri, è forza che la ragione ceda . . . che nasce una perturbatione di mente; laquale non senza giudicio di cecità di mente continua, & per lo continuare, diviene maggiore fino a tanto, che cade nell'effetto: il quale oprato senza ragione, necessariamente conviene parere furioso. Et così le furie nascono di Acheronte, & della Notte.

(*Della geneologia de gli dei* [Venetia, 1627], fol. 44$^{\text{r-v}}$).

The recollection of the Furies draws the *Discordia* iconography back into tight interaction with the stern justice of Overdo also, inasmuch as they figured as strict purveyors of justice notable for their disregard of mitigating circumstances; and as Boccaccio goes on to elaborate this aspect of tradition he ironically helps to equate the double chaos created by Ursula and by Overdo with his metaphor of "smoke":

Che poi stiano dinanzi a Giove, non è maraviglia; come che egli sia detto benigno, & pio: percioche al pio giudice è bisogno haver per ministri de'vindicatori delle scelerità, de quali se mancano, ò non tengono cura, l'autorità delle leggi, leggiermente và in fumo. Appresso, alle volte per li peccati, de popoli, dalla divinità è conceduto, che negli elementi si congiunga il furore, & che per la discordia di quelli s'infetti l'aere; onde nascono pestilenze mortali, per le cui noi infelici siamo ingiottiti.

(*Ibid.*)

The above discussion implies that I find the "vapours" central to *Bartholomew Fair* as does James E. Robinson, but in a more directly symbolic and less psy-

Now it should be easy to recognize that there is pattern in the apparent confusion of a play dominated from first to last with flytings and slapstick battles: those of Wasp in the Littlewit home, of the head knocking between Quarlous and Knockem, of Wasp's beating upon Overdo and Troubleall's scuffle with the watchmen, of the puppets' abrupt turn upon their maker Leatherhead, of the whore's thumping on Mistress Overdo. The vapors are the clouds of discord which rise from the passions of the pig booth hell, and they provide disastrously effective commentary upon that other cloud which enfolds the angry and arbitrary Jehovah, Justice Overdo, blinded by the smoke of battle in his ironically well-intentioned efforts to establish order in this modern Tyre through applying the letter of the law —properly considered, as the mythographers knew, as the symbolic property of *Discordia* herself. And it is this destructive, disordering effect of legalism which Troubleall embodies. He cannot be considered in this aspect of his dramatic function, however, apart from his counterbalance, the appropriately named Quarlous, whose efficiency gains him a dubious ascendancy in every exchange.

VI

Troubleall acts as a voice of conscience troubling all with whom he comes in contact, as well as serving in the role of destiny's agent. It is, indeed, this very conscientiousness, evoked by Overdo's justice, which has driven him mad and, as we have seen, finally draws a countering gesture of mercy from the justice himself when, overhearing the watchmen describe his angry willfulness and its effect upon Troubleall, he sighs, "I will be more tender hereafter. I see compassion may become a Justice, though it be

---

chological manner than he does in his study *"Bartholomew Fair:* Comedy of Vapors," *SEL,* I (1961), 65–80. It also implies rejection of Thayer's reading which focuses upon Ursula as "earth itself, the Great Mother, Demeter, and Eve, a great goddess with all her shapes combined in one great unshape—Ursa Major" (*Ben Jonson,* pp. 132–133; cf. 128–158, esp. 134–136, 142). My further reasons for flatly opposing Thayer's imaginative mythic interpretation of *Bartholomew Fair* will emerge in the discussion of sterility, section VII below. Closer to my view is Jonas Barish, *"Bartholomew Fair* and Its Puppets," *MLQ,* XX (1959), 8–10.

a weakness" (IV.i.77–78). But this is little, grudging, and ineffective; the only truly effective mercy which Troubleall receives emanating, in fact, from the hell booth itself when the coarse pimp Knockem forges Overdo's warrant in pure pity for the "mad child o' the Pie-powders" (IV.vi.1 ff.).[26]

Only Quarlous is entirely untroubled and unscrupulous toward this victim among victims, stripping him naked in the pig booth and assuming his clothes as a disguise (IV.vi.151–153; V.i.14–15; V.vi.52–67) which he utilizes to gain Purecraft's confidence and fortune, and also thus perverting Overdo's one attempt to offer merciful restitution: the warrant, which Quarlous employs to dispose of Grace at a price. In short, he uses the appearance of mad conscientiousness, the "face," to gain his ends much more effectively than even Busy had used his "lunatic conscience" as a masquerade for "the state of innocence . . . and childhood" (I.iii.136–141). The point is emphasized by the juxtaposition of Knockem's isolated and wholly disinterested act of mercy toward Troubleall with Quarlous' aloof, unfeeling "mercy" toward his other tool, Edgworth. When the latter, having stolen for Quarlous, invites him to share a friendly whore, Quarlous mocks Scripture in warning that he would beat his effrontery down, "If I had not already forgiven you a greater trespass" (IV.vi.15 ff.).

If Overdo is the Jehovah of the play, his mercy has been stolen by Quarlous in the misappropriation of the warrant, which emerges by inevitable allegory as the right to dispose of Grace. Quarlous, by name and by nature the most fully acclimatized denizen of this chaotic hell, is fast emerging as the natural challenger to the omnipotence of the bungling justice, who has inadvertently passed into his hands the only source of authority in the fair: possession. To leave matters here would have been for Jonson to deny not only law, but order in any form. There is yet another aspect of the drama which reverses any such tendency and establishes the ultimate new dispensation in the symbolic universe of *Bartholomew Fair:* the order of "flesh and blood."

---

26. That the infernal denizens of the fair seem the only characters capable of humane compassion is emphasized by the other roaring pimp, Whit, interceding in Cokes's behalf when he is about to be attacked during the puppet show: "No, I pre dee, captain, let him alone. He is a child i' faith, la" (V.iv.218–219). But the mercy of hell is strained, since it is Troubleall's champion, Knockem, from whom Whit here must rescue Cokes.

VII

Quarlous, of course, reveals through his manipulations that Overdo must accept frailty as he reduces this deity himself to "flesh and blood," making God into man, Overdo into Adam, in the most ironic manner. The other dramatic "conversion" is that of Overdo's hypocritical counterpart, Busy, who accepts the fair and its "enormities" precisely because the puppets—after all their perverse lasciviousness in the puppet-play within the play of "Hero and Leander"—turn out *not* to be "flesh and blood," and hence are not guilty of the traditional sins found in transvestite actors. But this inverted conversion is accomplished through mockery of the order imposed by *law:* What Busy finds that their sexlessness reveals is their "lawful" calling (V.v.14–110). The lawfulness of the sexless, sterile puppets affords comment upon Overdo's earlier insistence upon law (an insistence carefully mimicked in the arguments of puppet Dionysius): What he learns in being reduced by Quarlous, what we all learn from *Bartholomew Fair,* is that law, strict justice, is more and less than flesh and blood can either abide or profit from.

Overdo learns this lesson in part by discovering the prostitution which culminates his own wife's adventures in the pig-booth hell: The pig may be lasciviously sensual in its connotations, but the ultimate perversion of natural order is the fact that in this very center of sensuality one paradoxically discovers the transmutation of sexuality into sterile commercialism. It is an essential discord like that revealed by the lascivious puppets, who justify their bawdy playlet by revealing their wooden sterility. Intensifying the paradox which sterilizes in the name of the pig and the shilling, is the fact that Win-the-fight [27] Littlewit joins the ranks of the whores willingly, although it is her very pregnancy which was the original instrument for bringing the others of the Littlewit ambience to the fair, fearing lest she should long too stringently for roast pig and "miscarry, or hazard her first fruits" (I.vi.64). In fact, fruit as the emblem of sexuality has been made a very anatomy of the desirable, fertile young Win, whom Winwife compliments as a "garden" herself, "A wife here with a straw-

---

27. Fitting name, we see at last, for a woman who leads all the others into the booth of Discord.

berry-breath, cherry-lips, apricot-cheeks, and a soft velvet head, like a melicotton" (I.ii.13–15).

The plot sets Win's and Littlewit's scheme to use her pregnancy, her incipient "first fruits," to lead the family to the fair in immediate juxtaposition with Cokes's insistence upon taking Grace to "my Fair: I call't my Fair, because of Bartholomew; you know my name is Bartholomew" (I.v.62–64). Wasp argues and harangues against the pastime because of Cokes's vulnerability in special sort to fruit: "If he go to the Fair, he will buy of everything to a baby there. . . . Pray heaven I bring him off with one stone! And then he is such a ravener after fruit! You will not believe what a coil I had, t'other day, to compound a business between a Cather'ne-pear-woman and him" (110–116). Wasp's premonitions are more than justified when Edgworth and Nightingale employ the confidence game of spilling "Cather'ne pears," which Cokes scrambles to gather while they steal his very clothes (IV.ii). In the end, Cokes hurls his pears away in a pathetic pet:

I ha' paid for my pears, a rot on 'em. . . . Methinks the Fair should not have us'd me thus, an' 'twere but for my name's sake; I would not ha' us'd a dog o' the name, so. . . . I ha' lost myself, and my cloak and my hat; and my fine sword, and my sister, and Numps, and Mistress Grace (a gentlewoman that I should ha' married), and a cut-work handkerchief she ga' me, and two purses, today. And my bargain o' hobby-horses and ginger-bread, which grieves me worst of all.

(IV.ii.73–86)

The juxtaposition and conclusion suggest the catalogues which delimit the mentality of Pope's Belinda, and this is just the point. For Cokes, fruits are simply to be possessed and eaten, and his longing for the fruits of marriage is no more profound than that for the toys of the fair. Even as he is collecting his license to marry Grace, he glances up at Win and would possess her, too: "A pretty little soul, this same Mistress Littlewit! would I might marry her" (I.v.79–80), and this trivial possessiveness, the reduction of human relations to things to be bought and owned, is reflected in his delighted decision to furnish out his wedding masque and banquet with the toy people and gingerbread he finds on the stalls (III.iv.93–165). Thus, like the pregnant prostitute Win Littlewit, Bartholomew Cokes, the fair's most innocent child, accepts "face" value: sterility and the reduction of marriage to possession, of flesh and blood to mere toys. And in his gewgaw-seeking lust Cokes becomes the internal symbol for the larger symbolic action of the others who seek the possession of toys in the chaos of Vanity Fair.[28]

VIII

There remains now only to review the denouement which brings together the threads of imagery and of action into a coherent pattern.

Troubleall has invoked a double blessing throughout the course of his meandering appearances: "quit ye, and multiply ye"—a blessing which calls for mercy and fertility. It is clear that, from the fair's omnipotent deity, Overdo, to its most innocent child, Cokes, these are just the values which are least honored. And yet, as we have seen, even in this hell of their own invention men and gods can turn away for a moment from their self-seeking to feel love (and what other quality embraces mercy and fertility in human relations?) toward one another: Witness Overdo's or Knockem's pity for Troubleall, or Whit's gentleness toward Cokes, or Winwife's decision to pass up the rich widow for the more natural union with the young ward, Grace. All can turn aside, that is, except Quarlous, who knows only a mocking mercy and inverts Winwife's choice by selling the ward and marrying the widow. And it is Quarlous who caps the paradox of possession, for winning all, he marries himself indissolubly to hell, to the living, sterile image of that burning chaos in which the play has been enacted. As Littlewit warned, "the devil can equivocate, as well as a shopkeeper" in prophecy, and it is this diabolic equivocation (for what is the devil but shopkeeper when the Tyrronian Fair is hell and marriage goes by shillings and pence?) which brings Quarlous and Dame Purecraft together. The instrument of destiny has been Troubleall, and if Quarlous prefers to forget it when he accepts the hypocritical widow of wealth, he once knew that Troubleall's lottery-like choice of a husband for Grace "damn'd or sav'd." He lost the lottery, and compounded for the loss by selling away his right of election to Winwife: clear enough indication of

28. Contrast the fertility rite reading of *Bartholomew Fair* noticed above (Thayer, *Ben Jonson,* pp. 128–158), and Barish, *"Bartholomew Fair* and Its Puppets," pp. 4–5.

his bitter triumph, tasting, like that of Satan, of the ashes of brimstone. The worst punishment, though, is that Quarlous himself has known the geography of the pit which he elects with all the aplomb of a proud victor. Ursula, we remember, in her first imagistic identification of the pig booth as hell had cried out against her destiny: "Fie upon't: who would wear out their youth and prime thus, in roasting of pigs, that had any cooler vocation? Hell's a kind of cold cellar to't, a very fine vault" (II.ii.42–45). And by now we have realized how this lusty heat only burns to sterility all that enters the mouth of the passions' furnace. But this is macrocosm to what Quarlous himself had described earlier in warning Winwife away from that infernal microcosm, the aging Widow Purecraft:

I'll be sworn, some of them, that thou art or hast been a suitor to, are so old as no chaste or married pleasure can ever become 'em: the honest instrument of procreation has, forty years since, left to belong to 'em; thou must visit 'em, as thou wouldst do a tomb, with a torch, or three handfuls of link, flaming hot, and so thou mayst hap to make 'em feel thee, and after, come to inherit according to thy inches. A sweet course for a man to waste the brand of life for, to be still raking himself a fortune in an old woman's embers.

(II.iii.69–78) [29]

Quarlous, in toppling Overdo as the omnipotent authority in the world of the fair, has inherited hell—the hell of a commercial, self-serving, merciless world. Jehovah, tested and found wanting by that symbolic "fleshly motion of pig" whereby "the wicked Tempter . . . broacheth flesh and blood, as it were, on the weaker side" (as Busy early attests: I.vi.13–17), is reduced to "but Adam, flesh and blood" by the new Machiavellian. Neither old nor new deity seems effective, for all their paradoxical power.

But Winwife has Grace, not bought but won, albeit with the ambiguous aid of a mad destiny, and their concord alone has transcended the chaos of the fair which is to continue at Overdo's house. It is a fitting and promising close for the great humanist skeptic's last great play. For if Overdo has learned mercy only through his discovery of the weakness of literal justice in a human cosmos, and if Quarlous has continued and intensified the old errors in a new way by embracing sterility as if it were to be possessed, then

29. We may notice now that Overdo himself implied the analogy in calling the pig booth "the very womb and bed of enormity" (II.ii.107).

it is clear that all men, like Winwife, can obtain Grace only through the concord of flesh and blood living together to multiply in the mysterious, even mad, destiny of their union of love.

In *Every Man Out of His Humour* Jonson permitted his deity to blow away the actors as mere embodiments of the vapors of their own infernal stage. But in *Bartholomew Fair* man finally emerges from the vapors engendered by the discords of passion, of lust, and of litigation, to announce the ultimate benediction: "quit ye and multiply ye." In one sense, Jonson has here blasphemed the Scriptures and denied the very omnipotence of God himself. But, as he said in the Induction, it was not "profaneness," because deity has again announced his Grace through incarnation.

Chapman and an Aspect
of Modern Criticism

Thelma Herring

C HAPMAN HAS BEEN FORTUNATE in the scholars he has attracted. Such
"desertfull Commentars" [1] as F. L. Schoell and A. S. Ferguson have
labored with great learning to enrich our understanding of his
method of composition and the sources of some of his obscurest poetry.
He has not, it seems to me, been so fortunate in some of his recent critics.
The desire for pattern and order, for a theory which tidies everything up
and explains a man's work by a single formula—a tendency with which
we are all too familiar in modern criticism of Shakespeare—is apparent
also in much that has been written about Chapman. The dangerous over-
simplifications of Ennis Rees's study of the tragedies were quickly recog-

1. Epistle Dedicatory, "Achilles' Shield," *Chapman's Homer,* ed. Allardyce Nicoll
(London, 1957), I.543. References to Chapman's translations of Homer are to this
edition; those to the plays are to Thomas Marc Parrott's edition of *The Plays and
Poems of George Chapman: The Tragedies* (London, 1910) and *The Comedies*
(London, 1914).

153

nized, but the doctrinaire approach persists. The single-minded critic presents a Chapman who is misleadingly single-minded—a Stoic, or a Neoplatonist, or a Christian instead of a man in whose ethical and religious thought elements of Stoicism, Neoplatonism, and Christianity were blended, not always in the same proportions. Such a critic is also in danger of doing grave injustice to Chapman's versatility as an artist.

An admirer of "Senecal man," Chapman clearly fell far short of this chilly ideal. The combative instincts of the writer of the commentaries on Homer warred against the genuine yearning for a calm self-sufficiency; he was too explosive to be always the sober and noble moralist. So, too, his deeply felt conviction of the superiority of the contemplative life has to be weighed against his ardent patriotism, his admiration for the heroic virtues, his love of praising such active heroes as Raleigh and the Veres, even by means of similes in very unlikely contexts. This inner stress not only makes him more interesting as a person, but also, while clearly responsible for some blemishes, enriches his work, giving it an energy and complexity that tend to be overlooked when critics concentrate on only one aspect.

But the critic who approaches a play with preconceived ideas about the author's preoccupations is not only in danger of ignoring everything except what he is looking for; he is also in the worse danger of finding what is not there at all. This, it seems to me, is what happens in Irving Ribner's study of *The Tragedy of Chabot* [2] in his book on Jacobean tragedy,[3] and also in a recent article by Henry M. Weidner, "Homer and the Fallen World: Focus of Satire in George Chapman's *The Widow's Tears*." [4] (It is significant that Weidner remarks in a footnote: "I believe that my reading of Chapman's 'interests' parallels in many ways the recent work done by Irving Ribner on some of the tragedies." [5]) I intend to discuss the two plays in question, probably Chapman's last comedy and his last tragedy, in relation to these articles.

2. Originally printed in *MLR, LV* (1960), 321–331, with the title "The Meaning of Chapman's 'Tragedy of Chabot.'" There are a few trifling omissions and changes in the reprint.

3. *Jacobean Tragedy: The Quest for Moral Order* (London, 1962).

4. *JEGP*, LXII (1963), 518–532.

5. *Ibid.*, p. 520.

I

Rightly pointing to the importance of Tharsalio as the central figure in *The Widow's Tears,* Weidner suggests that he is the chief object of its satire, and he rejects the view of Chapman's editor, T. M. Parrott, that Tharsalio's judgments are proved right by the play,[6] with the remark: "If one follows this reading, one is put in the peculiar position of regarding Chapman, *the playwright most often seen as a doctrinaire neo-Stoic or neo-Platonist,* as an enunciator in this play of Machiavellian or even atheistic doctrines." In fact, Tharsalio stands for everything Chapman denounces. "Thus the apparent triumph of Tharsalio's cynicism is to be seen as Chapman's satiric commentary on the fallen world and one of its chief disciples. In the process of the satire Chapman *points by implication to the norms of idealism which are so crucial in this part of his dramatic career.* . . . Permeating all of Chapman's later comedies (and some of his tragedies) is the ideal of a Homeric 'golden age.' "[7]

To apply the term "golden age" to the Homeric world is itself somewhat misleading, but the meaning is clear enough. The increasing tendency to relate Chapman's plays, particularly his tragedies, to his translations of Homer is undoubtedly relevant, in view of his own estimate of the work that he was "born to do" (though it sometimes seems to be forgotten that his major preoccupation during the years when he was also writing for the stage was the *Iliad,* not the *Odyssey*). But whatever may be true of a comedy like *The Gentleman Usher,*[8] it is not helpful to invoke a Homeric golden age in discussing *The Widow's Tears;* for it is not there in the play at all—not even by implication. The critic, I suggest, finds it only because he is looking for it.

One cannot, of course, be sure of what Chapman's *intentions* were. He *may* have intended his audience, acquainted (perhaps) with earlier plays

6. Cf. also Samuel Schoenbaum, *"The Widow's Tears* and the Other Chapman," *HLQ,* XXIII (1960), 334–335.

7. "Homer and the Fallen World," p. 519. Italics are mine.

8. Discussed by Weidner in a previous article, "The Dramatic Uses of Homeric Idealism: The Significance of Theme and Design in George Chapman's *The Gentleman Usher,*" *ELH,* XXVIII (1961), 121–136.

of his and somehow equipped with a knowledge of Homer (though almost certainly he had as yet published only his *Seaven Bookes of The Iliades* and *Achilles' Shield*) to judge the characters and events of *The Widow's Tears* by the standards of an ideal heroic age; but if he has entirely failed to indicate this in the play, he has *not* made it relevant to the play's meaning. There are, it is true, two specific allusions to Homer (I.i.153; I.ii.9–15), but even Weidner does not claim that these amount to much; allusions to Penelope's conduct toward her suitors and to Ulysses' encounter with the Sirens are too common to attract special attention. Remarking, however, that the plot in which Tharsalio woos and wins the widowed Countess Eudora contains "an ironically radical inversion of many actions from the *Odyssey*," Weidner declares that Tharsalio appears to be "a fallen Ulysses," "a perverter of human knowledge" who has traveled much but understood little, "a scourger of decorous illusion and ceremony." [9]

This sounds ingenious, but is it not stretching the evidence? To begin with, if we are looking for parallels in the plot, Tharsalio is *not* a "fallen Ulysses" but, if anything, a successful Antinous. He *has* traveled and, according to Cynthia, been corrupted as a result: "Brother, I fear me in your travels, you have drunk too much of that Italian air, that hath infected the whole mass of your ingenuous nature . . ." (I.i.132–134). But of how many other characters in the drama of this period is this not true? Why should we attach symbolic significance to the brief allusions to Ulysses and Penelope and not to the three allusions to Dido and Æneas? Two of these are more striking than the Homeric references—Tharsalio's warning to Lysander:

Why, brother, if you be sure of your wife's loyalty for term of life, why should you be curious to search the almanacs for after-times, whether some wandering Æneas should enjoy your reversion, or whether your true turtle would sit mourning on a withered branch, till Atropos cut her throat?

(II.i.20–25)

and Ero's comparison of the meeting of the lovers in the tomb to that of Dido and Æneas in the cave (IV.iii.85–86). [10] Again, the one scrap of

9. "Homer and the Fallen World," p. 520.
10. Cf. also II.iv.203.

evidence in the dialogue to suggest that a contrast is deliberately being pointed between a "fallen world" and an earlier, more virtuous age occurs in III.i.167 ff., when Eudora's servant Lycus suggests that there *have* been young widows who remained faithful to their dead husbands, and Tharsalio replies: "Of the first stamp, perhaps, when the metal was purer than in these degenerate days. Of later years much of that coin hath been counterfeit. . . ." But this lightly spoken concession cannot be elevated into something thematically significant; the real stress falls elsewhere in this dialogue. When Lysander protests: "Not all, brother!" Tharsalio replies ironically: "My matchless sister only excepted; for she, you know, is made of another metal than that she borrowed of her mother." What Chapman is concerned with here is not the decadence of Cynthia's world, or even her mother's, compared with Homer's, but with Cynthia's pretensions to a superhuman virtue.

What *is* true of the world of this play is that it seems to be controlled by a number of blind deities. It opens with Tharsalio renouncing the blind goddess Fortune for Confidence, whom he later, however, addresses as "the third blind deity / That governs earth in all her happiness" (with Love and Fortune) (I.i.174–175); Lysander warns Cynthia not to heed "Opinion, the blind goddess of fools" (V.i.98); the denouement is presided over by a governor who prides himself on dispensing blind justice. But the world of comedy *is* commonly an irrational, topsy-turvy world. Chapman's is no doubt uncommon in degree, but none of this is sufficient to imply a Homeric golden age as a norm.

In opposing the view that Chapman, even if he is usually "a doctrinaire neo-Stoic or neo-Platonist," must always be filling that role, I certainly do not wish to suggest that he *is* to be regarded "as an enunciator in this play of Machiavellian or even atheistic doctrines." As Schoenbaum has stressed,[11] the Chapman of the comedies is often very different from the Chapman of the tragedies: He is capable both of "quick Venerian jests" and of "satirism's sauce";[12] and *The Widow's Tears* is not only a comedy in the technical sense but also a very funny play, though gentlemanly critics have been curiously unwilling to admit the fact (whether through chivalrous delicacy or a sneaking belief that suttee is a natural and

11. *"The Widow's Tears* and the Other Chapman," p. 322.
12. *All Fools,* Prologue.

desirable custom). He uses the cynic Tharsalio, not in order to enunciate Machiavellian or atheistic doctrines (Tharsalio himself cannot in any strict sense be labeled either a Machiavel or an atheist), but as the central figure in his comic design, the unmasker of comic pretensions. Technically, as has often been noted, Tharsalio plays the part of the intriguer who controls the action in the manner of the clever slave of New Comedy—the part sustained in earlier comedies by Irus, Lemot, Rinaldo, Vandome; but perhaps a more fruitful comparison may be made with the method of Old Comedy.[13] The relation of *Volpone* to Greek Old Comedy in its use of the two opposed types, the Impostor and the composite figure of the Ironical Buffoon, has been pointed out by P. H. Davison;[14] the likely closeness in date of this play to *The Widow's Tears* may have some significance. Certainly *The Widow's Tears* bears no such direct relationship to Greek models, but the type of the ἀλαζών or Impostor ("a person of absurd or extravagant pretensions")[15] may be traced in Eudora and Cynthia, and Tharsalio may be seen as a sophisticated development of the εἰρων or Ironical type who derides and exposes their pretensions.

In the first act it appears as though Tharsalio himself is destined for the role of Impostor as he is rebuffed in his audacious wooing of the countess. (His name is of course symbolic,[16] as is underlined by his taking Confidence as his patron deity.) Lysander's witnessing of his discomfiture, however, provides a motive for future action ("Well, out of this perhaps there may be moulded matter of more mirth than my baffling," I.iii.133–134) to bring about Lysander's discomfiture in retaliation: a comic turning of the tables like the gulling of Valerio in *All Fools*. First of all, though, Tharsalio achieves a personal triumph in the brilliant reversal of III.i, when, entering cloaked, he allows Lysander to suppose him rejected once more until he discards his cloak to reveal a splendid suit and casually

13. In the prologue to *All Fools* Chapman himself refers to "th'ancient comic vein / Of Eupolis and Cratinus."

14. *"Volpone* and the Old Comedy," *MLQ,* XXIV (1963), 151–157.

15. A. W. Pickard-Cambridge, *Dithyramb Tragedy and Comedy* (Oxford, 1927), p. 270, quoted by Davison, p. 153. Cf. Northrop Frye's discussion of these types in his *Anatomy of Criticism* (Princeton, 1957), pp. 172–174.

16. Cf. *Iliad* XVII, Commentarius, p. 370: "θάρσος, which signifies *confidentia* or *audacia.*" Note the quibbling on the word "confidence" in I.iii.38 ff., where Tharsalio's confidence (audacity) is opposed to Lysander's confidence (excessive trustfulness).

lets fall the words that confirm his changed status: "'Husband,' my Countess cried, 'take more, more yet'" (III.i.68).

The cynicism of Tharsalio's method of winning Eudora indeed needs no demonstration, but two things may be said: First, Parrott's relating him to the roués and fortune hunters of Restoration comedy [17] seems more pertinent than talk of "a fallen Ulysses"; there is a Middletonian realism in Tharsalio's pursuit of a profitable marriage (compare, for instance, Witgood in *A Trick to Catch the Old One*). Chapman the Neoplatonic idealist, the devotee of Night, had plenty of practical experience of the ways of the Elizabethan world, as his share in *Eastward Ho* suggests. In particular he knew the pressure of economic necessity: After all, the scholar who labored unpaid on the translation of Homer was also the playwright commissioned to write a play by one of the suitors involved in the extraordinary machinations for the hand of the heiress Agnes Howe.[18] Hymen states in the nuptial masque that Tharsalio's marriage will restore the fortunes of an ancient family, and with this we may link the reason which Tharsalio himself gives for his wish to disillusion Lysander:

> Truth is, I love my sister well and must acknowledge her more than ordinary virtues. But she hath so possessed my brother's heart with vows and disavowings, sealed with oaths, of second nuptials, as, in that confidence, he hath invested her in all his state, the ancient inheritance of our family; and left my nephew and the rest to hang upon her pure devotion; so as he dead, and she matching (as I am resolved she will) with some young prodigal, what must ensue, but her post-issue beggared, and our house, already sinking, buried quick in ruin.
>
> (II.iii.77–86)

This supplies him with a rational motive—quite rational enough for comedy. And, second, indelicate though his methods are, Tharsalio is *not* presented as an ineligible suitor. On the contrary, the diseased and boastful Spartan lord is introduced to show us that Eudora might do very much worse, and the conversation between Tharsalio and Lycus in II.iii makes it clear that Eudora's most sensible servant favors Tharsalio's suit. There is,

17. *Comedies,* p. 804.

18. See C. J. Sisson's account of the genesis of Chapman's lost comedy *The Old Joiner of Aldgate* in his *Lost Plays of Shakespeare's Age* (Cambridge, 1936), pp. 12–79.

after all, something engaging about the impudence of the man who can say: "No, madam, first let me be made a subject for disgrace; let your remorseless guard seize on my despised body, bind me hand and foot, and hurl me into your ladyship's bed"—which justifies the ambiguity of Eudora's response: "O gods! I protest thou dost more and more make me admire thee" (II.iv.233–238).

When Weidner speaks of "Chapman's satiric attack . . . on Tharsalio's unhealthy sense of the loss of the golden age," [19] it seems to me that he is not discovering the true focus of satire, but inventing one. Chapman's attack is directed at human excess, as expressed here in extravagant devotion to the dead, and Tharsalio is not unhealthy in refusing to be taken in. The chief objects of the satire *are* the two women—and (as has been less commonly noted) Lysander.

As Schoenbaum has observed,[20] there is a recurring (and traditional) strain of antifeminism in Chapman's comedies. Rinaldo in *All Fools* (I.i.56 ff.) pillages Juvenal's Sixth Satire in denouncing the whole sex, chaste and unchaste alike; in the earliest of all, Elimene, who despises the servingmen for being "such lifeless puppies, / Never to venture on their mistresses," [21] is too coarse even to dissemble her lust. But in most of these comedies Chapman juxtaposes two incompatible modes, a romantic mode which can accommodate his philosophical idealism and a realistic, satirical mode; thus, in *Monsieur D'Olive,* the finical behavior of the countess who withdraws from society because her husband has distrusted her honor is exposed to the ironical comments of the courtier Roderigue. In *The Widow's Tears,* however, he has achieved a unified tone by eliminating romance. Yet there is a thematic link between this play and the romantic plot of *Monsieur D'Olive,* one strand of which concerns the excessive grief of the Earl of St. Anne for his dead wife, whom he refuses to bury. Certainly there is a powerful contrast between "the hypocritical ostentation of Cynthia's mourning" and "the genuine sorrow" of the Earl; [22] nevertheless both plays show in their different ways the unnaturalness of such behavior: the Earl's wish to preserve a corpse, Cynthia's withdrawal to her husband's tomb, Eudora's vow not to take a second husband. Despite the

19. "Homer and the Fallen World," p. 520.
20. *"The Widow's Tears* and the Other Chapman," p. 329.
21. *The Blind Beggar of Alexandria,* scene i, 186–187.
22. Schoenbaum, p. 328.

prejudice against the remarriage of widows (not, of course, of widowers) which we know did exist in this period,[23] Chapman does not support it;[24] in these comedies, like Dr. Leavis, he is on the side of life.

From the beginning the unnaturalness of the women's behavior is indicated. "Chapman is concerned not with the ordinary run of women but with paragons," says Schoenbaum;[25] yes, but the ideals for which the paragons stand are not upheld by the play. Eudora's vow of widowhood is "placed" by the manner in which it is described by her waiting-woman Sthenia:

> I have been witness to so many of her fearful protestations to our late lord against that course; to her infinite oaths imprinted on his lips, and sealed in his heart with such imprecations to her bed, if ever it should receive a second impression; to her open and often detestations of that incestuous life (as she termed it) of widows' marriages, as being but a kind of lawful adultery, like usury permitted by the law, not approved; that to wed a second, was no better than to cuckold the first; that women should entertain wedlock as one body, as one life, beyond which there were no desire, no thought, no repentance from it, no restitution to it: so as if the conscience of her vows should not restrain her, yet the world's shame to break such a constant resolution, should repress any such motion in her.
>
> (II.iv.22 ff.)

So, too, the extravagance of Cynthia's comment on the news of Eudora's capitulation:

> CYNTHIA
> I am ashamed on't, and abhor to think
> So great and vow'd a pattern of our sex
> Should take into her thoughts, nay, to her bed
> (O stain to womanhood!) a second love.
> LYCUS
> In so short a time!
> CYNTHIA
> In any time!

23. Although its prevalence has been exaggerated, as Frank W. Wadsworth points out in his "Webster's *Duchess of Malfi* in the Light of Some Contemporary Ideas on Marriage and Remarriage," *PQ,* XXXV (1956), 394–407.

24. Cf. *Sir Giles Goosecap,* where there is no implied criticism of Eugenia's second marriage.

25. *"The Widow's Tears* and the Other Chapman," p. 325.

LYSANDER
No, wife?

CYNTHIA
By Juno, no; sooner a loathsome toad!

(III.i.119–124)

Later the mock-heroic tone of Lycus' description of Cynthia's reaction to the fictitious report of Lysander's death alerts us for an unmasking:

I never saw such an ecstasy of sorrow, since I knew the name of sorrow. Her hands flew up to her head like Furies, hid all her beauties in her dishevelled hair, and wept as she would turn fountain. . . . I assure you, sir, I was so transported with the spectacle, that, in despite of my discretion, I was forced to turn woman and bear a part with her. Humanity broke loose from my heart and streamed through mine eyes.

THARSALIO
In prose, thou wept'st. So have I seen many a moist auditor do at a play; when the story was but a mere fiction. And didst act the Nuntius well?

(IV.i.39 ff.)

The suggestion of acting is sustained in Lycus' ensuing narrative, which parodies a bombastic Nuntius speech. Surely Tharsalio is right:

This strain of mourning wi' th' sepulchre, like an overdoing actor, affects grossly, and is indeed so far forced from the life, that it bewrays itself to be altogether artificial. . . . Her officious ostentation of sorrow condemns her sincerity.

(IV.i.106 ff.)

If we disabuse our minds of prejudices against "Tharsalio the cynic," we recognize the voice of common sense in his final comment:

My sister may turn Niobe for love; but till Niobe be turned to a marble, I'll not despair but she may prove a woman.

(IV.i.136–138)

And what of Lysander? Is he the innocent victim of Tharsalio's experiment? Hardly. Lysander, too, has to be cured of excess—of the egoism indicated by Lycus' remark: "you know how strange his dotage ever was on his wife, taking special glory to have her love and loyalty to him so renowned abroad" (II.iii.50–52), and of "that spark jealousy, falling into his dry, melancholy brain, [which] had well near set the whole house on fire" (42–44). That sympathy for Lysander would be misplaced is proved by the comic violence of his reply: "By this hand, split her weasand!" when Tharsalio asks him: "But what would you say, brother, if you should find her married at your arrival?" (III.i.220 ff.). Both Tharsalio and Lycus warn him of the danger of curiosity, but he ignores them, and discovers the worst by cuckolding himself.

The comic tone is sustained up to V.ii, the scene in the tomb in which Cynthia offers her husband's "corpse" to save the life of the sentry, even though he professes to be Lysander's murderer (a twist in the plot for which Chapman himself was responsible). The incident shocks, and no doubt was meant to shock; but all the same I suspect that critics have taken it too solemnly. (Reading some of them, one is almost driven to suppose that they think Cynthia should indeed have starved herself in the tomb.) Weidner's comment that she is "heartsick at this knowledge"[26] is an unnecessary concession. When, a few lines later, she says:

> Love must salve any murther; I'll be judge
> Of thee, dear love, and these shall be thy pains,
> Instead of iron, to suffer these soft chains.
>   (*Embracing him*)—

and Lysander replies ironically:

> O, I am infinitely oblig'd—
>
>   (V.ii.41–44)

what response could be expected from an audience but laughter? Cynthia's reckless conduct is in scale: A woman who behaves so immoderately in one direction is liable to err just as far in the opposite. Like Florilla, like Marcellina, Cynthia needs to become aware of her self-deception. That her "awareness" at the end is intellectual rather than moral as she quick-wittedly turns the tables on Lysander is a weakness, perhaps, but of a kind often found in the conclusions of comedy; certainly in the last scene Chapman is not concerned with serious criticism of the women. It may not

26. "Homer and the Fallen World," p. 528.

be fanciful to detect a parody of *Macbeth* [27] in V.iii, when Cynthia snatches up the "crow," exclaiming:

Nay, then, I'll assay my strength; a soldier, and afraid of a dead man! A soft-roed milk-sop! Come, I'll do't myself.

LYSANDER

And I look on? Give me the iron.

CYNTHIA

No, I'll not lose the glory on't. This hand, *etc.*

(V.iii.129–133) [28]

Chapman was fond of parody, as is shown in *The Blind Beggar of Alexandria* on an extended scale,[29] in *May-Day* in isolated lines, in *Monsieur D'Olive* in the parody of the November Eclogue.[30] And it is possible to see a kind of parody of the conclusion of *Measure for Measure* in the final scene of *The Widow's Tears* when the foolish governor dispenses his blind justice, promising "I will whip lechery out o' th' city. . . . I will hunt jealousy out of my dominion." That the reconciliation of Cynthia and Lysander is presided over by this ass in office does not, perhaps, make the resolution any more unsatisfactory than that presided over by Vienna's duke, since the situation in Cyprus has never seemed so close to reality.

I would argue, then, that the tendency has been to underestimate the vivacity of *The Widow's Tears*. Yet it is true that "to a greater degree than the earlier comedies the play seems to owe its being to some profoundly felt inner necessity," [31] and this impression is produced chiefly by the vigorous

---

27. The date of composition of both plays is uncertain. If I am right in detecting an allusion to *Macbeth*, and if the argument of H. L. Rogers in "An English Tailor and Father Garnet's Straw," *RES*, N. S., XVI (February 1965), 44–49, for moving the date of *Macbeth* to late 1606 or early 1607 is accepted, the date most commonly favored for *The Widow's Tears* is at least a year too early; but as the *terminus ad quem* is 1609, this affords no difficulty.

28. Parrott in his textual notes (p. 820) says: "The *etc.* in the Q. denotes that the speech was cut here, or perhaps that Chapman left it unfinished." Perhaps it marks an ad-libbing parody of the "hand" theme in *Macbeth*.

29. Cf. Ennis Rees, "Chapman's *Blind Beggar* and the Marlovian Hero," *JEGP*, LVII (1958), 60–63.

30. IV.ii.137–140.

31. Schoenbaum, p. 323.

and challenging personality of Tharsalio. Whence does he derive this peculiar vitality? He has been described as the "comic" counterpart of Bussy D'Ambois; [32] certainly one feels that a degree of creative energy went into the imagining of these two protagonists, each in his own way impelled by "this insatiate spirit of aspiring," [33] which cannot be found in any other of Chapman's characters. Perhaps it is unnecessary to look beyond the history of his development as an artist to see Tharsalio as anything but the culmination of a series of representations of the comic intriguer, studied in greater depth as his powers matured; but if we do look beyond the evidence of the play itself, it need not be to seek explanations in ideas which Chapman has refrained from expressing in the text. Modern criticism is rightly chary of explaining literary works in terms of biography, and when as little is known of a writer as is known of Chapman, the method is particularly hazardous. Of course, however, some works do grow more directly out of their authors' personal experience than do others. Bertram Dobell's suggestion [34] that *The Widow's Tears* may be connected with the letters to and about a widow in the letterbook that he believed to be Chapman's [35] has not won universal acceptance, but if we do accept Chapman as the writer of the letters, we have, in the light of new information about his life, more reason than Dobell to perceive a possible relationship to the play. For Chapman himself, like Tharsalio, was the needy younger son of a good family whose elder brother had inherited the family estate. Like him, he had spent his youth serving in the household of a man of rank, and most scholars believe that he, too, had traveled on the Continent and been for a time a soldier.[36] If Dobell is right, he had also courted a wealthy widow who was not easily won, but unlike Tharsalio he evidently failed in his suit.

I hasten to add that I am *not* suggesting that the cynical Tharsalio who so shocks Weidner is a self-portrait. The relationship, if it does exist, is not

32. *TLS*, May 10, 1934, p. 329.

33. Lysander's phrase (III.i.34–35).

34. "Newly Discovered Documents of the Elizabethan and Jacobean Periods," I, *Athenæum*, March 23, 1901.

35. Folger Manuscript V.a.321.

36. For the early life of Chapman see Jean Robertson, "The Early Life of George Chapman," *MLR*, XL (1945), 157–165, and Mark Eccles, "Chapman's Early Years," *SP*, XLIII (1946), 176–193; also Reginald L. Hine, *Hitchin Worthies* (London, 1932).

as simple as that. But it is interesting to remember that critics *have* been inclined to accept an element of self-portraiture in another (and of course very different) character—Clarence, the poor scholar of *Sir Giles Goosecap* who marries the rich Eugenia. Jean Jacquot, for instance, though he is skeptical about Chapman's authorship of the letters to the widow, comments: "Clarence est une image embellie de Chapman lui-même, et son heureuse aventure satisfait le désir d'être aimé, admiré et compris, dont le *Banquet d'Ovide* contenait déjà l'aveu." [37] If, however, one does accept those letters as Chapman's, it is tempting to believe that it is no accident that Eugenia, like Eudora, is a widow. It is true that Chapman has drawn on Chaucer's *Troilus and Criseyde* in this play, but he has significantly transformed both the story and the characters of the lovers: Certainly the learned Eugenia is not like the faithless Criseyde, whereas some resemblance might be found between the women in *The Widow's Tears* and another Cressida, Shakespeare's. If indeed Chapman addressed to the widow he courted a letter [38] which begins:

Save him (Sweete wydowe) y^t lyves at youre mercie, and seekes no favours but onlie youres; that holdes you deare, and loves you muche, yea ten tymes more than he or they who soever they be that love you most:

(fol. 84^r)

and another which ends:

I finde a Page, or a gentlemanvsher may wth a good face, and omnipotent golde, make an honest woman a whoore, but to make a whoore an honest woman, is beyonde the laboures of Hercules. / but let experience teach you youre error. / I enuie not him that shall possesse you. if you have wrongd me, let youre owne inconstancye punish it selfe; ffor I can not wish you worsse then to be what you are—

(fol. 93^r)

he had clearly undergone an experience which would explain both the idealized presentation of Eugenia and the relish with which Tharsalio

37. *George Chapman (1559–1634), sa vie, sa poésie, son théâtre, sa pensée* (Paris, 1951), p. 89.

38. Quotations from the letters are from photostats supplied by courtesy of the authorities of the Folger Shakespeare Library. An article on the letterbook is in preparation.

exposes the hypocrisy of the real and the supposed widow. It may be noted that Momford, Eugenia's uncle, expresses a faith in "confidence" similar to Tharsalio's while indicating Eugenia's superiority to other women:

Audacity prospers above probability in all worldly matters. . . . Why should a man desiring to aspire an unreasonable creature, which is a woman, seek her fruition by reasonable means? . . . I tell thee, friend, the eminent confidence of strong spirits is the only witchcraft of this world. . . . this were enough to make thee hope well, if she were one of those painted communities that are ravished with coaches, and upper hands, and brave men of dirt; but thou knowest, friend, she's a good scholar, and like enough to bite at the rightest reason. . . .

(I.iv.123 ff.)

It is only in externals, of course, that Tharsalio bears any resemblance to Chapman; but if Chapman had been an angry and disappointed suitor (and the author of the "Invective Written against Mr. Ben Jonson" was not a man to suppress his resentment), there may have been an element of wish fulfillment in his presentation of Tharsalio's triumphant progress and the tarnishing of the proud widow's noble image which is the consequence of his success, a perhaps unconscious projection of himself into a personality diametrically opposed to his own.

This, however, is only a suggestion. The difference between *The Widow's Tears* and *Sir Giles Goosecap* is no more startling than that between *Troilus and Cressida* and *Twelfth Night*, and other explanations than the events of the dramatist's life are possible. It is not my concern to argue that Tharsalio is a persona through whom Chapman avenged himself, but to deny that he is a fallen Ulysses, reminding us of a lost golden world.

II

Irving Ribner shares Weidner's obsession with the contrast between the world of the play and that of a vanished "golden age," but he sees it in different terms—not Homeric but Christian. His book on Jacobean tragedy contains many references to the fall of man, and it is this emphasis, especially, in the section on *The Tragedy of Chabot* that seems to me open to the same kind of objection as I have made to Weidner's article. Before Ribner's criticism is discussed, however, a comment on the problem of dating *Chabot,* as it bears on the problem of authorship, seems necessary, though a full argument is not possible here.

With Ribner's desire to escape from the preoccupation with historical allegory resulting from Mrs. Solve's monograph [39] and to concentrate on the permanent aspects of the theme, one must sympathize; but his reconstruction of the history of the play is not very convincing. He thinks that Chapman probably first wrote it in 1614 [40] and that "some time after 1621, Shirley . . . probably decided to revise Chapman's old play because of its topicality, and Chapman . . . joined with him in revamping the play so that it might reflect more closely upon the Somerset affair. . . . Most of the revision must have been by Chapman himself." [41]

To this I would reply, briefly:

1. There *are* grounds for favoring a date between 1612 and 1614 for the first writing of the play. It has close thematic links with preceding tragedies (a point I shall consider later). There are parallel passages in the poems published (not, however, necessarily written) in 1612, notably the passage borrowed from Ficino's commentary on Plato's *Symposium* [42] in "A Hymn to Our Saviour on the Cross," ll.221–248, and again, more briefly and in a less similar context, in *Chabot,* I.i.96 ff. (which at least suggests that *Chabot* is the later of the two). Another small point is the use of the names Allegre and Asall for two minor, unhistorical characters. It has not, I think, been noted that Chapman probably took them from Grimeston's *A General Inventorie of the Historie of France,* which he had been using c. 1610 for *The Revenge of Bussy D'Ambois.* "Alegre, an adventurous and wise captaine," and Balthazar, "called the Chevelier d'Azzal," are mentioned in the war in Piedmont in 1536. [43] But none of these points is at all

39. Norma Dobie Solve, *Stuart Politics in Chapman's Tragedy of Chabot* (Ann Arbor, 1928).

40. Silently altered from 1612 or 1613 in his article in *MLR.*

41. *Jacobean Tragedy,* p. 37.

42. Oratio Sexta, cap. XVII.

43. *General Inventorie,* 2nd ed. (London, 1611), p. 652; cf. p. 663, where the names appear as "Allegre" and "the knight Assal."

conclusive; for instance, parallel passages do occur in works demonstrably far apart in date.

2. If we accept that the play was revised to make it more topical during the Somerset affair, it is inconceivable that Shirley was the prime mover. Surely it would be Chapman who would try to help the patron to whom he had dedicated *Homer's Odysses* and in whose defense, at the outbreak of the Overbury scandal, he had already written his tactless but wholeheartedly loyal poem, *Andromeda Liberata*. In any case, this is an improbably early date for Shirley, whose first independent play was licensed in 1625.

3. The researches of C. J. Sisson and Robert Butman [44] have provided us with an excellent reason for Chapman's sudden disappearance from the London stage, a reason which could also explain what has seemed strange to some scholars, his reemergence as a playwright according to Mrs. Solve's dating of *Chabot,* i.e., after March 1621 (the conviction of Bacon) and before December 1624 (when Somerset received a full pardon). Since he was apparently living at Hitchin (to avoid imprisonment for debt) from the autumn of 1614 to the autumn of 1619, his silence was natural; but from October 1619 onward he was engaged in litigation which ultimately led to a decree in his favor (the final hearing was in February 1622), and he was then free to reenter the world of the theaters if he wished.

4. In fact, everything points to Shirley's having revised the play shortly before it was licensed on April 29, 1635, probably *after* Chapman's death on May 12, 1634—as Parrott suggested in his edition. Parrott rightly indicates that there are significant points of resemblance in Shirley's *The Duke's Mistress* (licensed in January 1636).

5. Since Mrs. Solve shows convincingly that the most likely explanation of the fictitious role played by Montmorency and the unhistorical treatment of his character is that he was modeled on George Villiers and the story of Chabot adapted to refer to the arrest and trial of the Earl of Somerset, it seems clear that if *Chabot* were first written about 1613 it must have undergone a radical revision by Chapman about a decade later and a further revision by Shirley about 1634. This adds greatly to the complication; it is not impossible, since Chapman does appear to have reworked some of his plays. I am inclined myself to think that he did recast a play on

44. "George Chapman, 1612–22: Some New Facts," *MLR*, XLVI (1951), 185–190.

which he had been working—perhaps only meditating—during the years in Hitchin. Otherwise one is driven to conclude that Shirley revised a twenty-year-old play, altering it considerably to provide a parallel with events and characters "in the news" more than a decade before, not because it would still be topical but because he saw some dramatic gain in the change.

That Shirley's presence *is* visible in the play has been shown conclusively by Parrott, who also indicates the kind of effect his revision has on Chapman's work. This is not the place to argue over details; I would merely state that it seems to me hazardous to say of any scene in the play that it is *wholly* Shirley's.

The fact that Shirley's work is superimposed upon Chapman's makes it difficult to speak confidently of the responsibility of either for what seems distinctive in *Chabot* compared with the other tragedies, though the many affinities may be safely attributed to Chapman. One notices at once the more obviously "theatrical" quality of this play and the reduction in speeches of a philosophical or doctrinal kind. This *might* be due to Chapman's trying to conform to the tastes of the twenties but is much more likely to be an effect of Shirley's revising hand. There are far fewer borrowings from ancient philosophers: Plutarch is not drawn on as in *Byron* and *Caesar and Pompey,* nor Epictetus as in *The Revenge of Bussy D'Ambois*. Should we therefore conclude with Ribner that Chapman seems to have renounced Stoicism,[45] or is Wieler right in regarding *Chabot* as "fashioned from Stoic influences"?[46] Obviously Shirley may have excised passages; it does not follow that the basic philosophy is different. I shall revert to this: It is relevant to my view that the Christian myth of the fall of man, which figures so largely in Ribner's argument, has nothing to do with Chapman's theme.

I quote key passages from Ribner's book:

Chabot would live by a principle of perfect, unwavering justice. His tragedy is also his education, for he comes to learn that such an ideal is impossible in an imperfect world. Human justice, Chapman is saying, can only reflect the justice of the cosmos, and this has been corrupted by the fall of man (p. 39). He

45. *Jacobean Tragedy,* p. 19.

46. John William Wieler, *George Chapman: The Effect of Stoicism upon His Tragedies* (New York, 1949), pp. 116 ff.

prides himself upon his ability to overcome his human frailty and to mete out perfect justice, looking to his own innocence to shield him from a hostile world. . . . But no man is truly innocent, for to live is to share in the general corruption of mankind, and Chabot's fall is Chapman's ironic commentary upon the power of such belief in innocence to preserve him. . . . (p. 42). Chabot, . . . by his pursuit of an absolute justice, must deny those qualities of human frailty which are the property of fallen man and which make perfect justice impossible. Chabot's very devotion to justice becomes the source of pride, and it is also a source of delusion (p. 43). This very challenge to the king's authority makes necessary Chabot's destruction. His affirmation of complete innocence is a denial of the fall of man, and thus of the necessity of kingship and of all human institutions which proceed from kingship, including the courts of law themselves (p. 44). When the king offers to pardon Chabot he is asserting that the salvation of man depends not upon justice but mercy (p. 45). Man's only hope in a fallen world is the love and mercy of his king and his fellow men (p. 49).

No doubt if the play really did say these things it would be a more orthodox tragedy, but it surely says nothing of the kind. Ribner is reading into the text his own moral commentary on the action.

Chabot is not essentially a tragic study of the pride and delusion of fallen man. Throughout his career as poet and tragic dramatist, Chapman wrestled with the problem of the good life—more specifically, in his tragedies, the problem for the individual of preserving one's inner integrity while living an active public life in a corrupt world, the problem of the reciprocal obligations of king and subject, of allowing the self-fulfillment of the individual great man while containing him within the bounds of organized society. That he sometimes recalls the golden age of Saturn, stressing the idea that kings and laws are the result of man's degeneracy, is indeed true. Ribner quotes the *locus classicus,* the king's speech on "Man in his native noblesse" in *Bussy D'Ambois* (III.ii.90 ff.), and Strozza's statement of the same idea in *The Gentleman Usher* (V.iv.56 ff.). The stress falls, however, not on the Christian conception of the fall of man but on the Stoic belief that even now the truly virtuous man is a law unto himself (e.g., Strozza's "A virtuous man is subject to no prince,/ But to his soul and honour, which are laws / That carry fire and sword within themselves"); Bussy, Byron, Margaret all make this claim.[47] Byron, of

47. *Bussy D'Ambois,* II.i.194 ff.; *Byron's Conspiracy,* III.iii.140 ff.; *The Gentleman Usher,* IV.ii.132 ff.

course, does not reveal the inner worth needed to justify it; but in portraying his true "Senecal man," a Clermont or a Cato, Chapman is certainly not concerned with the imperfection of fallen man [48] but with that "excitation to heroical life" of which he speaks in the dedication of *The Revenge of Bussy D'Ambois,* the fact that the spiritual freedom of man in the golden age is still recoverable. It is always the *extraordinary* in man that interests him. In *Chabot* he does not introduce the image of the world of Saturn at all, though Allegre in the first scene discourses on "this vile, degenerate age"; but in the portrayal of his protagonist there is implicit emphasis on the typical Stoic virtue of "constancy," based on right reason, which Lipsius had glorified,[49] rather than on pride and delusion.

The themes of all Chapman's tragedies are closely related, though none is a mere restatement of an earlier play. *Byron* is a rethinking of the problem of the Renaissance great man treated more sympathetically but with some moral confusion in *Bussy D'Ambois; The Revenge* is a kind of recantation. Out of the problem of the relations between the king and his most eminent subject in *Byron* grows the treatment of the same problem with the attitudes of the characters reversed in *Chabot,* while the latter play is also closely connected with *Caesar and Pompey* in its treatment of the nature of justice and the question whether it is possible to maintain virtue while engaging in public life.

Without falling into the trap of assuming that Chapman's ideas never underwent change, we can at any rate say that elsewhere he certainly does not suggest that the pursuit of absolute justice can lead only to pride and delusion; nor should we expect this of a writer so deeply influenced by Platonic and Stoic ideas, since to both Plato and the Stoics a love of justice was fundamental to the good life. Henry IV's reference to "the religious sword of justice" in his prayer for the dauphin and the concern for justice

48. In his deeply Christian poem, "A Hymn to Our Saviour on the Cross" (published 1612), Chapman characteristically stresses man's perfectibility through grace despite the fall, and chides the "hypocritical humility" of those who plead that they are men and must err.

49. Lipsius (*De Constantia,* Book I, Chap. iv) distinguishes between Constancy and Obstinacy, "which is a certain hardnesse of a stubberne mind, proceeding from pride or vaine glorie" (Stradling's translation). Cf. the king's acknowledgment that he has never known Chabot to be obstinate in his views when convinced of error (IV.i.172 ff.).

expressed in his prayer before Byron's arrest[50] are crucial in defining his relations with Byron and shaping our attitudes toward both men. The king is justified by the play, not because he happens to hold authority, but because he exercises it with reverence for justice. The epigraph to *Caesar and Pompey* ("Only a just man is a free man") sums up the importance of justice in the Stoic scale of values. It would be absurd to suspect irony in I.ii.27 ff., when the Sixth Citizen says, "being just,/ Thou mayst defy the gods," and Cato replies, "Said like a god"; for Cato's career is designed to illustrate precisely this view. In the argument on suicide (IV.v.66 ff.) his words, "is not every just man to himself / The perfect'st law?" point to the inward nature of this conception of justice. Finally, I would cite a comment by Chapman himself in his notes to his translation of *The Georgics of Hesiod*:

He persuades his brother to the love of justice by argument taken from the true nature of man, that, by virtue of his divine soul, naturally loves it; because God infused into that divine beam of his, being immortal, a love to that that preserved immortality, without that immortal destruction affected in injustice.[51]

Pasquier, Chapman's source[52] for the story of *Chabot,* says nothing specifically about Chabot's devotion to the ideal of justice, which in the play reflects Chapman's own moral preoccupations (one cannot believe it to have been the distinguishing characteristic of Somerset). The opposition between "justice" and "policy" is symbolized in the figures of Chabot and his enemy Poyet, the chancellor, who in a Machiavellian speech uses Chapman's Neoplatonic vocabulary with quibbling irony to justify the supple conduct of a "politician":

> our soul motion is affirm'd
> To be, like heavenly natures', circular;
> And circles being call'd ambitious lines,
> We must, like them, become ambitious ever,

50. *Byron's Tragedy,* I.i.135; IV.ii.63 ff.

51. *The Works of George Chapman: Poems and Minor Translations,* ed. R. H. Shepherd (London, 1875), p. 219.

52. Estienne Pasquier, *Les Recherches de la France* (1611, Book V, Chap. 12, or 1621, Book VI, Chap. 9).

And endless in our circumventions;
No tough hides limiting our cheverel minds.

(I.i.188 ff.)

But the main conflict is between Chabot and the king, and here Robert Ornstein's interpretation of the play as concerned with "the conflict between absolutist prerogative and the medieval ideal of the rule of law," [53] though too narrowly political, is much more to the point than Ribner's; this contemporary problem is certainly an issue in the play. In *Basilikon Doron* the future James I had lectured his son (who was to be Chapman's patron) on justice ("the greatest vertue, that properly belongeth to a kings office"), advising him to "Vse Iustice, but with such moderation, as it turne not in Tyrannie: otherwaies *summum ius,* is *summa iniuria*" [54] (a maxim echoed by King Francis in *Chabot:* "who knows not that extreme justice is (By all rul'd laws) the extreme of injury . . ." II.iii.17–18). But unfortunately, James's absolutist claims involved a conception of justice which sanctioned arbitrary actions like Francis' arrest of Chabot.

The rightness of Chabot's stand is indicated in several ways: by the direct witness of his servant Allegre, by the negative evidence of Poyet's hostility, by the impression which his wife's faith in him makes on the queen, and by the tributes of the vacillating but fundamentally good-natured Montmorency, who, like Poyet, illuminates an aspect of Chabot's character by contrast, in this case between the man who cares nothing for what others say when pursuing what he believes to be right and one "wrought on with the counsels and opinions / Of other men" (I.i.84–85)— a contrast, incidentally, which suggests the Stoical cast of Chabot's mind. It is true that Chabot's father-in-law, though he also attests to his virtue, by his warning to leave the court raises the problem of combining "goodness" with "greatness"; his attitude is similar to that of Athenodorus as reported by Seneca in his *De Tranquillitate Animi:*

"quia in hac" inquit "tam insana hominum ambitione tot calumniatoribus in deterius recta torquentibus parum tuta simplicitas est et plus futurum semper est quod obstet quam quod succedat, a foro quidem et publico recedendum est."

(Bk. 9, Chap. 3, 2)

53. *The Moral Vision of Jacobean Tragedy* (Madison, 1960), p. 76.
54. ΒΑΣΙΛΙΚΟΝ ΔΩΡΟΝ; *or His Maiesties Instructions to His Dearest Sonne, Henry the Prince* (London, 1603; STC No. 14350), p. "58" [85].

Like Seneca himself, Chabot thinks this complete withdrawal unnecessary. As the favorite of an absolute monarch, he is more deeply involved in
public life than either Clermont or Cato, who also face this problem; and
Chapman chose him from a historical context which enabled him to focus
on the kind of situation that could arise under James I (whether or not he
specifically had in mind the trial of Somerset and the devious manipulations of the law by James and Bacon in connection with it).

When the king threatens Chabot with arrest, Chabot accepts the
challenge in the words, "I'll endure the chance, the dice being square"
(II.iii.112); but of course the dice are *not* square. That Chabot should
discover that the king is an imperfect instrument of justice, and that what
his legal ministers dispense in the courts with the object of pleasing him is
not justice, does not mean that Chabot was mistaken in his pursuit of the
ideal of justice, still less that he is guilty of pride. Ribner does not seem to
distinguish here between justice and law; "in Chabot's very victory is also
his defeat, for the open corruption of the court . . . is now revealed, and the
faith in justice by which he had lived is shattered"; [55] but Chabot has never
had any illusions about the administration of law, as shown by his
reference in II.iii.144–145 to "the certain ruin / Of men shot into law from
kings' bent brow" and by his defiance of lawyers' misrepresentations:
"these grave toys I shall despise in death" (151). Arguing that Chabot's
pride and delusion are implicit in his first conflict with the king over the
tearing of the unlawful bill, Ribner quotes his speech:

> if the innocence and right that rais'd me
> And means for mine, can find no friend hereafter
> Of Him that ever lives . . .
> > let my fabric ruin,
> My stock want sap, my branches by the root
> Be torn to death, and swept with whirlwinds out—
> > > (II.iii.29 ff.)

with the comment:

This is foreshadowing of Chabot's end, for his final knowledge that his supposed innocence cannot protect him, that the king's whim may have power
to destroy him, for "A great man, I see, may be / As soon dispatch'd as a

---

55. *Jacobean Tragedy*, p. 46.

common subject" (IV.i.80–81) will kill in him the will to live. Chapman then will use this very symbol of the tree to remind the audience that the fate which Chabot here thinks impossible has in fact come upon him.[56]

This is misleading. As Ribner uses them, the words on the dispatch of a great man appear to be Chabot's disillusioned comment on his own fate; in fact they are the king's sarcastic comment on the news of Chabot's condemnation. Certainly at the time Chabot's innocence does not save him, but his name *is* finally cleared; as Allegre puts it, ". . . you were rescued / By the great arm of Providence" (V.iii.40–41). Ribner's argument about the symbol of the tree seems at first sight cogent, but, after all, the transplanted tree of V.iii.52 ff. is not the same as the deracinated tree of the passage quoted, and its withering is due not to the desertion of heaven, but to an inevitable decay after injury, in spite of the beneficence of sun and dew. Chapman is so fond of this tree symbol that I am not even sure that the repetition is deliberate.[57]

When the plot against Chabot is exposed, the king reflects:

> the seed of all
> Man's sensual frailty may be said to abide,
> And have their confluence in only pride.
>
> (IV.i.370–372)

He is speaking of Poyet; the charge is in no way turned against Chabot, whom he proceeds to exalt in the speech on "blessed justice" which Ribner ignores:

> as in cloudy days we see the sun
> Glide over turrets, temples, richest fields,
> All those left dark and slighted in his way,
> And on the wretched plight of some poor shed,
> Pours all the glories of his golden head:
> So heavenly virtue on this envied lord
> Points all his graces . . .
>
> (IV.i.426 ff.)

56. *Ibid.*, p. 43.

57. Cf. the contrast between the hollow tree and the solid tree uprooted by the wind, like Bussy blown over by blind chance (*Bussy D'Ambois,* V.ii.37 ff.).

Where, here, is the suggestion of the pride and delusion of fallen man?

This preconception about Chapman's theme confuses Ribner's approach to the central incident, the king's offer and Chabot's refusal of a pardon, which he passes over very quickly with the extraordinary statement that the king "is asserting that the salvation of man depends not upon justice but mercy." [58] Francis has no such theological motive: He welcomes Chabot's sentence so that he can get a moral advantage over him by pardoning him. To Chabot's justified resentment at the implication of guilt in a pardon, Ribner shows a strange lack of sympathy; but this theme of the unsought pardon is common in Chapman—e.g., Bussy after his duel craves the right to be above pardon (II.i.190 ff.), Cato refuses to receive his life from Caesar. The question was a delicate one for both innocent and guilty in an era of autocratic sovereigns and the rise and fall of great favorites; the situation repeats itself in life and in art. In *The Tragedy of Byron* Henry IV is prepared to pardon Byron if he confesses (and here Chapman follows Grimeston's account). James I desired the conviction of Somerset, intending to pardon him; at the trial the Lord High Steward, urging Somerset to throw himself on the king's mercy, quoted the case of Byron, who appealed for mercy too late,[59] but Somerset steadily refused to admit guilt.[60] His adherence to assertion of his innocence seems to have been impressive; nevertheless, his case was not needed to draw Chapman's attention to the subject. That Chabot refuses to accept pardon even when it is offered is proof of his integrity, not "of the pride which causes him to reject the mercy all men need." [61] Francis may have considered himself God's deputy, but he was certainly not God, and to equate his capricious pardon with divine mercy is to distort the meaning of Chabot's action.

Act V, which Ezra Lehman in his edition of the play called an excrescence, has always presented a difficulty. Ribner and others have pointed out that it doesn't fit the historical allegory very well,[62] though

58. *Jacobean Tragedy*, p. 45.

59. See William McElwee, *The Murder of Sir Thomas Overbury* (London, 1952), p. 253.

60. As Mrs. Solve points out, it was probably a *reversal of judgment* rather than a pardon that Somerset sought.

61. Ribner, p. 46.

62. Ribner's remark, "A real allegorist would have had Chabot live, as Somerset actually lived, several years longer than Chapman himself" (p. 36), is comic as it stands. Chapman was not clairvoyant.

Chapman may in any case have felt obliged to pay some attention to history at this point.[63] From the dramatic point of view, compared with the endings of his other tragedies, there is a softening strain of pathos, for which Shirley was probably responsible. It seems to me simply true that there *is* a falling-off in this act, just as in the play as a whole; though there is greater variety and liveliness than in most of the other tragedies, there is also a thinning of texture, a loss of philosophical weight.[64] Ribner, however, attempts to salvage Act V as a tragic conclusion by seeing in Chabot's death "a dramatic symbol of the collapse of the ideal of justice for which Chabot had stood." [65] On the contrary, the *ideal* remains, and the "moral" that Ribner draws (from lines probably written by Shirley), "Man's only hope in a fallen world is the love and mercy of his king and his fellow men," is a striking misrepresentation of the relations between Chabot and Francis. But if Shirley has sentimentalized the execution of the ending, the conception does seem to me symbolically appropriate, though not in terms of the collapse of justice. Ribner, in insisting on the guilt of fallen man, ignores the role of conscience or, in Stoic terms, of right reason; Chapman does not. Justice depends not only on external law but also on the spirit within a man, that "apter light" which, as Asall says (I.i.102 ff.), the Almighty Wisdom has given each man within himself to guide his acts. The Wife's Father, however, was right to this extent, that it is much easier to follow that "apter light" away from the world of policy. As Chapman put it in the poem which he appended to *The Crowne of All Homers Workes:*

> As Night the life-enclining starrs best showes,
> So lives obscure the starriest soules disclose.[66]

Ribner cannot understand why Chabot should die after being thoroughly vindicated. He takes the king's words immediately after the trial:

63. The historical Chabot died two years after his arrest, as a result of his ordeal. Chapman may have been warning the king of the danger of delaying full exoneration.

64. II.iii, which appears to be wholly written by Chapman, is, however, a superb debate between Chabot and the king, in which the dialogue has more dramatic "bite" than usual, without any sacrifice of seriousness.

65. *Jacobean Tragedy*, p. 47.

66. *Chapman's Homer*, II.615.74–75.

> . . . now you feel how vain is too much faith
> And flattery of yourself, as if your breast
> Were proof gainst all invasion; 'tis so slight,
> You see, it lets in death—
>
> (IV.i.215–218)

as evidence of Chabot's frailty, but the irony works against the king himself: It is *his* lack of faith in Chabot that inflicts the wound that lets in death. To Chabot, who had said "Death is the life of good men" (II.ii.64), dying is not difficult, as it is to Byron. Chapman's "Senecal" heroes embrace death willingly—Clermont with a not altogether convincing defense of his suicide, Cato (as though Chapman wished to offer a better example of justified suicide) blending Stoicism and Christianity in his elaborate argument for the right of all just men to kill themselves and so "enlarge their lives." [67] Chabot, a more human and imperfect example of "Senecal" man, slips out of life in a manner that avoids offending both Christian and Neoplatonic objections to suicide but implies a willing relinquishment of earthly existence.

The two studies discussed are, I believe, examples of a kind of criticism which distorts the work that it is examining to fit it into a pattern. Weidner imposes on *The Widow's Tears* ideas that he has derived from other works of Chapman; Ribner attributes to *The Tragedy of Chabot* a point of view that is not characteristic of Chapman at all. The one approach tends to discover a false uniformity, the other eviscerates Chapman's faith by translating it into what he might have termed the language of "hypocritical humility." That Chapman was committed to certain central beliefs, passionately and tenaciously held, is true; that his robust, assertive personality informs all that he wrote is true also; but the beliefs were eclectic, the work diverse, the artist an adaptable Elizabethan who contemplated eternity but lived vigorously in the temporal world.

67. *Caesar and Pompey*, IV.v.57 ff.

Juan del Encina's Carnival Eclogues and the Spanish Drama of the Renaissance

Charlotte Stern

O N Shrove Tuesday in 1494 two Carnival plays by the Salmantine poet-musician Juan del Encina were performed in the ducal palace of the House of Alba for the entertainment of the duke and duchess. First published in 1496 in Encina's *Cancionero,* the plays are to-day readily accessible in a new critical edition by Humberto López Morales (Madrid, 1963), but unfortunately the editor has not yet provided the indispensable notes and commentary. In a history of the Spanish theater, Encina's Carnival eclogues are particularly significant because they represent the first notable literary effort at secular drama for which a stage performance can be definitely established. In addition, the plays reflect Encina's almost complete liberation from the classical idyllic tradition and his exclusive involvement with the contemporary Salmantine shepherd. An analysis of the purpose and dramatic structure of the eclogues is, furthermore, important for an appreciation of the sudden and rapid evolution of the Spanish theater in the early Renaissance after centuries of seeming inertia.

Like the majority of Encina's plays, the Carnival eclogues were performed as a pair. The first play depicts a contemporary scene in which the shepherds Bras and Beneyto discuss the duke and duchess, and lavish praise on the House of Alba. At the same time they express grief over the impending departure of the duke for France. Their good humor is quickly restored, however, when Pedruelo returns from town to inform them that a peace treaty has been negotiated and the war between France and Spain avoided. Finally, Bras, Beneyto, and Pedruelo are joined by Lloriente, and all four offer a prayer for peace in the closing *villancico*. The play is a *loa,* a eulogy of the duke and duchess, and at first glance would seem comparable to the *loas* of later sixteenth-century dramatists. J. Richard Andrews has, however, suggested that it is an example of "epideictic or panegyric oratory," a piece of cajoling flattery which really conveys not praise but hostility toward the duke. Andrews further proposes that the mention of Lent in the middle of the play "would be a sly hint that the irritating Duke was a symbolic parallel with the hateful figure of Doña Cuaresma" (Lady Lent), while in the second play, "Encina would be symbolically complaining that life under Ducal protection was a continual Lent in secular form." [1] The Carnival plays, then, would seem further to strengthen Andrews' characterization of Encina as a man of notable poetic endowment but one whose personal frustrations and lack of professional recognition and social acceptance led him to express, on occasion, a deep resentment toward his patron.

While I recognize the general validity of Andrews' main thesis, it seems to me that in his interpretation of the second Carnival play particularly, he has stretched his point beyond belief. In any case, the first eclogue is clearly rhetorical, whether its eulogistic tone is interpreted ironically or not. Its function, moreover, is immediately apparent. It is a prologue that serves to introduce the audience to the rustic Carnival scene that follows. The interdependence of the two plays is achieved through the brief summary in the prologue (ll. 161–190) of the action of the Carnival scene and through the reappearance in the second play of the same four actors. In this respect the first Carnival eclogue is comparable to the *introitos* of Torres Naharro and the *loas* of other sixteenth-century dramatists.

Encina's second Carnival piece, by far the more important work for the study of the early theater, is the dramatization of a traditional Shrove

---

1. *Juan del Encina: Prometheus in Search of Prestige* (Berkeley, 1959), pp. 123–125.

Tuesday feast. It opens on a truly boisterous note as the shepherd Bras bursts into the drawing room where the performance takes place, shouting "¡Carnal fuera, carnal fuera!" In Encina's time this was the traditional cry, a peremptory and ungracious farewell to Carnival, who, after a jubilant welcome and several days of absolute rule, was summarily expelled from the village amid raucous shouts and unrestrained pandemonium. The hullabaloo terminated generally with the smashing of worthless pots and pans that the peasants had saved throughout the year for the occasion. Today in northern Spain the villagers still hasten from door to door, shouting "Antroxu fuera, que rompí la cazuela," as they smash their wooden bowls, thus signaling the end of Carnival and the dramatic arrival of the Lenten season.[2] But in Encina's play, Beneyto, whose hunger is not yet assuaged, hastens to prevent Bras from putting this premature damper on his pleasure: "Espera, espera," he pleads, "que aun no estoy repantigado!" to which Bras quickly retorts, "¡Ya estoy ancho, Dios loado!" and prepares to hurl his pitcher or bowl (ll. 1–4).

The importance of these opening lines cannot be overstated. The ritual shout "¡Carnal fuera!" establishes both the content and mood of the play. The piece is the dramatization of a fifteenth-century rustic Carnival celebration. Spanish folklore and ritual are its essence, while the noisy gaiety of the initial lines becomes its dominant mood. In subsequent Carnival plays the spirit remains one of rollicking good fun—as, for example, in the *Entremés famoso: el abadejillo* by Quiñones de Benavente, where a villager cheerfully reflects: "No hay más alegre tiempo en todo el año / que las Carnestolendas . . . / todo grita y porrazos,/ mazas, tizne, salvado y naranjazos, / con mucho huevo huero."[3] Today in northwestern Spain, Galician *Entruido* (dialectal form of *Antruejo*) means not only "Carnival" but, by extension, any type of noisy revelry.[4]

The ritual spirit of Encina's play is reinforced almost immediately when Beneyto and Bras swear by the patron saint of Carnival, *San Gorgomellaz* (l. 20), also called on occasion *San Gargantón,* Saint Big Throat, appropriately named for his Gargantuan appetite. *Gorgomellaz,* like the other

---

2. Constantino Cabal, *Contribución al diccionario folklórico de Asturias* (Oviedo, Instituto de Estudios Asturianos, 1958), V, 102.

3. *Colección de entremeses, loas, bailes, jácaras y mojigangas,* ed. E. Cotarelo, *NBAE,* XVIII (Madrid, 1911), 581–582.

4. Cabal, IV, 105.

Sayagués form *gorgomillera* (l. 6), is clearly an augmentative, derived from the extremely rare *gorgomilo, gargamelo,* "throat." [5] But *gorgomellaz* not only means "big throat" but, like Provençal *gargamèlo,* has logically acquired the additional connotation of "big eater." Consequently, it most fittingly expresses the Carnival spirit of "swilling and guzzling," and obviously belongs to the same festive European tradition from which Rabelais derived the names for his giants: *Gargantua, Grandgozier, Gargamelle, Badebec,* and *Pantagruel,* all prodigious consumers of food and drink.[6] *San Gorgomellaz,* then, is a burlesque saint, one of the many *santos populacheros* found in the sixteenth-century drama.

Georges Cirot has further observed that in Encina's play one of the shepherds is appropriately named *Bras* (western Spanish variant of the Castilian *Blas*) in honor of Saint Blaise, whose feast day is celebrated on February 3, near the beginning of Carnival. Saint Blaise, Cirot emphasizes, "est ce qu'on appelle sur les calendiers espagnols 'abogado de la garganta,' et cette spécialité ne lui est pas attribuée qu'en Espagne." [7]

In the final song of the play, however, the shepherds toast *San Antruejo* (l. 204), Saint Carnival himself, whose colorful career reaches back into the Middle Ages and forward to the present day. Indeed, who can forget Sir Carnival's ignominious defeat at the hands of Lady Lent in Juan Ruiz's *Book of Good Love* (sts. 1067–1127), followed, however, by his triumphal reentry into the village on Easter morning (sts. 1210–1222), when the town's butchers, herdsmen, and cattle all turn out to greet him and his no less distinguished companion Sir Love, to the strident music of shepherds' pipes, flutes, and flageolets! In contemporary Carnival celebrations a direct descendant of Encina's *San Antruejo* still figures prominently in the dramatic activities of the folk. In some Galician villages he continues to be called *San Entruido,* while elsewhere he may be *el Meco, el Vello, el Felo, el Judas, Pero-Palo,* or *Carnistolles.* Regardless of his name, he is either a young boy disguised as a cantankerous old man (*el viejo*) or a stuffed doll

5. For Spanish *gorgomilo,* see W. Meyer-Lübke, *REW,* 3685; V. García de Diego, *Diccionario etimológico español e hispánico,* 3046, p. 782; J. Corominas, *Diccionario crítico etimológico de la lengua castellana,* II, 681–682.

6. See P. Albarel, "Origine du mot 'Gargantua,'" *RER,* IV (1906), 390–393, and Marcel Bataillon, "Sur le nom de Gargantua," *Miscelánea de Estudos a Joaquim de Carvalho,* IV (1960), 377–381.

7. "Le théâtre religieux d'Encina," *BH,* XLIII (1941), 28–29.

(*pelele*), a straw man in ragged attire but usually sporting a fine hat. He is drawn in a cart to the outskirts of town, where villagers rain blows upon him while a pompous judge recites in mock-heroic verse Carnival's last will and testament. Finally the straw man is burned or drowned. Thus Carnival is expelled from the village, and since he is the village scapegoat, the townsfolk believe they have expelled with him all the sins and vice committed during the year.[8] It is obvious, then, that the Spanish ceremony described here belongs to the widespread European ritual of "burying the Carnival."

San Gorgomellaz or *San Antruejo* was the incarnation of the Carnival spirit, just as the English puppet Jack-of-Lent personified the Lenten season. Would it be too farfetched, then, to assume that a straw man representing *San Gorgomellaz* or *San Antruejo* was an actual stage prop in Encina's play? Certainly its presence would remind the audience of all the noisy fun and games associated with folk Carnival celebrations. The rustics toast *San Antruejo* and honor him so that he in turn will befriend them when times are bad. In the closing carol the shepherds make their purpose clear: "onrremos a tan buen santo/porq*ue* en ha*m*bre nos acorra" (ll. 211–212), while in another carol from the same period the shepherds also express their devotion to Saint Big Throat: "comamos tocino / por San Gargantón / qu'es gran devoción / hartarnos de vino."[9] In Encina's eclogue there is clearly the suggestion of religious parody characteristic of the Carnival season as the rustics address their entreaty to a burlesque saint, in striking contrast with the sixteenth-century nativity plays in which the shepherds dance, sing, and pray to the Virgin, their patroness and intercessor before God.

Encina's Carnival scene is given over entirely to the animated depiction of the ritual feast, eaten by the shepherds with a gustatory delight worthy of Saint Big Throat himself. The Rabelaisian orgy is the essence of Encina's play precisely because it was the most authentic and perhaps the most ancient expression of the Carnival spirit. The traditional names for the days comprising Carnival clearly imply that the festival was synonymous with abundant food and drink. If in the fourteenth century Juan Ruiz mentions only *jueves lardero*, in a contemporary Asturian jingle the

8. Cabal, V, 123–127.

9. No. 394 in the *Cancionero musical de los siglos XV y XVI,* ed. F. Asenjo Barbieri (Madrid, 1890).

accent is definitely on eating: "Sábado freixoleiro, / domingo lardeiro, / lunes gordo, / martes Antroido." Saturday, then, is marked by an unprecedented consumption of *freixolos,* a kind of ceremonial cake; Sunday means pork or bacon, hence *lardeiro;* Monday, more of the same (*gordo* = fat; compare French *Mardi gras*), and finally Tuesday is *Antroido,* the feast to end all feasts—*Martes Antroido*—without further designation because "Antroido es sinónimo de hartazgo, y basta la palabra para que surja, como en un conjuro, una mesa pantagruélica con multitud de platos repletísimos."[10] Modern dialectal dictionaries from Galicia corroborate the meaning of *hartazgo,* "bellyful," for *antroido, entruido.* In the same region one also hears the verb *entruidar,* "eat to excess," and the colloquial expression *e un entruido,* used to describe a person given to intemperate eating.[11] The Castilian proverb "Antruejo buen santo, Pascua no tanto" likewise stresses the hedonistic spirit of the folk.[12] Although in the Carnival play by Quiñones de Benavente the rustic feast itself is not dramatized, a village girl regales the audience with a jocular description of it:

> Llámole al tiempo yo, en Carnestolendas,
> mar de comidas, golfo de meriendas,
> Flandes de los lechones,
> general avenida de roscones,
> sanguinolento estrago de morcillas,
> plaga de quesadillas,
> convalecencia en que mujeres y hombres
> tantas ganas sacamos,
> que hasta las herraduras nos tragamos. . . .
>
> (p. 582)

In Calderón's *Entremés de las Carnestolendas,* however, the *vejete* (old man) is more cynical in his appraisal of Carnival:

> ¡Oh loco tiempo de Carnestolendas
> diluvio universal de las meriendas

10. Cabal, IV, 225.

11. Antonio Fraguas Fraguas, "Máscaras y sermones de Carnaval en Cotobad (Galicia)," *RDTrP,* II (1946), 436, and Vicente Risco, "Notas sobre las fiestas de Carnaval en Galicia," *RDTrP,* IV (1948), 163–164.

12. Gonzalo Correas, *Vocabulario de refranes y frases proverbiales* (Madrid, 1924), p. 55.

feria de casadillas y roscones,
vida breve de pavos y capones,
y hojaldres, que al doctor le dan ganancia
con masa cruda y con manteca rancia! [13]

Because the shepherds' Carnival meal is a ritual feast, it is communal in character. Bras needs little urging before agreeing to share Beneyto's wine and bacon (ll. 9–20), and when the shepherds see two companions out in the fields, they immediately invite them with whistles and shouts to partake of the traditional Carnival fare (ll. 109–130). Furthermore, in keeping with the communal spirit, Beneyto supplies the wine and bacon, while Pedruelo provides a bowl of fresh goat's milk (ll. 127–130). It should be stressed that the ritual meal eaten in common was probably "looked upon both as a sacrament and as an oath of mutual help and support." [14] The shepherds' liberality also recalls the primitive potlatch, a solemn feast in which the host displays extreme prodigality. [15]

The ritual nature of the Carnival feast is also apparent in the rustic victuals. Bacon is a special Carnival delicacy, in keeping with Mediterranean folk tradition. Even today in Spanish-speaking countries pork continues to enjoy special prominence on certain feast days. The wine is equally important, since Carnival demands not only excessive eating but drinking as well. Finally, the shepherds all share Pedruelo's goat's milk after first suggesting that he may have stolen it from Antón (ll. 155–160) and, second, that it may not be goat's milk but cow's milk (ll. 165–170). Again the reader finds himself enmeshed in folk tradition. Stealing bowls of milk is one of the special licenses permitted during Carnival in northern Spanish villages. [16]

The Saturnalian feast, at which overeating was definitely a magic rite, was celebrated in early spring. Most probably it had its beginnings in agricultural and pastoral festivals of pre-Christian origin that were designed to prepare the farmer for the planting season. According to Sir James Frazer, the peasant believed that there existed a sympathetic

13. *Entremés de las Carnestolendas, BAE*, XIV (Madrid, 1945), 632.
14. Sir James Frazer. *The New Golden Bough*, ed. Theodor H. Gaster (New York, 1959), pp. 480–481.
15. Johan Huizinga, *Homo Ludens* (Boston, 1950), pp. 58–62.
16. Cabal, IV, 215.

connection between himself and his seeds. While they were in his possession, his behavior directly affected their vitality, which in turn determined the success or failure of the summer crops. "What wonder, then," muses Frazer, "if the simple husbandman imagined that by cramming his belly, by swilling and guzzling, just before he proceeded to sow his fields, he thereby imparted additional vigour to the seeds?" After they were sown, he would naturally observe a period of abstinence, depriving himself in order to encourage their germination and growth in the soil. Frazer therefore offers the following explanation for the Christian celebrations of Carnival and Lent: "In modern times the indulgence of the Carnival is followed immediately by the abstinence of Lent; and if Carnival is the direct descendant of the Saturnalia, may not Lent in like manner be merely the continuation, under a thin disguise, of a period of temperance which was annually observed for superstitious motives by Italian farmers long before the Christian era?"[17] With the Christianization of pagan spring festivals, the Carnival season remained a period of incontinence that was designed to fortify the peasant against the long, lean days of Lent.

Apart from the ritual feast itself, another Carnival rite is alluded to in Encina's play. Beneyto entertains his companion with an animated account of the mock-heroic battle he has witnessed between the opposing forces of Carnival and Lent (ll. 52–100). Beneyto has actually *seen* Lady Lent chase Sir Carnival to the outskirts of town in a scene reminiscent of Brueghel's famous painting (1559, Kunsthistorisches Museum, Vienna). Beneyto's narrative implies that the battle was an authentic Spanish folk ritual in the fifteenth century. The shepherd describes with singular verve the animals, fish, and vegetables that comprise the two armies. In reality, village boys, armed with pots and pans and decked out in animal skins and masks depicting pigs, roosters, and sardines, together with other boys wearing strings of sausages, onions, scallions, and doughnuts around their necks, made up the forces of Carnival and Lent. But Beneyto, like his descendant

17. *The New Golden Bough,* pp. 570–571. For the Christianization of the English festival of Plough Monday, see E. K. Chambers, *The Mediaeval Stage* (Oxford, 1903), I, 114, 120–143, and, by the same author, *The English Folk Play* (Oxford, 1933), pp. 216–229; for the origins of the German *Fastnachtsspiel,* see Maximilian J. Rudwin, *The Origin of the German Carnival Comedy* (New York, 1920), pp. 1–23.

the Argentine *gaucho,* refers to the actors not as actors but as the animals or vegetables they are impersonating. His narrative is, consequently, more entertaining, but it also illustrates the characteristic limitation of the popular mind in grasping the nature of dramatic impersonation. The medieval folk ritual described in the eclogue survived into the seventeenth century. In 1599 in a performance given in Valencia at the wedding of Philip III and Margarite, Archduchess of Austria, Lope de Vega, disguised as Sir Carnival and weighed down with Carnival delicacies, was chased across the stage by another actor dressed as Lady Lent.[18]

Encina terminates his play in the same ebullient spirit that has characterized it from the beginning. The four shepherds join in singing a boisterous carol (*villancico*) toasting Saint Carnival probably for the final time that year:

> Oy comamos y bevamos,   embutamos estos panchos,
> y cantemos y holguemos   recalquemos el pellejo,
> que mañana ayunaremos.   que costumbre es de concejo
> Por onrra de santantruejo,   que todos oy nos hartemos
> paremonos oy bien anchos,   que mañana ayunaremos.
>   (ll. 201–210) [19]

The song, reminiscent of the raucous tavern songs of the medieval Goliardic poets, was an original composition, but inspired by folk tradition. This is confirmed by the presence in a Renaissance songbook of two comparable songs (*Cancionero musical,* Nos. 37, 394). The second one, in particular, is amazingly similar to Encina's in both form and content:

> Comer y beber   pues no hay regocijo
> hasta reventar,   do falta comer.
> después ayunar.   Comer y beber
> Hayamos placer   hasta reventar,
> en Sant Antruijo,   después ayunar.

Encina's song is clearly a carol, having the initial three-line verse (*estribillo*) followed by several stanzas (*mudanzas*), each terminating with the two-line burden (*vuelta*). Furthermore, it is a polyphonic

18. Félix Lecoy, *Recherches sur le Libro de Buen Amor* (Paris, 1938), p. 252.
19. Music published by Barbieri, *op. cit.,* pp. 529–530.

roundelai, as were the other Renaissance *villancicos* composed by the court musicians. But in keeping with peasant tradition, Encina's carol was probably accompanied by a traditional shepherds' dance, either a line or circle dance similar to the English hornpipe and characterized by strenuous leaping and jumping steps that further assured the richness of the summer harvest and the vigorous growth of newborn animals and children.[20] Like the other features of Encina's play, the Renaissance Carnival songs have twentieth-century counterparts. One Galician carol described as a *cantiga de Carnaval* salutes *San Entroido:*

> Este é o Santo Entroido,   o que quere o Santo Entroido
> é o Santo verdadeiro,   é que lle enchan o.

Another, classified as a *cantiga de despedida del Entroido,* bids a fond farewell to Shrove Tuesday:

> Adiós Martes de Entroido,   hastra o día de Pascua
> adiós meu queridiño;   non se come mais touciño.[21]

The analysis of Encina's second Carnival play clearly establishes the poet's indebtedness to, and appreciation of, native pastoral tradition. The rustics are pure Spanish types and contrast sharply with the ambivalent shepherds found earlier in Encina's free adaptation of Vergil's *Eclogues,* where the Salmantine poet's dual allegiance—classical and Spanish—is immediately apparent in the shepherds' double names and in many curious interpolations. In the Carnival plays, however, the only remnant of classical influence is found in their designation as *églogas.* Here Encina's use of the Vergilian term implies a rather flimsy attempt to give status to a genre obviously not yet recognized as worthy of a distinguished court poet.

The performance of the Carnival eclogues in the ducal palace suggests that in the late fifteenth century the upper classes were entertained by Encina's interpretation of folk tradition because they vicariously enjoyed

---

20. Compare the acrobatic feats, games, and dances performed by the shepherds in the *introitos* of Torres Naharro. See Joseph E. Gillet, *Torres Naharro and the Drama of the Renaissance* (Philadelphia, 1960), Chap. I, "Primitivism," pp. 21–24.
21. Risco, *op. cit.,* pp. 357–359.

the rustic simplicity, the rare good humor, the spontaneous *joie de vivre,* and the sprightly country songs and dances that characterized the rural festivals of the nomadic Salmantine shepherds. One is tempted to compare the Spanish piece with the English *Merriment of Christmas at the House of the Right Worshipfull John Salusbury of Lleweni.* In Robert Chester's celebration honoring his distinguished patron, the shepherds express their appreciation to their "frolique freind of Arcady" on Christmas Eve. They would have presented as "newe yeares homely gifte / peares Apples fildbieres or the hazell nutt," but "nipping winter and a forward spring" deprived them of their offering. So they settle for a lively song and dance:

> A homely cuntry hornepipe we will daunce,
> A sheapheards prety Gigg to make him sport
> and sing A madringall or roundelay
> to please our Lordlike sheapheard lord of vs
> take hands take hands our hartes lett vs Advaunce
> and strive to please his humour with A daunce.[22]

Brueghel, too, comes to mind. Like the Flemish master, Encina reflects the Renaissance interest in the contemporary scene and the sharpened awareness of the picturesque world of peasants and townsfolk. What better way to catch a visual impression of Encina's Carnival scene than to view the communal meal in Brueghel's *Harvesters* (1565, Metropolitan Museum of Art, New York) or the lively musical festival in the *Peasant Dance* (1568, Kunsthistorisches Museum, Vienna)?

The spirit of Encina's play is, indeed, Renaissance. The poet focuses almost exclusively on Carnival, and depicts the unbridled peasant delight in food and drink that in turn reflects the growing enthusiasm for the pleasures of this world. The shepherds savor with a true gourmand's delectation the delicacies that comprise their rustic fare; they are reluctant to welcome the Lenten season, fretting and grumbling over its imminence (ll. 102–104, 137–138). Encina's play looks forward to Rabelais rather than backward to the Middle Ages. With the emphasis on Carnival, it is a welcome respite from those deadly moralizing *coplas* by the fifteenth-

---

22. *Poems by Sir John Salusbury and Robert Chester* (London: Early English Text Society, 1914), Extra Series, No. CXIII, pp. 19–20.

century *cancionero* poets that cast a pall of gloom over the joys of here and now, condemning the pleasures of the body and exhorting man to abstinence and restraint. Encina's play, then, was designed to give a final lift to the human spirit before all Spain was plunged into the inevitable gloom of the Lenten season.

Since Encina's literary prestige rests largely on his distinction as the father of the Spanish stage, special attention must be given to the theatrical merits of the Carnival eclogues. The decidedly rhetorical nature of the first play implies that Encina has diverted the drama from its true purpose. His concern with a political subject clearly links the piece with the earlier pseudo-dramatic *Coplas de Mingo Revulgo* (*c.* 1464) and with a later Renaissance festival play by Francisco de Madrid (*c.* 1495).[23] The first eclogue, however, is only a prologue. Its subject matter can be at least partially justified because the play serves as a transition to the special realm of theatrical illusion created in the second Carnival play. In the prologue the actors involve themselves in the duke's affairs, and although they do not address him directly, as was done in Encina's first Christmas eclogue, their conversation about him draws him and his retinue into the special realm of dramatic illusion by bridging the boundary between reality, which is the duke's drawing room, and theater, which is the rustic Carnival scene. Encina, then, is experimenting with the complex phenomenon of theatrical illusion in his transitional prologue piece.

The clever manipulation of the real and imaginary worlds is further developed in the second eclogue. The Carnival play, in its performance in the palace, reflects a historical reality, an authentic custom of the time. Bruce W. Wardropper has observed that in Spain during the pre-Lenten season, as in the Roman Saturnalia, the shepherds and the aristocracy reversed their roles. The shepherds actually held their Carnival feast *in the royal palace* and parodied the customs of the nobility.[24] The tradition is suggested in the play itself. Beneyto, in extending an invitation to Bras to join him for supper, comments that they will simply be imitating their master: "Estiendete, Bras, y ayamos / gran solaz / oy, qu'es san gorgomellaz / que assi hazen *nuestros* amos" (ll. 27–30). Apparently the "temporary suspension of normal social life," which in Encina's time was

23. See Joseph E. Gillet, "Egloga hecha por Francisco de Madrid (1495?)," *HR*, XI (1943), 275–303.

24. "Metamorphosis in the Theatre of Juan del Encina," *SP*, LIX (1962), 45.

characteristic of the topsy-turvy Carnival season, permitted the shepherds to indulge in coarse jokes, horseplay, and pranks that would not have been tolerated normally.[25] Wardropper concludes that "the shepherds for a brief span were metamorphosed into courtiers aware that they soon would be disenchanted" (p. 46). But Encina has not simply painted in dialogue form a social practice of the time. He has created a comedy that unfolds in that peculiar sphere of theatrical illusion which is both distinct and removed from the real world. The stage rustics are not real Spanish herdsmen but professional actors, friends or colleagues of Encina, who impersonate the Salmantine shepherds, aping their actions and burlesquing their rustic speech in a spirit of rollicking good humor designed to entertain a courtly audience. But the inescapable fact remains that the second Carnival play dramatized a custom on the very day when that custom was a historical reality. The title of the play, *Egloga representada en la mesma noche de Antruejo o Carnestollendas*, emphasizes not its Carnival content but its performance on Shrove Tuesday. In this complex situation the spectators remain constantly bewildered. Are they witnessing Spanish shepherds parodying their lord and lady and indulging themselves in the ducal palace, or are they watching professional actors impersonate rustics at their traditional Carnival feast?

The performance of Encina's plays on Shrove Tuesday has additional implications. It would appear that in Encina's time drama was still intrinsically associated with certain annual celebrations. This may well be the persistent influence of the Nativity and Resurrection plays which were indissolubly tied to the two great Christian feasts. Or it may simply be evidence that Encina's comedy is still close to its ritual and festival origins, and therefore associated particularly with the carefree Carnival spirit. After all, comedy is an art form that develops naturally "whenever people are gathered to celebrate life in spring festivals, triumphs, birthdays, weddings or initiations."[26] But it should be emphasized that, although Encina's second Carnival piece is performed on the day of a popular folk festival and its content inspired by folk customs, it is not a *Volksstück*, since what is authentic folk drama—the battle between Carnival and Lent —is not dramatized in Encina's play but narrated by Beneyto. This is an

25. Huizinga, pp. 12–13.
26. Susanne K. Langer, *Feeling and Form* (New York, 1953), p. 331.

interesting phenomenon, particularly since the dramatic form of the battle was probably older and more widespread than the narrative version.[27] In this respect Encina's Carnival play is like his second Christmas eclogue, which also leaves off where the traditional folk drama of the Nativity begins. Was this because folk games and ritual were not yet recognized as essentially *dramatic* in the early sixteenth century?

Encina's Carnival eclogue is clearly a farce in which the humorous possibilities of the subject are fully exploited. The theme of eating, although not in itself laughable, is comic when transferred to the stage, particularly when it is not just a question of eating but of overeating. Encina capitalizes on the comic aspects of the situation much more effectively than the later sixteenth-century playwrights, who fail to maintain their predecessor's festive, ribald spirit. Encina's play is, in effect, a string of comic moments in which each new incident is more hilarious than the one before, in accordance with the requirements of truly good comedy. A talented actor would enjoy portraying Bras's initial dilemma. The shepherd's uncomfortable feeling of satiety is an admonition against further indulgence, but Beneyto's wine and bacon are most tempting. Beneyto's description of the battle between Carnival and Lent would be extremely funny if the mock-heroic language in which it is written were carried over into appropriate pantomime. Still more hilarious are two comic incidents near the end of the play. The shepherds' protestations of moderation in food and drink (ll. 144–146) are laughable and ironic, especially on Shrove Tuesday, when excessive eating was not only the order of the day but a ritual obligation. They are quickly belied by the guzzling scene that follows. In that final incident (ll. 171–190), by far the most entertaining, Pedruelo censures his companions' noisy slurping and their drinking out of turn, but his criticism, alas, has the opposite effect from that intended. In this scene the humor is double edged: The actors as shepherds burlesque the peasants' noisy drinking habits, but the shepherds in their brief moment as courtiers are also ridiculing the polished Renaissance manners of the nobility: "Beneyto, pues sos humano, / sorve llano" (ll.181–182). The spectators unwittingly laugh at the rustics when they

27. See Gregoire Lozinski, *La bataille de Caresme et de Charnage* (Paris: Bibliothéque de l'Ecole des Hautes Etudes, 1933). Lozinski publishes the complete text of the French *conte à rire* and studies thoroughly the dramatic and narrative versions of the theme in European tradition.

themselves are the butt of the humor. While all these incidents are inherently comic, it is in their artistic function as structural elements within the farce itself that Encina has created the spirit of vitality and zest that is the essence of comedy.

In accordance with the farcical nature of the eclogue, Encina's use of the rustic jargon called Sayagués is more intense than in his earlier works. Apparently he has intuitively divined its theatrical effectiveness in the comic portrayal of the stage rustic. Moreover, the accumulation of picturesque augmentatives meaning "gluttonous" (*beverrón, comilón, mamillón,* and *papillón*) and of several expressions meaning "eat greedily or excessively" (*comer a muerde y sorbe, comer a calcaporra, cenar hasta traque restraque, rehinchar* or *embutir el pancho,* and *aguzar el pasapán*) reinforces Encina's depiction of the stage yokel as a prodigious eater.

Encina's remarkable sense of the comic and his awareness of the new literary opportunities that the theater offered have earned for him his distinction as the father of the Spanish drama. With his noisy Carnival farce, he has broken with the medieval liturgical tradition and has ushered in an exciting new era in the history of the theater.

The Rise of Cinquecento Tragedy

Lienhard Bergel

U NTIL RECENTLY, the critical evaluation of Italian Renaissance tragedy
has been almost exclusively determined by the negative judgments
of romanticism. In an essay on "Imitation and Originality in Cinquecento Tragedy,"[1] I have tried to demonstrate the unreliability of these
adverse opinions, which rest not only on a very limited or even nonexistent
knowledge of the literature they condemn, but are also untenable in the
light of modern literary theory. The question now arises: What principles
are to guide a different, nonromantic approach to the Italian tragedy of the
Renaissance, an approach that avoids mere philological description, but
aims at a truly historical interpretation?

Several sporadic attempts have been made in this direction. Benedetto
Croce undertook to distinguish the "poetic" from the "nonpoetic" in a
select group of tragedies, and arrived at the conclusion that little genuine

---

1. In *Proceedings of the Fourth Congress of the International Comparative
Literature Association* (The Hague, now in press). An essay that criticizes some
of the basic romantic assumptions on tragedy from within the romantic camp is
Egidio Gorra, "Delle Origini del Dramma Moderno," in *Fra Drammi e Poemi*
(Milan, 1900), pp. 488–526.

poetry could be garnered from them. Yet the fact that Croce discovered some scattered fragments of poetry at all was a first important refutation of the romantic disparagements. Croce demonstrated here the same freedom from romantic prejudices that enabled him to recognize the aesthetic significance of the tragedies of Della Valle and De' Dottori, two poets whose dramatic "systems" are essentially identical with those of their sixteenth-century predecessors.[2]

Yet it is unlikely that extending further the aesthetic scrutiny practiced by Croce will yield a rich harvest. It is easy to demonstrate that the Italian tragedy of the Renaissance is not great art. But what is it, then? If certain works of literature are aesthetically unsatisfactory, they still remain part of the total literary production of a period and therefore pose questions for the literary historian. These questions demand an answer, particularly if they deal with a branch of literature that was as flourishing and influential as was Cinquecento tragedy. At the time, such a literature must have filled genuine needs, and their nature calls for investigation. Thus the problem of Italian Renaissance tragedy shifts from the aesthetic field to that of cultural history. A literature that is aesthetically unrewarding can nevertheless provide considerable insight into the intellectual currents, the emotional climate, and the taste of the time. In the history of dramatic literature there is an almost exact parallel to Italian Renaissance tragedy: the drama of German preromanticism, the *Sturm und Drang*, which is aesthetically questionable but culturally important.

The significance of such documentary literature is usually twofold: It contributes to what modern Italian criticism aptly terms *civiltà letteraria*, an expression that in Anglo-Saxon criticism roughly corresponds to "conventions," [3] and it cultivates special modes of sensibility. In Cinquecento tragedy, the first of these aspects has not only been studied but overstudied, to the extent that it has paralyzed other approaches. It is now generally agreed that Italian Renaissance tragedy served the useful function of replacing diffuse medieval theatrical practices with a more concentrated form of dramatic structure, culminating in the French classicism of the seventeenth century. This "technical" approach occupied most of the

2. About the antiromantic tendencies in Croce's studies in Italian Renaissance literature, see Mario Puppo, *Il Metodo e la Critica di Benedetto Croce* (Milan, 1964), pp. 116 ff.

3. The concept is closely related to that of "tradition" discussed in Puppo, Chap. 9.

attention of the older critics. The Italian Renaissance tragedies were looked upon mainly as school exercises in practicing the prescriptions contained in Aristotle's *Poetics* and in the interpretations which that text had received in the sixteenth century. The plays were tested in regard to their faithfulness to the famous three unities and other technical details; the texts themselves were discussed only in passing.[4]

There were, however, besides Croce, literary historians who directed their attention to the texts as such and interpreted them.[5] These tendencies received their most programmatic expression in an essay by Luigi Russo that was undoubtedly intended as an introduction to a series of studies on Cinquecento tragedy; death prevented him from carrying out his plans.[6] Russo asked why, after sporadic experiments in composing tragedies, in the sixteenth century the interest in the genre increased enormously. He refused to see in this sudden outburst of dramatic activity a purely literary phenomenon, because he was convinced that the roots must be sought in a shift in sensibility. Russo was not interested in the genre "tragedy" as such, but in exploring the intellectual and emotional climate that favored the writing of tragedy; and he searched for a connection between the rise of tragedy and the "crisis of the Renaissance." Thus an investigation of Cinquecento tragedy was placed in the broadest possible framework.

The shift in sensibility with which Russo was concerned can be observed in the prologues to their plays written by two of the leading tragic poets of the time, Giraldi Cintio and Ludovico Dolce. For them the writing of

4. An extreme example of recent date for this tendency is Edouard Roditi, "The Genesis of Neo-classical Tragedy," *South-Atlantic Quarterly,* XLVI (1947), 93–108.

5. Useful, though sketchy and sometimes unreliable, is Giuseppe Toffanin, *Il Cinquecento* (Milan, 1941), pp. 448 ff., and "Il Teatro del Rinascimento," in *La Religione degli Umanisti* (Bologna, 1950), pp. 39–81. Most comprehensive and always stimulating is Mario Apollonio, *Storia del Teatro Italiano* (Florence, 1951), Vol. II, Chap. 4. An important essay by Apollonio that has received little attention is "Note sulla Storia del Teatro Italiano . . . ," *Studi Urbinati di Storia, Filosofia, e Letteratura,* II, Series B (1938), 95–125. Important recent publications are Raffaello Ramat, *"Il Re Torrismondo,"* in *Torquato Tasso,* Comitato per le Celebrazioni di Torquato Tasso, Ferrara 1954 (Milan, 1957), pp. 365–413, and P. R. Horne, *The Tragedies of Giambattista Cinthio Giraldi* (London, 1962).

6. Luigi Russo, "La Tragedia nel Cinque e Seicento," *Belfagor,* XIV (1959), 14–22.

tragedies is not a learned game in which a classical genre is to be imitated under the guidance of Aristotle's *Poetics;* both frankly express their distrust of the Greek philosopher.[7] Both are practical playwrights who wish to maintain contact with their audience, but at the same time they feel an obligation to educate the public. For Giraldi it is not the function of the dramatic author to entertain, but to present a true image of reality, and for this reason he will not hesitate to destroy flattering illusions about the world that the audience may nurture. He knows that theatergoers are accustomed to comic entertainment consisting largely of love intrigues. Instead what will be offered in his play are "tears, sighs, anguish, cares, and cruel deaths," because this "corresponds to our hard lot and to the miserable condition in which we find ourselves."[8] Dolce confirms Giraldi's views with specific arguments. Fortuna, who rules the world, has changed her character—she has become hostile and unjust. Plays must therefore deal with misfortunes of all kinds; tragedy must replace comedy.[9]

In another prologue, Dolce develops a full-fledged theory of the origin and nature of tragedy, and there again he emphasizes that tragedy, not comedy, is the genre most appropriate for his time. Dolce links the birth of tragedy with classical myths about the ages of man, as found in Hesiod, Ovid, and other poets, and he simplifies these myths for his purposes. Tragedy was born when the Iron Age began, when Jupiter dethroned his father Saturn. At that time tyranny began to rule; faith, honesty, and

7. Dolce, in the prologue to *Marianna,* makes Tragedia speak: "I do not wish to turn to the great disciple of Plato, who wrote laws and prescriptions for me; though he was a famous philosopher, he was not a poet." (". . . volle accostarsi . . . non al gran discepol di Platone, Il quale ha di me scritto ordini e leggi; Che, se ben fu filosofo di tanto Sonoro grido, egli non fu Poeta.")—"If one were to weigh the tragic poets on the scale of Aristotle's *Poetics,* none would be found worthy of the title 'tragic poet.'" ("E chi vuol por le poesie di quanti Tragici fur dentro le sue bilancie, Non sarà degno di tal nome alcuno.") *Teatro Italiano Antico* (Milan, 1808 f.), V, 199.—Giraldi, in the dedicatory letter preceding *Orbecche,* complains of the many obscurities in Aristotle's *Poetics,* so that he finally gave up trying to understand it (*ibid.,* IV, 118 ff.).

8. ". . . Non amorosi piaceri, o abbracciamenti, Ma lagrime, sospiri, angoscie, affanni, E crude morti."—". . . in queste angoscie Convenienti a la nostra aspra sorte, Et al misero stato in che noi semo." Prologue to *Orbecche,* in *La Tragedia Classica,* ed. Giammaria Gasparini (Turin, 1963), p. 148.

9. Ludovico Dolce, *Le Tragedie* (Venetiae, 1566), Prologue to *Medea.*

truthfulness disappeared. From then on the weak, neglected by fortune, were exploited and abused by the strong and fortunate, and Astraea, the goddess of justice, left the earth.[10]

For an understanding of Dolce's explanation of the birth of tragedy, one must probably turn to Seneca's *Medea*. If Seneca's plays are arranged "chronomythologically," i.e., according to the historical sequence of the mythical events presented, *Medea* is the earliest.[11] *Medea* is not only a personal tragedy, but has also historical implications, because its heroine is the first person who suffered a tragic experience. Medea is the victim of the end of the Golden Age, which was terminated when Jason violated its ethical code. According to Seneca, the representative act of this violation is seafaring. Navigation leads to plundering foreign shores and thus opens a wide field to human avarice, the sin that destroyed the innocence of man's primitive existence. Medea's misfortunes are only incidental to this comprehensive catastrophe.

Dolce's manner of connecting the birth of tragedy with the end of the Golden Age carries an interesting implication. The rise of tragedy in the sixteenth century in Italy is accompanied by the rise of the pastoral. In different ways both reflect the same change in attitude toward reality: tragedy, by facing without illusion the Iron Age in which man is now living; the pastoral, by looking back with longing toward the Golden Age which is past. The tragic strain in the great pastoral poetry of the late sixteenth century, particularly in Tasso's *Aminta,* has frequently been observed. Dolce's views on the birth of tragedy show its inner link with the pastoral.

After this mythical prehistory of tragedy, Dolce gives a brief sketch of its historical development: the tragic muse, who first inspired the Greek poets from Aeschylus to Euripides, later emigrated to Italy, where she guided the dramatists from Trissino to Aretino. For Dolce, there is no difference between "Grecians" and "Senecans," a distinction made by several writers on Italian Renaissance tragedy.[12] For him, the supposed leader of the "Senecans," Giraldi Cintio, is as much a true heir to the Greek dramatic

10. *Ibid.*, Prologue to *Ifigenia* (*in Aulis*).

11. See Francesco Giancotti, *Saggio sulle Tragedie di Seneca* (Roma-Napoli-Città di Castello, 1953), pp. 77–81.

12. See Ferdinando Neri, *La Tragedia Italiana del Cinquecento* (Florence, 1904); Marvin Herrick, *Italian Tragedy in the Renaissance* (Urbana, 1965); *et al.*

tradition as Trissino, and we must assume that Dolce himself, the translator and imitator of Seneca, who made sarcastic remarks about Aristotle's *Poetics,* considered himself a "Grecian" of the same kind as Giraldi.

The study of Cinquecento tragedy should be guided by Dolce's view-point: What matters is the intellectual and emotional content, not the degree of conformance with Aristotelian "rules"; not the theatrical form, but the tragic essence. Here the characteristic which has usually been considered the main defect of Italian Renaissance tragedy can prove to be most helpful. The principal objection that the romantic critics had raised against Cinquecento tragedy was that it was largely "imitation" of classical authors. It is exactly by examining closely the nature of this imitation that one can hope to obtain an insight into the character of Italian Renaissance tragedy. This applies particularly to the plays of the early sixteenth century which are usually grouped together as "Grecian."

The relative independence from Aristotle of the early Cinquecento tragic poets is indicated by their choice of plots. If these playwrights had been actually interested in writing "perfect" tragedies according to Aris-totle's *Poetics,* one would assume they would have tried to "imitate" the great model held before them, Sophocles' *Oedipus.* The fact is, however, that the Oedipus subject was taken up rather late, in Dolce's *Giocasta* of 1549 and in Dell'Anguillara's *Edippo* of 1565.[13] The tragic fables that attracted the earliest writers of the Cinquecento had nothing to do with the Oedipus theme: Trissino's *Sofonisba,* Rucellai's *Rosmunda* and *Oreste,* Alamanni's *Antigone,* Pazzi's *Didone,* Martelli's *Tullia.* Of these six plays, three have their immediate source in Livy and Vergil; two use Greek plays discussed in the *Poetics,* but only as secondary sources (*Rosmunda, Tullia*). If any preference for a Greek tragic subject is discernible at all, it is one mentioned in the *Poetics* only once, and then with disapproval: *Antigone.*[14] Alamanni adapted Sophocles' play freely, and Rucellai used it as a secondary source in *Rosmunda.* Thus the beginning of our investiga-

13. See Herrick, p. 44.

14. "That situation in which someone is in full consciousness about to do some-thing, and then does not do it, is the worst possible to be imagined, because this is repugnant and not tragic, for it does not lead to a catastrophe . . . as Antigone who does not kill Haemon." *Poetics,* Chap. XV, 1435b–1454a.

tion confirms René Wellek's doubts about the alleged close interdependence between Renaissance literary theory and practice.[15]

Since Sophocles' *Antigone* served twice as a model in early Cinquecento tragedy, it is convenient to begin our analysis with these "imitations." Of the two, Alamanni's adaptation is closer to the Greek text than Rucellai's *Rosmunda*; it seems therefore justified to reverse the chronological order and begin with *Antigone*.

This tragedy is, to my knowledge, the only Cinquecento play based on a classical model that has received a detailed analysis in which the Greek text is compared with the Renaissance version and conclusions are drawn from the differences between them. In his comprehensive work on Alamanni, Henri Hauvette pointed out many details in which the Italian poet diverges from Sophocles, but he did not grasp their full significance. Nevertheless the French scholar made one significant discovery: He observed that the character of Antigone has undergone a change; she appears "avec un héroisme plus soutenu . . . plus théâtral, que dans la tragédie grecque";[16] her sister Ismene has been similarly transformed. Hauvette puts these changes in a historical perspective: He sees in the play a forerunner of French classical tragedy, not because of the observance of the three unities, but because the Italian *Antigone* anticipates some inner qualities characteristic of the classical French theater: "une prédilection pour les expressions les plus générales et surtout les plus nobles."[17] Perhaps one of the reasons why Hauvette was so much more perspicacious than the other older critics of Cinquecento tragedy is that he did not read *Antigone* as a specialist in the drama, but studied Alamanni's writings as a whole; his reading of Alamanni's heroic epic poem *Giron il cortese* probably sharpened his awareness of similar features in the play. The analysis that follows will make use of Hauvette's findings and supplement them.

Sophocles' *Antigone* has justly been called by H. D. F. Kitto a problem play, similar to the middle group of Shakespeare's plays because of the uncertain point of view with which the poet evaluates his characters.[18]

15. See René Wellek, *A History of Modern Criticism* (New Haven, 1962), I, 6.
16. Henri Hauvette, *Un Exilé Florentin à la Cour de France au XVI° Siècle: Luigi Alamanni* (Paris, 1903), p. 247.
17. *Ibid.,* p. 246.
18. H. D. F. Kitto, *Greek Tragedy* (Garden City, 1954), p. 132.

Gilbert Norwood, though not using the same term, agrees with Kitto: Sophocles fully approves or disapproves of neither Antigone nor her antagonist Creon.[19] If the balance finally swings definitely in favor of Antigone, this is because Creon goes too far in upholding a position which is in itself not wrong. Alamanni eliminates this ambiguity completely. He disregards it because his Antigone is from the beginning conceived as a person of heroic stature; this stature would be diminished if there were the slightest doubt about the righteousness of the cause for which she is willing to die. Sophocles' Antigone is a young girl driven by her ethical instinct; she is a "beautiful soul," who resembles Goethe's Iphigenia but is younger and more impetuous and self-willed.[20] Alamanni's Antigone, on the other hand, is more mature; her convictions are based not on instinct but on careful deliberation.

The most far-reaching and most significant transformations of Sophocles' poetry are, however, found in Alamanni's versions of the choruses. In Sophocles the chorus, representing the citizens of Thebes, is naturally inclined to side with Creon, the ruler defending the city against the assaults of a foreign army, and only slowly do the Thebans turn against their king, when they observe his excesses in punishing a violator of civic discipline. In Alamanni, the chorus is divided from the beginning. For them, both brothers are equally in the wrong, driven by the same false *libido regnandi*. For this reason the members of the chorus are much more ready to express their admiration for Antigone than in Sophocles' tragedy. In both plays the chorus criticizes Antigone for her stubbornness and her foolish pride. Alamanni, however, adds a stanza in which the citizens pray for her life and praise her: "Even though she was arrogant and tactless in dealing with the king, she feels in her heart how much can be accomplished by compassion, indignation, and sorrow." [21] The word *pietà* that the chorus uses here is one of the key terms of the tragedy of the time; it is

19. Gilbert Norwood, *Greek Tragedy* (New York, n.d.), p. 140.

20. One of the most famous lines spoken by Goethe's Iphigenie: "Nicht mitzuhassen, mitzulieben bin ich da," corresponds to a Sophoclean passage thus rendered by Alamanni: "Per ambo amar, non per odiargli nacqui." *Teatro Italiano Antico,* II, 170.

21. "Che se ben fu superba/Contr'al Re nostro, e di dolcezza ignuda,/Pensa in femminil core/Quanto possa pietà, sdegno, e dolore." *Ibid.,* p. 175.

difficult to translate because it comprises at the same time compassion, piety, and the humanist concept of *humanitas.*

Yet in Alamanni's version this admiration for Antigone's *pietà* is not the dominant emotion. More powerful is the awareness of irresistible *Fortuna,* who destroys even a noble being like Antigone. Thus Alamanni deviates radically from the basic conceptions underlying Sophocles' tragedy. Sophocles presents his theme, the conflict between the individual and the state, in two different aspects. First he upholds the authority of the state, represented by Creon; then he condemns this power when it turns into tyranny. The metaphysical problem of the rule of *Fortuna,* Fate, is subordinated to conflicts on the human level. In Alamanni the order is reversed. The Renaissance poet is overwhelmed by the feeling of human vanity; he expresses this through the choruses of his invention. This sentiment is voiced very early in the play, when the chorus reflects on the conduct of the two brothers: their overweening ambition is not only hubris but folly, because it attaches too much importance to earthly things. It is this Christian conviction of the unsubstantiality of worldly matters which makes Alamanni alter completely the spirit of the next chorus. There Sophocles celebrates the achievements of which man is capable in collaboration with his fellow citizens; the link with the play is the thought that war interferes with man's noble tasks. While Sophocles praises the civilizing activity of man, which transforms the earth, Alamanni condemns it. Man is the most obnoxious of all living beings; when he changes his surroundings, he seeks danger for himself and harm for others. His ambitious undertakings are folly, because he dies long before he can complete them. In sharpest contrast to Sophocles' "Nothing is greater than man," Alamanni observes, "He who considers himself a human being, is only an animal." [22] Here the Horatian-Senecan theme of moderation, of *aurea mediocritas,* is transformed into a condemnation of all human enterprises reaching beyond the fulfillment of immediate needs.

Alamanni develops this theme in another chorus, again substituting his own for Sophocles' thoughts. In the Greek play, the chorus speaks of others who, like Antigone, were condemned to be buried alive. This is the will of Fate, but Fate is not always unjust. Thus the individual misfortune of

22. "Deh, com'è fera, che esser uom si crede!" *Ibid.,* p. 164.

Antigone is generalized. No radically pessimistic conclusions are drawn; on the contrary, the chorus wishes to console Antigone by pointing out that life is a mixture of good and evil. In Alamanni's version, however, the chorus returns to the theme of the folly of human aspirations and therefore seems to address itself to Creon rather than to Antigone: Ambition is the chase after an illusion, in which man exchanges his liberty and peace of mind for worthless things; he should free himself from emotions and let nature be his guide.[23] Thus it is not excess of worldly ambitions, but worldly aspirations altogether that are condemned. The chorus combines Stoic and Christian thoughts, a synthesis that retained its significance throughout the sixteenth and seventeenth centuries.

In the next chorus, also his own invention, Alamanni gives another reason for *contemptus mundi*. Life is worthless not only because human enterprises are vain, but because of the injustice of *Fortuna*. That goddess always destroys the righteous, worthy, and wise, and favors fools and wrongdoers.[24] The whole chorus gives the impression of being more than a literary exercise in repeating a classical *topos;* it has the ring of sincerely felt personal grief.[25]

Thus Alamanni gives his play a somber metaphysical background absent in Sophocles. One cannot assume that for the poet the philosophy expressed in the chorus is without significance for his conception of the main character; the two must be related, as in Sophocles. If to the Greek Antigone life seems no longer worth living, this feeling is in the nature of an emotional outburst. She reacts strongly against what she instinctively feels to be disregard for the divine law; but this violation is only an individual case, and life as such is not condemned. To Alamanni's Antigone, however, the world offers nothing of true value. The only value

23. "Ma se'l misero mondo/Volesse ben pensar come fallace/È quel ch'ei tanto apprezza,/In odio allora avria quant'or gli piace. . . ./Oh, quanto è dolce, oh quanto/Il cor disciolto aver d'ogni altra cura,/E'n bando por desio, timore, e spene . . ." *Ibid.*, p. 190.

24. "Tu i giusti sempre, e i degni,/E i saggi, oh Dea fallace,/Calchi, e sollevi al Ciel gl'ingiusti, e i folli:/Con povertade spegni/Gli alti intelletti, pace/Dando, e gioja, e ricchezze a'bassi, a'molli." *Ibid.*, p. 197.

25. R. Ramat's interpretation is unsatisfactory. He sees in the play mainly the work of a humanist who has not yet become aware of the great tensions of his time. It is difficult to perceive any "visione tranquilla" in Alamanni's *Antigone* (see Ramat, p. 380).

that exists is within her—namely, the awareness of *pietà;* and if she dies for her conviction, she will give up something not worth keeping. Antigone, as conceived by Alamanni, anticipates the figures of Christian martyrs in baroque tragedy, for whom sacrificing themselves for their faith is made easy because they are convinced of the unsubstantiality of this world. Such feelings are foreign to Sophocles' Antigone. When Alamanni strengthened the heroic traits in Antigone's character, he did so because his whole conception of life differed from that of Sophocles; the heroism and the pessimism pervading his play are inseparable.

Yet compared with his predecessor, Rucellai, Alamanni's modifications of Sophocles' play were relatively conservative. The changes in external detail inevitable when Rucellai fused the Sophoclean plot with an episode of early Langobardic history are less important than the shifts in conception. Rosmunda surpasses Alamanni's Antigone in lucidity. She is only fifteen years old, yet she is capable of refuting the cautious, practical advice of her nurse, and she defines the issues with great precision. For the nurse the practical—"l'utile, la prudenza"—consists of respecting social reputation— "gloria ed honore." To these Rosmunda opposes her own concepts of honor and fame: "il bel morire," a death that receives its beauty from being a sacrifice for *pietà.* The whole first part of Rucellai's play centers around this concept of a "beautiful death." The immediate occasion for this self- sacrifice, Rosmunda's desire to bury her father against the wishes of the victorious Alboin, is almost forgotten; she is possessed by the frenzied urge to die a beautiful death, whatever the cause may be. Even more than with Alamanni's play, the reader has the impression of living in an atmosphere of religious exaltation characteristic of the martyr plays of the baroque and of Bartoli's *History of the Jesuit Order.* Heroism and "il bel morire" are for Rosmunda one. When searching for the body of her father, she encourages her companions: "Remain constant and strong, for a noble death is first among the beautiful things." The chorus echoes her sentiments: "Happy are those who adorned their lives with a beautiful death, but miserable those who prefer to live their lives to the last in such harsh serfdom." [26] If death is unattainable, then the stoic restraint of both hope and despair is

26. "Siate constanti e forti,/Che generosa morte/Ha'l primo loco fra le cose belle." —"Oh felici coloro/Che con sì bel morire/Avete adorno la passata vita!/Ma miseri costoro/Che 'n sì duro servire/Staranno 'nsino all'ultima partita!" *Teatro Italiano Antico,* I, 152, 149.

the only way to make bearable a life that is constantly disturbed by the whims of *Fortuna*. What is particularly significant in these passages is that the ethical ideal of greatness, of generosity, is here joined with the aesthetic concept of beauty.[27] The union of the two is not found in Alamanni.

There are other differences between Alamanni's *Antigone* and Rucellai's *Rosmunda*. The religious pessimism, so clearly formulated in Alamanni's play, is replaced by a deep, groundless melancholy that has taken hold of Rosmunda, and this mood seems to be independent of the external events that led to the defeat and death of her father. The futility of living overwhelms her; to lose all hope is a desirable thing.[28] This motif is only touched upon in the early part of the play, but will become of great importance later.

Like Alamanni, Rucellai is not principally concerned with the problem dominating Sophocles' *Antigone,* the power of a ruler and the justification for opposing it. Thus Alboin is presented without the ambiguities surrounding the role of Creon. The Langobard king is the typical brutal, egotistical tyrant of sixteenth-century tragedy, and the maxims he voices are stripped of the subtleties that are an integral part of Machiavelli's theory of power. However, Rucellai introduces a dramatic complication and an ethical issue that are not found in either Sophocles or Alamanni. This new motif is closely associated with the figure of the watchman who surprises Rosmunda searching for the body of her father. Falisco, the guard, represents a tyrant's servant who is not deaf to the demands for *pietà*. Faced with a conflict between his orders and Rosmunda's appeal to his humanity, he resolves it by deciding to arrest her but to plead with Alboin for her life. This seems to him the best way out, not as a compromise but because he sincerely desires to save Rosmunda. He understands that heroic resistance to superior power can only lead to death, and he wishes to

27. A recent study of the concept of "greatness" is Georg Weise's book *L'Ideale Eroico nel Rinascimento* (Naples, 1961). As reviewers have pointed out, the volume has many weaknesses, but at least it attracts attention to a neglected problem. Important in this context—and philologically more reliable than Weise —are Chaps. IX and X of Camillo Guerrieri Crocetti's *G. B. Giraldi ed il Pensiero Critico del Secolo XVI* (Milano-Genova-Roma-Napoli, 1932). Weise does not discuss the link between the "heroic" and the "beautiful."

28. "E in la miseria desiar la vita/È grave mal consperso di dolcezza:/E buon acquisto è perder la speranza." *Teatro Italiano Antico,* I, 170.—The last line is worthy of Alfieri.

preserve life. Thus a counterweight is provided to the clamor for "il bel morire," and heroic idealism is questioned at least by implication. Falisco is the suitable person to introduce these doubts, because he is not of noble birth and the code of heroism does not apply to him. Perhaps there is in him a touch of the Spanish *villano gracioso*, but without cynical or comical features. Falisco possesses no greatness, but his attempt to reconcile the demands of the practical with those of *pietà* is not base, and he demonstrates courage when he faces the king. First he admonishes his master not to sully his reputation with an act of cruelty. After this attempt has failed, he proposes a surprising resolution of the conflict: Instead of killing Rosmunda, Alboin should marry her and thus enlarge his kingdom. To the modern reader this must appear a ridiculous and improbable suggestion. Yet Rucellai is not concerned with psychological verisimilitude, but with an ethical and religious problem, however clumsily he may present it: Is life to be thrown away lightly under the influence of the emotions? His task is twofold: to overcome the fury of Alboin, who sees his orders transgressed by both Rosmunda and his servant, and to dissuade the young girl from her irrational determination to die; the second of these tasks proves to be the more difficult. Rosmunda is longing for death because she wants to escape the rule of *Fortuna*. Falisco tries to impress her with the standard argument: Life is a mixture of good and bad luck; Fortune's wheel is constantly turning. But she remains unmoved. This deep melancholy appears to Falisco unworthy of her greatness, because true greatness demands control of the emotions. He tries to impress upon her that her wish to die under any circumstances means actually yielding to the emotions, to *furor*.[29] Rucellai contrasts one kind of greatness, "il bel morire," with another, the Stoic-Senecan ideal of the control of the passions, and he sides with the latter. Yet the conflict between the two principles is presented with considerable finesse. Rosmunda proves herself to be a skillful debater, in full command of the lucidity characteristic of her from the beginning. Only a few of the many examples can be given here. Her determination to die is also a form of wisdom: "He who does not

---

29. "L'animo grande è sempre da lodare,/Ma non quel che se stesso non conosce:/Perocchè l'uno innalza il possessore,/L'altro l'abbassa, e spesso lo ruina." *Ibid.*, pp. 168–169. "Furor," "passione," "ira" denote the irrational, the emotions in general, not only love, desire for revenge, ambition, and similar impulses. About mastery of the emotions as a form of "greatness," see Weise, pp. 221 ff.

know how to die knows little." [30] She defends *furor, ira,* as an integral part of courage, the courage to die.[31] The nurse rejects this unorthodox defense of the emotions and urges Rosmunda to accept what *Fortuna* offers, life with all its limitations. But the final argument that wins over Rosmunda is one that appeals to both her *pietà* and her greatness as a ruler: If she insists on refusing to marry Alboin, her faithful attendants will suffer at the hands of the king's soldiers; she owes it to her subjects to subordinate her wishes to their welfare. Thus reason prevails over subjective feelings.

Yet the pendulum swings back once more. The king's barbarism—he made her drink from the skull of her father—has crushed her completely. Her former betrothed recognizes that revenge is a necessity for her in order that her will to live may return, and he urges her: "Let the furor of revenge overcome your pain." [32] Thus furor becomes an approved instrument in the service of a just cause. Heaven shows its *pietà* by permitting the revenge to succeed.

In spite of its crudity and many contrived situations, *Rosmunda* is a play that deserves to be taken seriously as a document illuminating the moral questions that must have agitated Rucellai's time. He examines the nature of greatness from two different points of view; he condemns and approves furor, the emotions; he tests the value of prudence and practicality. In the shifting attitudes toward these issues, Rosmunda is a rudimentary problem play.

In his *Oreste* Rucellai continues the themes of his earlier play, *pietà* and "il bel morire." Now, however, he no longer doubts the value of uncompromising heroism. *Oreste* is in essence one long-drawn-out contest for the honor of dying a beautiful death. More clearly than in *Rosmunda,* the heroic yearnings arise from a feeling of absolute pessimism, making death appear preferable to life on this earth. Again it is the chorus that expresses these convictions; nothing corresponding is found in the choruses of Rucellai's source, Euripides' *Iphigenia in Tauris.* The spirit of these hymns is practically identical with that of the original choruses in Alamanni's *Antigone:* the blindness of man in not recognizing the vanity

---

30. "Che ben sa poco, chi non sa morire." *Teatro Italiano Antico,* I, 170. This is another line that reminds one of Alfieri.

31. "Vero è che ho aggiunto l'ira alla ragione,/. . . poscia a quello somministra l'ira/Incitamento e spron della fortezza." *Ibid.,* p. 171.

32. "L'ira del vendicare/Vinca il grave dolore." *Ibid.,* p. 186.

of human ambitions, which are epitomized in the lust for power. *Pietà* is not found in the pomp of royal palaces, but in the simplicity of country life.

Orestes, Pylades, and Iphigenia are convinced of these truths; the fate of Agamemnon is a vivid example. In Rucellai's version the mythical core of Euripides' play, the efforts to free Orestes from the Furies, is practically forgotten. Except for occasional brief relapses, Orestes is in complete possession of his mental faculties, and the plan to return the statue of Diana to Greece serves here mainly as a framework for creating situations in which *pietà* can assert itself heroically. It is the chorus which first sounds the theme of "il bel morire," when the people of Tauris offer themselves to die for the foreigners condemned by the barbaric laws of the island: "Ch'un bel morir tutta la vita onora." [33] This theme, "Death is the real life," is varied throughout the play; Orestes expresses most forcefully its Christian character: "Man dies the day he is born and begins to live when he dies. . . . The soul which is a foreigner in this hostel wishes to return home." [34] More explicitly than in *Rosmunda, pietà* and heroism are seen as one: "Che pietade e fortezza son sorelle." [35]

This new conception of the play is evident from the manner in which Euripides' characters are changed. In the Greek play the theme of one friend wishing to sacrifice himself for the other is of only minor significance; the principal reason why neither wants to return to Greece, thus allowing the other to let himself be sacrificed in Tauris, is the fear of disgrace at home, not heroic *pietà*, as in Rucellai's play. The character of Iphigenia undergoes a similar transformation. The Greek Iphigenia is full of resentment against her countrymen who decided on her death for the good of the country, and therefore she feels at first no hesitation toward killing the strangers. The Italian Iphigenia, however, is always ready to sacrifice herself and thus to set an example of *pietà* by dying with fortitude.

---

33. *Teatro Italiano Antico,* II, 56.

34. ". . . l'uom muor dal dì che nasce,/E ch'ei comincia a viver, quando e'muore. . . ./L'alma, che in questo albergo è peregrina,/Desia di ritornar là donde venne." *Ibid.,* p. 95.

35. *Ibid.,* p. 71.—To the older critics, this reshaping of Greek tragedy according to the sentiments of the late Renaissance appeared as a distortion in bad taste. Thus Creizenach finds *Oreste* by "die geschmacklose Entfaltung deklamatorischen Edelmutes entstellt" (*Geschichte des neueren Dramas* [Halle, 1901], II, 390).

With Rucellai begins the transformation of the figure of Iphigenia, culminating in Goethe's drama.

The three remaining Cinquecento tragedies usually called "Grecian" use Latin rather than Greek sources. Among the three, Pazzi's *Didone* is better suited for our purposes than the other two because it gives a better opportunity for following the transformation of a classical model and drawing from the differences conclusions about the nature of Italian Renaissance tragedy. Like Alamanni and Rucellai, Pazzi had before him a text in which the characters and the point of view of the author are fully developed, while Livy provided for Trissino and Martelli only outlines.[36] *Didone* is also of particular interest because here a strong admirer of Aristotle—Pazzi was among the first Renaissance translators of the *Poetics* —transforms an episode from a Latin epic poem into a tragedy. The question is: To what extent are his theoretical knowledge and his practice in agreement?

The opening of the play makes it obvious that Aristotle is for Pazzi of no particular importance; he feels much closer to Seneca than to the author of the *Poetics*. The ghost of Dido's murdered husband is driven from the underworld by pity for his widow; he knows that her encounter with Aeneas will lead to catastrophe. Thus a Senecan atmosphere is created from the beginning—not, as might be assumed, in order to produce the famous "Senecan horror," but, in the words of Pierre Grimal, "à dessiner par avance les grandes lignes de la situation morale, indépendamment des événements qui en marqueront le déroulement." As Grimal pointed out, Seneca wishes to make clear from the beginning that his characters are doomed.[37] This weakens or eliminates the effect of Aristotle's main tragic device, the peripety that unexpectedly ends a state of presumed happiness and security. Sichaeus is not the spokesman for a divine world order, like the Delphic Oracle and Tiresias in *Oedipus;* he sees in what is coming the working of "celestial fraud." Thus the metaphysical framework within

36. For *Sofonisba* the relationship to Livy is complicated by the role Petrarch may have played.

37. Pierre Grimal, "Les Tragédies de Sénèque," in *Les Tragédies de Sénèque et le théâtre de la Renaissance,* ed. Jean Jacquot (Paris, 1964), pp. 7 ff.—Grimal's essay is the best brief presentation of the modern conception of Seneca the dramatist; he makes full use of recent Italian scholarship that is mainly responsible for the new image of the Roman poet.

which the tragedy unfolds is close to the irrational Senecan *fatum—fortuna*.[38] This Senecan viewpoint made it possible for Pazzi to detach the Dido episode from its Vergilian context. Aeneas' divine mission is for Pazzi a matter of indifference, and therefore he is free to change the character of the Roman hero. In Vergil, Aeneas feels sorry for Dido, whereas in the Italian version he is troubled with guilt and criticized by Achates for his lack of compassion and decency. The Vergilian Aeneas proves his greatness by leaving Dido; Pazzi presents him as a reprehensible, faithless lover. Thus the sufferings of the Renaissance Dido are no longer part of a vast religious-patriotic structure; she stands alone, like the central figure of a modern drama. This isolation makes possible a greater stress on reflections about individual conduct, either by the characters themselves or by the chorus. Such a procedure is characteristic for Seneca, but it widens the distance from Aristotle, for whom the center of tragedy is the plot.

Sichaeus' appearance to his widow from the world of the dead sharpens the moral issue from the start, because thus Dido is reminded of her pledge not to remarry. To leave no doubts, the chorus impresses on her that she is faced by a conflict between conscience and pleasure. Vergil, by contrast, is much more tolerant and understanding, not wishing to draw distinctions too clearly. He therefore analyzes Dido's sentiments very little, preferring to describe the external manifestations of her inner turmoil, and hardly ever does he explicitly evaluate her conduct. Pazzi's Dido, on the other hand, has an unrelenting capacity for self-analysis, like Seneca's Phaedra and so many heroes and heroines of Cinquecento tragedy. It is particularly noteworthy that the terms she uses in her effort to understand herself are the same as will later be found in French classical tragedy. Thus she complains that she is unable to maintain her inner "order," that she lost, forgot herself ("scordata di me stessa"); she is ashamed of the impotence of her reason ("il ceco intelletto").

In Vergil the fact that Dido is a ruler, the founder of Carthage, is mentioned only in passing. Pazzi's heroine, however, is weighed down by

---

38. Grimal points out that Seneca tends to identify *fatum—fortuna* with character. This relationship only strengthens the irrational character of *Fortuna*, because the determination of character is left to her whim.—For biographical explanations of the pessimism that pervades Seneca's tragedies, in contrast to his philosophical writings, see the conclusion of Grimal's essay and F. Martinazzoli, *Seneca* (Florence, 1945), p. 151.

the awareness of her "greatness"; she knows that in the past she has shown "più che feminil core." The chorus sees in Dido's behavior a fall from greatness. Even great souls can commit grave errors; Dido, whose intellect reaches to the stars, is unable to possess herself. Thus the fall from greatness is not limited to external misfortunes; it can also be the destruction of the moral self. She is criticized by the chorus, not for having fallen in love, but because in her love she was unable to keep control of herself, to the detriment of her greatness.

Yet there are moments in which Dido reveals her former grandeur. When Aeneas' departure has become a certainty, the chorus praises her for not allowing the servants to witness her pain: "This great soul considers it below her dignity to exhibit her miserable condition before those who revere her. Oh, how under all circumstances the royal blood and the nobility of her ancestors prove themselves!" [39] Thus Pazzi uses every opportunity for measuring Dido's conduct against the code of greatness.

In the *Aeneid* Dido finally becomes the helpless victim of speechless furor: she is *demens*. Vergil describes her in a detached manner, with a mixture of puzzlement and disapproval, comparing her with mythical figures in similar mental disarray. The distance between him and his character is so great that Dido's conduct reminds him of a stage performance: "Aut Agamemnonius scaenis agitatus Orestes." Pazzi's Dido, however, reveals her feelings in a long soliloquy; she is far from being demented. Vergil briefly states that Dido is now determined to die; Pazzi's heroine slowly and logically works her way toward that decision. Here Pazzi invents details of marvellous psychological finesse. He makes Dido first convince herself that it is hopeless to restore her relationship with Aeneas. Then she dreams that she could simply wipe out what has happened and return to the life she led before his arrival: "resurga la prima gloria." But she realizes that this is impossible; her regal splendor—a moral quality—has been blemished forever. She deserved to be punished by Aeneas' desertion, because she had broken her pledge to her dead husband. In this state of moral humiliation she recalls the *virtù* of her ancestors. This

39. "L'animo generoso/sdegna il miser suo stato/aprir maxime a quelli/da i quali è reuerito./Oh come in ogni sorte/appar la regia stirpe,/e'l nobil de i passati /per sin al fin si scorge." Alessandro Paccio de' Medici, *Le Tragedie Metriche,* ed. Angelo Solerti (Bologna, 1887), p. 92.

thought will give her the strength to die with calm and dignity, and it would be unworthy of her to change her mind. She therefore represses a momentary temptation to weaken, when hope rises anew with the return of Anna from her mission to Aeneas, and she reprehends herself: "You let yourself again be overcome by cowardice." [40] In the *Aeneid* Dido is merely a woman destroyed by love, and her suicide is an act of despair. In *Didone* it is the loss of *gloria* that forces her to die, and her voluntary death is a means of recovering her greatness; Pazzi anticipates here the ending of Alfieri's *Saul*.

It is regrettable that Pazzi does not stop at this point. Instead he continues with some freely invented variations on the theme of greatness, whose artificiality contrasts disagreeably with the relatively simple contours of the preceding scenes. Dido's old suitor Jarba hopes to win her hand now that his rival has disappeared. Jarba is the heroic lover who believes that love justifies the commission of crimes; he therefore does not hesitate to turn against his ally, Dido's brother. Dido accepts the marriage proposal because thus she will be able to revenge the murder of her brother. Ingeniously she relates this desire for revenge to her present predicament: If her husband were still alive, she would never have been attracted to Aeneas. Yet she does not forget her responsibilities as a ruler: The death of her brother will break the siege of Carthage. Jarba, in carrying out the revenge, proves to be a truly noble mind; the similarity with the revenge theme in *Rosmunda* is obvious.

However, Dido's decision to die has not been abandoned; its execution has only been delayed. This suicide raises a question in the mind of Pazzi: Can this act of furor be reconciled with her greatness? He does not pursue the problem; the final impression is that Dido died a heroic death.

This uncertainty in dealing with the tragic-heroic is more clearly pronounced in the preface Pazzi wrote for his tragedies. He discusses the nature of tragedy: it should be "una imitatione . . . un documento della vita heroica." [41] In *Didone* Pazzi carried out his program; however, he felt uneasy about his play because of "quella crudelissima et acerbissima morte di Didone." He prefers the fable of *Iphigenia in Tauris* which, to be true,

40. "Oh anima inferma/ancor ti lasci da uiltà solleuare?" *Ibid.,* p. 95.
41. *Ibid.,* p. 43.

is "lacrymosa e funesta," yet it has a happy ending. Thus Pazzi's position resembles that of Rucellai in *Rosmunda*; the tragic-heroic attracts and frightens them at the same time.

Hesitations of the kind found in Pazzi and Rucellai, occasionally leading to outright contradictions, are not rare in Cinquecento tragedy. Sometimes they are due to conflicts between the classical source and modern attitudes, conflicts that remained unsolved; sometimes to ambiguities that the authors themselves introduced. It is an unhistorical oversimplification to ascribe perplexing details of this kind to immaturity and inexperience in writing plays. One should not forget that the period in which these tragedies were composed was one of refined literary culture. Why should the authors of tragedy have been excluded from it and be condemned as immature? It would seem more accurate to assume that the passages which present puzzles reflect uncertainties that were felt at the time, unresolved moral and metaphysical problems.

Modern research has taught us to see the Italian sixteenth century not as a period of classical harmony, but as one of crisis.[42] The earliest Cinquecento tragedies are among the first works of literature to reflect this crisis. In these plays there is present a pessimism of Christian-Senecan character that has no counterpart in the secular literature of the time; the hesitations with which this pessimism is presented only prove that the new ways of feeling and thinking were most disturbing. The worship of heroic, beautiful death was an attempt to overcome this anguish; the traditional concept of greatness received a new meaning when it was joined with the ideal of *pietà*.

The rise of tragedy in the Cinquecento is therefore not an exclusively literary development, based on an interest in Aristotle's *Poetics* and in Greek tragedy as a genre. As we have seen, essential features of the *Poetics* were disregarded, and the Greek plays that served as models were greatly transformed. The real classical influence was that of Seneca, and this long before Giraldi's sponsoring of the Latin poet.[43] As has recently been

42. See the programmatic article by Giorgio de Blasi; "Problemi Critici del Rinascimento," in *Letteratura Italiana. Le Correnti* (Milan, 1956), I, 205 ff.

43. In *The Senecan Tradition in Renaissance Tragedy* (Manchester, 1946), H. B. Charlton challenges the validity of the distinction between "Grecian" and "Senecan" tragedies. Yet Charlton still tends to equate "Senecan" with "startling incidents" (p. 48), and he does not understand the nature of "imitation" of classical models

demonstrated, more convincingly than ever, the tragedies of Seneca were rarely imitated in the Middle Ages and in the early Renaissance, not because they were inaccessible, but because they were not understood.[44] If Seneca became of such decisive importance for the playwrights of the sixteenth century, the reason cannot have been the humanistic desire to imitate a classical author; if this were true, imitation on a large scale could have set in much earlier. The rapid rise of tragedy in the Cinquecento is only incidentally a chapter in the history of a genre; it must be understood as part of a broad shift in taste and sensibility. Symptomatic of these changes was a lessening of the importance of Cicero, Vergil, and Livy and a strengthening of the interest in Seneca, both "morale" and "tragicus," and in Tacitus.

Tragedy flourished in the Cinquecento largely because it spread Senecan ideas, or ideas that had some affinity with those of Seneca, such as certain aspects of Christianity. This fact has been obscured by the undue attention paid to the least significant feature of Seneca's tragedies: the famous "Senecan horror," consisting of ghosts, mysterious rituals, and barbaric behavior. What is usually overlooked is the amount of "Senecan horror" that can be found in classical literature before Seneca and that was readily accessible. Serious doubts about the nature of the traditional "Senecan horror" have recently been voiced by Manlio Pastore-Stocchi, who points out that the cruelty described in late medieval and early Renaissance tragedy need not necessarily have been drawn from books, but could very well be based on concrete observations of the realities of the time; there was no need for classical models.[45] In Cinquecento tragedy "Senecan horror" has become a completely stereotyped procedure for contrasting barbaric behavior with *pietà* or for demonstrating just punishment; these clichés must have lost all concrete significance. The core both of the tragedies of Seneca and of the Cinquecento is *pietas, humanitas*.

---

in Renaissance tragedy. On the other hand, he recognizes that the heroes of Cinquecento tragedy often do not meet the prescriptions of Aristotle's *Poetics* (p. 56).

44. See Manlio Pastore-Stocchi, "Un Chapitre d'histoire littéraire au XIV⁰ et XV⁰ siècles: 'Seneca poeta tragicus.' " *Les Tragédies de Sénèque et le théâtre de la Renaissance*, pp. 11 ff.

45. *Ibid.*, p. 25.

Reviews

CLUBB, LOUISE GEORGE. *Giambattista Della Porta, Dramatist*. Princeton, New Jersey: Princeton University Press, 1965. Pp. xvi, 359. $8.50.

I N CANTO XIV of the *Gerusalemme Liberata* Tasso describes the visit of Carlo and Ubaldo to a magician who reveals the circumstances of Rinaldo's ensnarement by Alcina. This *mago* is versed in the secrets of nature, which he studies as a revelation of the power and glory of God. He is familiar with the principles of alchemy, with the peculiar virtues of plants and streams; he records the movements of the stars and the forces of the elements; and he possesses second sight.

The figure of the *mago naturale*, as he became known to Tasso's readers, was in all probability inspired by the Neapolitan scientist and playwright Giambattista Della Porta, whose sobriquet was the *Mago della Natura* and who published the first edition of his *Magiae naturalis* in 1558, five years before Tasso began to compose the *Gerusalemme*. Alchemy fascinated Della Porta, as did astrology, physiognomy, and prognostication; to these semioccult studies he added a profound knowledge of the natural sciences, and published in some seventeen volumes the results of his research in varied fields. He was a peripatetic collector, and his "cabinet of curiosities" was so famous that as late as 1742 Dézallier d'Argenville, when compiling his *Conchyliologie*, wrote to Don Mateo Egizion, librarian of the King of the Two Sicilies, to find out whether it still existed in Naples and might be listed among the extant Italian collections. Unfortunately the Inquisition had not shared Tasso's faith that the secrets of nature are learned by the will of God and that the process of revelation is a continuous one. Della Porta, a friend of such dangerous philosophers as Sarpi, Campanella, and Galileo and at least an acquaintance of Bruno, was regarded by the Holy Office with constant distrust. After his death his collection and library were dispersed, and, as Don Mateo regretfully wrote, no one in Naples carried on his tradition.

Professor Clubb's excellent book, the first serious study of Della Porta in English and the only complete study in any language, begins with a carefully documented biography, though even she has not been able to fill in the mysterious eight years after 1593. She establishes a more satisfactory and precise dating of the plays than has hitherto been attempted—a difficult task because Della Porta's comedy *Olimpia* may have been written as early as 1555, but was not published until 1589. It was his first drama to appear in print. Professor Clubb then passes on to a detailed study of the plays individually, and closes with an account of Della Porta's influence on the theater in France, England, Spain, and Germany.

From 1580 to 1587 Della Porta enjoyed the protection of Tasso's patron, Cardinal Luigi d'Este, and his lasting fame was to be inspired by that great poet who had also served the house of Este, Lodovico Ariosto. For it is as a dramatist, not as a scientist, that Della Porta's name has survived, and Ariosto's influence is clear in all his work. His Olimpia takes her name from the *Furioso,* and that this was apparent to Della Porta's generation is evident, for when Angelo de Fornaris adapted the play for a French audience he gave it the name of another heroine from the same epic, *Angelica.* The name of Ariosto's evil hag, Gabrina, is used for two disagreeable old women in Della Porta's *La Turca* and *La Trappolaria,* and in the latter play two characters take their names from prototypes in Ariosto's *Cassaria.* Della Porta's tragicomedy in verse, *Penelope,* is a refutation of Ariosto's charge that Ulysses' wife owed her reputation for chastity to Homer, a slander which apparently caused a good deal of debate in the sixteenth century. The episode of Ginevra in the *Orlando Furioso* is used in *I due fratelli rivali,* though Della Porta was also familiar with Bandello's version. The central situation of *La Tabernaria* is borrowed from *La Scolastica. L'Astrologo,* probably composed to appease the Inquisition, is indebted to Ariosto's more spontaneously satirical *Il Negromante*, and Professor Clubb thinks that it may originally have borne the same title. Minor plot borrowings from Ariosto are numerous.

Other traces of Ferrarese influence may be seen in the plays. A pedant in *La Tabernaria* is called Tito Strozzi, like the well-known poet. Della Porta's only surviving *tragedia sacra* is *Il Georgio,* and St. George was the patron saint of Ferrara, whose encounter with the dragon is paralleled in the *Furioso* and recalled in the *Gerusalemme.* An incident from the *Aminta* seems to have inspired one in *La Furiosa.* Stylistically Della Porta adopts Ariosto's favorite use of a hendecasyllable composed of five verbs, and in *Il Georgio* writes, describing the dragon, "Avvolge, sbrana, uccide, infetta, e tronca."

The year of Della Porta's birth, long in doubt, has been established as 1535. During his long lifetime, for he did not die until 1615, he witnessed, and shared in, an important development in the theater. A new type of comedy took shape, which, retaining the complicated Plautine intrigue adapted by Ariosto, added a stronger love interest, a more important part for the heroine, greater psychological realism, and a strain of romantic feeling which had been unknown to earlier comedy. The new tone of high-minded sentiment was, however, owing to the equally increasing popularity of the *commedia dell'arte,* offset among the comic characters by farcical, even vulgar scenes, often in dialect. Della Porta was influenced by the changing tastes of his times, but it is difficult to establish a consistent development in his comic style, particularly as some of his later plays may have been adapted from works written at a much earlier date. Professor Clubb suggests that Spanish influence may have affected Della Porta; this seems unlikely, for when he began to write, the Spanish theater was still embryonic, and when Lope de Vega's first plays were performed Della Porta was already a veteran dramatist. The Spanish references which appear in the comedies beginning with *La Trappolaria* (whose original title was possibly *La Spagnuola*) are natural local color in a Neapolitan setting of that period, and the Spanish viceroy before whom many of the performances took place was probably gratified by these allusions to his native land. The developments in the Italian theater between 1550 and 1614 which Professor Clubb traces in Chapter III are sufficient to account for Della Porta's dramatic style.

His lively mind, his skill in handling complex plots and a multiplicity of

characters, formed only a part of his endowment as a dramatist. He gives
timeworn themes new vitality and a contemporary flavor by enriching
them with his own experience of society, as when he recalls the dishonest
fringes of occultist circles, the Neapolitan hangman whom he had met in
the course of his research on physiognomy, the academies and the popular
taverns which he and his friends frequented, the Turkish raids which had
taken place in his childhood. His dialogue is supple and natural; the
conversation of his lower class characters abounds in popular sayings.

Della Porta's influence abroad was important, and such dramatists as
Middleton and Molière were indebted to him. Knowledge of his works
was diffused both by the printed plays and by the *scenari* based on them,
which Professor Clubb describes in an interesting appendix. Some of his
comedies, like those of such other Renaissance dramatists as Machiavelli
and Beolco, have been revived in Italy in this century. Appropriately
enough, since Della Porta himself was the victim of censorship, a version of
the *Due fratelli rivali* appeared in the "liberation number" of *Il Dramma*
(August 15–September 1, 1943), which also contains an editorial rejoicing
at the end of an era when only innocuous works (including, presumably,
sixteenth-century revivals) could be performed on the Italian stage.

Professor Clubb has written an admirable book, both readable and
scholarly, which in examining the life and work of an important figure of
the late Renaissance illuminates as well the world in which he worked. She
provides lively English translations for all passages in Italian, including
two long scenes translated in an appendix. Her bibliography and index are
models of completeness and clarity, and Italian scholars as well as students
of the Elizabethan theater are much in her debt.

                                                         BEATRICE CORRIGAN

NICOLL, ALLARDYCE. *The World of Harlequin.* New York: Cambridge University Press, 1963. Pp. 243. $18.50.

T HE heavy paper and gaudy pictures of the jacket on this handsome volume suggest that it has been designed as a gift book. It is regrettable that one of the eloquent portrayals of the *commedia dell' arte,* by an artist who knew it at first hand, was not selected for the dust wrapper design. Once we are past the jacket, Professor Nicoll returns us to more familiar ground. He tells us that he is going to attempt to account for the strength of Harlequin, pointing out that he and Hamlet are among the most enduring of theatrical creations. His second aim is to explore and explain the "potent force" of the *commedia* and "wherein its virtue consisted." The book is actually a brief history of the *commedia* with an emphasis on its more interesting theatrical types. And in recounting this history, Nicoll has had the advantages of a generous publisher and the most recent pictorial discoveries about the *commedia.*

Unfortunately the format interferes with the usefulness of the pictures to the student, for he must go to the front of the book for detailed information about the chronological order of the illustrations. And not to look at the list of "Illustrations" could cause serious misunderstandings of the sequence of events in the Italian theater, for the pictures are thrown in higgledy-piggledy with the text. In the first eleven pages, for example, we find reproductions in this order: a chapter heading with figures from a late sixteenth-century fresco, a title-page to Scala, a sketch by Degas, a water color by Cézanne, a woodcut of 1601, two engravings of 1728, a frontispiece of 1694, a late seventeenth-century engraving, two engravings after Gillot (no date given), another chapter heading from a late sixteenth-century fresco, and a Pantalone dancing by G. D. Tiepolo (also undated). Dates are given quite at random throughout the list, and anyone but an art historian with an encyclopedic memory would have to check several reference works to get any sequential information.

The generalizations that Nicoll supplies about the various stock characters of the *commedia* are frequently as bewildering as his pictures. To be sure, he emphasizes the diversity of roles played by the stock character of Pantalone, but he certainly overemphasizes Cecchini's statement (p. 48) that the role "is always a serious part" when he tells us (p. 49) that "Pantalone's behaviour should not be of a kind to arouse raucous laughter, should not depart from the serious norm." The illustrations on pp. 48–49 deny his point, for the exaggerated posturings of Pantalone show that if he took himself seriously, he certainly was the butt of the actors' jokes and the audience's laughter, whether he was a Polonius or a Shylock. And surely we must find it hard to perceive in Pantalone "a vigorous and downright middle-aged merchant, with a fine career behind him, who has become involved in an emotional world with which he cannot always cope" (p. 52).

In describing the iconography of Pantalone, Nicoll speaks accurately enough of the tights, jacket, hat, gown, slippers, and mask, and the "occasional" addition "of spectacles" (p. 44). But when he remarks on "a pouch, sometimes so placed as to suggest a phallus" as one of these "occasional additions," he neglects to take into account the exaggerated codpieces of Pls. 27–28–29, the bloomingly suggestive handkerchiefs of the chapter headings, and the obvious phallus of the Callot drawing (Pl. 128) entitled "Pantalone and the Capitano." A more serious lapse, however, is Nicoll's failure to indicate the emphasis on the uneuphemized phallus among most of the early portraits of Pantalone, for he thus ignores the chronological development of Pantalone from an unabashedly lecherous old goat to a more refined and more hypocritical elderly admirer, involved in an emotional world with which he hopes to cope.

Inevitably, too, the more shocking portrayals of the *commedia* are suppressed. One must guess, then, that in the choice of plates from the "Recueil Fossard" only the neutral scenes are selected in which the abundantly furnished phallic Pantalone conceals his abundance with an arm or a cloak; as a result the raucously sexual play from which the scenes seem to derive loses its flavor. Indeed it is in this collection that one finds the most grotesquely phallic of all Pantalones, sprouting an emblematic rose (Pl. XXXVIII). It would be hard to reconcile these Pantalones with Nicoll's genteel old merchant.

Nowhere in *The World of Harlequin* does Nicoll explain the reasons for his change of mind about the nature of *commedia* from his earlier and more useful *Masks, Mimes, and Miracles* (London, 1931), where he says that Pantalone was often distinguished by "a phallic appendage only a little less prominent than that worn by the ancient mimes" (p. 254), and that Pantalone and the Dottore are usually together, sometimes as lovers' fathers, courtiers, or little better than servants, but always made fun of for their "tremulous age, pedantic affectations, blundering folly" (p. 253).

Professor Nicoll places himself in an equally awkard position in discussing the *commedia* representations of Callot, which he feels are not representative of the more regular theater in Italy, but more probably of the carnival (p. 76). Elsewhere, nonetheless, he reluctantly admits the general accuracy of Callot's drawings of Francatrip, Captains, and Scaramuccia, and his description of Pulcinella exactly tallies with Callot's delineation. His most direct attack on Callot comes with his discussion of the figure of Trastullo. "In no wise," he tells us (p. 82), is he "distinguished from any other of his zanni." He adds that Callot may have seen "fit to dress all his comic servants alike, or . . . was depicting a non-theatrical figure, or else that the Neapolitan actors had abandoned all nice differences in their parts." Yet in Pl. 128 (p. 216) Nicoll calls the preliminary drawing for this Trastullo a Pantalone. Since a similar figure peers through the curtain of the stage in the introductory plate to the *Balli di Sfessania,* Trastullo may have been the name of a particular Pantalone rather than an incorrect delineation of a stock character developed elsewhere. I must regretfully report that other generalizations made about the *commedia* in *World* are inaccurate. The Zannis, for example, are no more similar to one another in Callot than they are in representations by other artists, the captains are not uniformly dressed despite Nicoll's assertion that they are (cf. Captains Mala Gamba and Bellavita with Captains Csgangarato and Cocodrillo), and the Harlequins in the background of Callot's *Balli* are much like early Harlequins portrayed elsewhere despite Nicoll's opinion that they are not.

Professor Nicoll wants to turn Callot's representations into carnival figures, but the theatricality of the representations is borne out by the gestures and stance of the dancers, the professional skill of the jugglers and acrobats, the *lazzi* of an involved sort being acted out in the backgrounds, and the opening plate of a stage with a play in progress. Surely these are theatrical rather than carnival activities. It is interesting to compare the electric grotesqueries of the *Balli* with an actual carnival figure that Nicoll shows elsewhere (and apparently accepts as a reasonably accurate dramatic representation), the portrait of Coviello singing (Pl. 38). The masks worn by the two figures of this plate suggest the Dottore or Pantalone and are out of keeping with the costumes. The picture is taken from Bertelli's *Carnevale Italiano Mascherata* (1643). I think one must agree with Nicoll that the Neapolitan figures of Callot occasionally differ from other representations of the *commedia,* and one must always keep in mind the artistic shaping of the pictures as they were drawn and etched (and Callot was not a photographer). But to deny them validity for these reasons is to eliminate most of the representations of the *commedia* from consideration for similar reasons and to forget that Callot has other *commedia* plates which need to be taken into account in making such a judgment, among them the infrequently reproduced ones from *Les Caprices.*

In a broader view of *The World of Harlequin,* what can be said of its usefulness as an introduction to the *commedia dell' arte?* For the general reader or the undergraduate, it might be a useful introduction to a complex topic. For the professional theater person, Professor Nicoll's accounts of the origin and development of the various characters of the *commedia* will provide a lively and reasonably comprehensive survey of the rise and decline of the *commedia dell' arte* in various parts of the western world. The color and black-and-white pictures are reproduced carefully, and the book is printed in a readable type. Besides the List of Illustrations, there are a Bibliography, Notes (I found a note indicated on p. 82 but absent in Notes), and an Index. And Professor Nicoll carries through on his promise to use illustrative material which "has not been reproduced or which is to be found only with difficulty," although he does not warn us of his concern to protect us from coarse pictures. But the serious student looking for precise information or the scholar wanting a dependable secondary source had better look elsewhere. For this critical assessment, by attempting to appeal to a "popular" audience, loses much of its value for a scholarly one.

CHARLES S. FELVER

Notes on Contributors

LIENHARD BERGEL, who teaches German and Comparative Literature at Queens College of the City University of New York, has written articles on Croce, Pavese, and other subjects; he is at present engaged in a reevaluation of sixteenth-century Italian tragedy and its influence on European tragedy.

RUBY CHATTERJI, who has degrees from Calcutta and Leicester universities, teaches English at Shri Shikshayatan College in Calcutta. She plans further studies of Middleton's use of language and imagery.

JACKSON I. COPE teaches Renaissance drama at The Johns Hopkins University. His books include *Joseph Glanvill, Anglican Apologist* (1956) and *The Metaphoric Structure of* PARADISE LOST (1962).

BEATRICE CORRIGAN is Professor of Italian at the University of Toronto. In addition to articles and reviews, she has published a *Catalogue of Italian Plays, 1500–1700, in the Library of the University of Toronto* (1961).

INGA-STINA EWBANK (née EKEBLAD), Lecturer in English Literature at the University of Liverpool, has published articles on Shakespeare and Elizabethan drama. She is author of a book on the Brontës, to be published soon, and is preparing editions of *The Duchess of Malfi, The Humorous Lieutenant,* and *Glausamond and Fidelia.*

CHARLES S. FELVER, Chairman of the Division of Language Arts of Chico State College, is author of *Robert Armin, Shakespeare's Fool* (1961).

WERNER HABICHT, Privatdozent in English at the University of Munich, has published *Die Gebärde in englischen Dichtungen des Mittelalters* (1959), and articles on Elizabethan literature and modern English drama.

THELMA HERRING, who has degrees from Sydney and Oxford universities, is Senior Lecturer in English at the University of New South Wales. She is engaged in other studies of Chapman.

G. K. HUNTER, Professor of English Literature at the University of Warwick, has edited *All's Well That Ends Well* for the New Arden Shakespeare, and is the author of *John Lyly: The Humanist as Courtier* (1962).

HARRY LEVIN is Chairman of the Department of Comparative Literature at Harvard University. His many books include *The Overreacher: A Study of Christopher Marlowe* (1952), *The Question of Hamlet* (1959), and *The Gate of Horn: A Study of Five French Realists* (1963).

DIETER MEHL is in charge of the administration of the Department of English at the University of Munich. His publications include *The Elizabethan Dumb Show: The History of a Dramatic Convention* (1965), and a number of articles and translations.

CHARLOTTE STERN is Assistant Professor of Modern Languages at Lynchburg College. She has contributed several articles and reviews on the early Spanish theater to *Hispanic Review,* and is presently completing a book, *Estudios sobre el sayagués,* to be published in Spain.

Books Received

The LISTING of a book does not preclude its subsequent review in *Renaissance Drama*.

BARTHES, ROLAND. *On Racine,* trans. RICHARD HOWARD. New York: Hill and Wang, 1964. $1.75 (paper).

CHAPMAN, GEORGE. *Bussy D'Ambois,* ed. NICHOLAS BROOKE. The Revels Plays. Cambridge, Mass.: Harvard University Press, 1964. Pp. lxxvi + 169. $4.00.

————. *Bussy D'Ambois,* ed. ROBERT J. LORDI. Regents Renaissance Drama. Lincoln: University of Nebraska Press, 1964. Pp. xxxii + 128. $1.00.

CHECKSFIELD, M. M. *Portraits of Renaissance Life and Thought.* New York: Barnes & Noble, 1965. Pp. x + 244. $5.00.

COGHILL, NEVILL. *Shakespeare's Professional Skills.* Cambridge: Cambridge University Press, 1964. Pp. xvi + 224. $7.50.

Critical Essays on the Theatre of Calderón, ed. BRUCE W. WARDROPPER. New York: New York University Press, 1965. Pp. xvi + 239. $6.00.

DANE, CLEMENCE. *London Has a Garden.* New York: W. W. Norton & Co., 1964. Pp. 211. $5.95.

ELIZABETH I. *The Poems of Queen Elizabeth I,* ed. LEICESTER BRADNER. Providence: Brown University Press, 1964. Pp. xx + 91. $4.50.

ENGLAND, MARTHA WINBURN. *Garrick's Jubilee.* Columbus: Ohio State University Press, 1964. Pp. x + 273. $6.25.

English Literary Criticism: The Renaissance, ed. O. E. HARDISON, JR. Goldentree Books. New York: Appleton-Century-Crofts, 1963. Pp. xii + 337. $2.95 (paper).

GRANT, W. LEONARD. *Neo-Latin Literature and the Pastoral.* Chapel Hill: University of North Carolina Press, 1965. Pp. x + 434. $8.00.

GREAVES, MARGARET. *The Blazon of Honour: Studies in Medieval and Renaissance Magnanimity.* New York: Barnes & Noble, 1964. Pp. 142. $3.75.

HALLIDAY, F. E. *The Poetry of Shakespeare's Plays.* New York: Barnes & Noble, 1964. Pp. 194. $1.50 (paper).

HARRIS, WILLIAM O. *Skelton's Magnyfycence and the Cardinal Virtue Tradition.* Chapel Hill: University of North Carolina Press, 1965. Pp. xii + 177. $5.00.

HEILMAN, ROBERT B. *This Great Stage: Image and Structure in King Lear.* 2nd printing. Seattle: University of Washington Press. 1963. Pp. xii + 339. $5.00.

His Infinite Variety: Major Shakespearean Criticism Since Johnson, ed. PAUL N. SIEGEL. Philadelphia: J. B. Lippincott Co., 1964. Pp. xii + 432. $4.95.

HOLMES, MARTIN. *The Guns of Elsinore.* New York: Barnes & Noble, 1964. Pp. 188. $4.50.

JONSON, BEN. *Bartholomew Fair,* ed. EDWARD B. PARTRIDGE. Regents Renaissance Drama. Lincoln: University of Nebraska Press, 1964. Pp. xx + 187. $1.00.

KIMBROUGH, ROBERT. *Shakespeare's Troilus & Cressida and Its Setting.* Cambridge, Mass.: Harvard University Press, 1964. Pp. xiv + 208. $4.75.

KLEIN, DAVID. *The Elizabethan Dramatists as Critics.* New York: Philosophical Library, 1963. Pp. xii + 420. $6.00.

KNIGHT, G. WILSON. *Shakespearian Production.* Evanston: Northwestern University Press, 1964. Pp. 323. $6.95.

LAPP, JOHN C. *Aspects of Racinian Tragedy.* Toronto: University of Toronto Press, 1964. Pp. xii + 195. $5.50.

Le Lieu théâtral à la renaissance, ed. JEAN JACQUOT, ELIE KONIGSON, and MARCEL ODDON. Paris: Éditions du Centre National de la Recherche Scientifique, 1964. Pp. xii + 532. NF 98,00.

MARLOWE, CHRISTOPHER. *The Jew of Malta,* ed. RICHARD W. VAN FOSSEN. Regents Renaissance Drama. Lincoln: University of Nebraska Press, 1964. Pp. xxx + 122. $1.00.

Marlowe: A Collection of Critical Essays, ed. CLIFFORD LEECH. Twentieth-Century Views. Englewood, N. J.: Prentice Hall, 1964. Pp. vi + 186. $3.95.

MARSTON, JOHN. *Antonio and Mellida,* ed. G. K. HUNTER. Regents Renaissance Drama. Lincoln: University of Nebraska Press, 1965. Pp. xxii + 88. $1.00.

————. *Antonio's Revenge,* ed. G. K. HUNTER. Regents Renaissance Drama. Lincoln: University of Nebraska Press, 1965. Pp. xxii + 94. $1.00.

————. *The Dutch Courtesan,* ed. M. L. WINE. Regents Renaissance Drama. Lincoln: University of Nebraska Press, 1965. Pp. xxviii + 128. $1.00.

————. *The Fawn,* ed. GERALD A. SMITH. Regents Renaissance Drama. Lincoln: University of Nebraska Press, 1965. Pp. xx + 123. $1.00.

————. *The Malcontent,* ed. M. L. WINE. Regents Renaissance Drama. Lincoln: University of Nebraska Press, 1964. Pp. xxvi + 125. $1.00.

MASSINGER, PHILIP. *The City Madam,* ed. CYRUS HOY. Regents Renaissance Drama. Lincoln: University of Nebraska Press, 1964. Pp. xx + 108. $1.00.

MEHL, DIETER. *The Elizabethan Dumb Show.* London: Methuen & Co., 1965. Pp. xiv + 207. 30s.

MIDDLETON, THOMAS. *A Mad World, My Masters,* ed. STANDISH HENNING. Regents Renaissance Drama. Lincoln: University of Nebraska Press, 1965. Pp. xx + 111. $1.00.

NICOLL, ALLARDYCE. *British Drama* (5th ed., rev.). New York: Barnes & Noble, 1963. Pp. 365. $5.50.

POWELL, ANTHONY. *John Aubrey and His Friends* (rev. ed.). New York: Barnes & Noble, 1964. Pp. 342. $7.50.

SHAKESPEARE, WILLIAM. *The Most Excellent and Lamentable Tragedie of Romeo and Juliet,* ed. GEORGE WALTON WILLIAMS. Durham: Duke University Press, 1964. Pp. xviii + 170. $6.50.

Shakespeare 1564–1964: A Collection of Modern Essays by Various Hands, ed. EDWARD A. BLOOM. Providence: Brown University Press, 1964. Pp. xiv + 226. $6.50.

Shakespeare in Germany 1590–1700, with Translations of Five Early Plays, ed. and trans. ERNEST and HENRY BRENNECKE. Curtain Playwrights. Chicago: University of Chicago Press, 1964. Pp. viii + 301. $7.50.

Shakespeare in His Own Age. Shakespeare Survey 17, ed. ALLARDYCE NICOLL. Cambridge: Cambridge University Press. Pp. x + 277. $9.50.

SHIRLEY, JAMES. *The Cardinal,* ed. CHARLES R. FORKER. Bloomington: Indiana University Press, 1964. Pp. lxxii + 142. $6.00 (paper).

————. *The Traitor,* ed. JOHN STEWART CARTER. Regents Renaissance Drama. Lincoln: University of Nebraska Press, 1965. Pp. xviii + 111. $1.00.

SMITH, IRWIN. *Shakespeare's Blackfriars Playhouse: Its History and Design.* New York: New York University Press, 1964. Pp. xx + 577. $15.00.

T<small>OMLINSON</small>, T. B. *A Study of Elizabethan and Jacobean Tragedy*. Cambridge: Cambridge University Press. Pp. viii + 293. $6.00.

W<small>EINBERG</small>, B<small>ERNARD</small>. *The Art of Jean Racine*. Chicago: University of Chicago Press, 1963. Pp. xvi + 355. $7.50.

W<small>ILSON</small>, J<small>OHN</small> H<small>AROLD</small>. *Mr. Goodman the Player*. Pittsburgh: University of Pittsburgh Press, 1964. Pp. x + 153. $4.00.

DATE DUE

FEB 29 '68	FEB 17 72		
MAR 13 '68	NOV 16 72		
SEP 30 '68	N 2 6 73		
P 5 68	DEC 9 74		
NOV	FE 8 '77		
NOV 23 '68	FE 21 77		
DEC 10 '68	MR 9 '77		
Dec N	DE 6 78		
APR 2	MR 6 '79		
APR 24 '69	FE 16 81		
OCT 29 69			
DEC 2 '69			
OCT 1 '70			
NOV 5 74			
DEC 9 '70			
APR 6 7			
FEB 2 72			
FE 16 '72			
GAYLORD			PRINTED IN U.S.A.